Dramatherapy

Clinical Studies

of related interest

Dramatic Approaches to Brief Therapy
Edited by Alida Gersie
ISBN 1 85302 271 1

Persona and Performance
The Meaning of Role in Drama, Therapy and Everyday Life
Robert J Landy
ISBN 1 85302 230 pb
ISBN 1 85302 229 2 hb

Dramatherapy for People with Learning Disabilities
A World of Difference
Anna Chesner
Foreword by Sue Emmy Jennings
ISBN 1 85302 208 X

Art Therapy and Dramatherapy
Masks of the Soul
Sue Jennings and Åse Minde
ISBN 1 85302 181 4 pb
ISBN 1 85302 027 3 hb

Storymaking in Education and Therapy
Alida Gersie and Nancy King
ISBN 1 85302 520 8 pb
ISBN 1 85302 519 4 hb

Post Traumatic Stress Disorder and Dramatherapy
Treatment and Risk Reduction
Linda Winn
Foreword by Alida Gersie
ISBN 1 85302 183 0

Play Therapy with Abused Children
Ann Cattanach
ISBN 1 85302 193 8 pb
ISBN 1 85302 120 2 hb

Play Therapy
Where the Sky Meets the Underworld
Ann Cattanch
ISBN 1 85302 211 X

Dramatherapy
Clinical Studies

Edited by Steve Mitchell

Jessica Kingsley Publishers
London and Bristol, Pennsylvania

The right of Steve Mitchell to be identified as author of this work has been asserted by him in accordance with the Copyright, Designs and Patents Act 1988.

First published in the United Kingdom in 1996 by
Jessica Kingsley Publishers Ltd
116 Pentonville Road
London N1 9JB, England
and
1900 Frost Road, Suite 101
Bristol, PA 19007, U S A

Copyright © 1996 the contributors and the publisher

Chapter 10 by Ditty Dokter is reproduced in part from her (1994) contribution to
Arts Therapies and Clients with Eating Disorders: Fragile Board.
London: Jessica Kingsley Publishers.

Library of Congress Cataloging in Publication Data
Dramatherapy : clinical studies / edited by Steve Mitchell.
p. cm.
Inlcudes bibligraphical references and index.
ISBN 1–85302–304–3 (pbk.: alk. paper)
1. Psychodrama. 2. Psychodrama--Case studies. I. Mitchell.
Steve, 1949-
RC489.P7D726 1995
616.89 1523--dc20

British Library Cataloguing in Publication Data
A CIP catalogue record for this book is available from the British Library

ISBN 1–85302–304–3

Printed and Bound in Great Britain by
Athenaeum Press, Gateshead, Tyne and Wear.

Contents

Acknowledgements   viii

Preface   ix
Steve Mitchell

1. Dramatherapy and Personality Disorder:
   Echoes of Abuse   1
   Chris Appolinari

2. Dramatherapy with People with Learning Disabilities   15
   Jocelyne James

3. Dramatherapy and Out-patient Support Groups   33
   Lorraine Fox

4. Dramatherapy with Children in an Educational Unit:
   The More You Look, The More You See   50
   Di Grimshaw

5. The Ritual of Individual Dramatherapy   71
   Steve Mitchell

6. Exploratory-level Dramatherapy within a
   Psychotherapy Setting   91
   Judy Donovan

7. Therapeutic Theatre   108
   Madeline Andersen-Warren

8. Dramatherapy in Acute Intervention   136
   Pete Holloway

9. The Seeds of the Pomegranate:
    Images of Depression   151
    Brenda Rawlinson

10. Dramatherapy and Clients with Eating Disorders:
    Fragile Board   179
    Ditty Dokter

11. Cues to the Dramatherapist From the Group   194
    Katerina Couroucli-Robertson

12. The Life Cycle   218
    Jayne E. Liddy

13. The Business: One Dramatherapist's View
    of a Business Plan   240
    Lorraine Fox

    The Contributors   255
    Index   257

Dedication

This book is dedicated to all our teachers, particularly our clients, who in sharing their journeys, have allowed us to evolve and define, as well as to refine, our dramatherapy practice.

Acknowledgements

I must thank three people in particular for the help they have given me with this enterprise:

First, my wife Sue, who has patiently supported me all the way, from endless debates on dramatherapy to reading drafts and for giving up time on the family computer.

Second, Fiona Allen, Head Occupational Therapist at Lancaster Health Priorities Trust, my line-manager, who gives me time to engage in researching dramatherapy practice.

Third, Jessica Kingsley, who from the first has encouraged the work, supported its growth and responded with care.
I thank you all.

Preface

My hope is that this collection of 'clinical studies' will be helpful to students who are starting out and also to seasoned campaigners who discover themselves faced with a new clinical population. I also hope that these studies will be informative to those new to dramatherapy and give some understanding as to what dramatherapists actually do. In recent years there have been a number of publications investigating the philosophical and theoretical considerations that underpin dramatherapy practice. The purpose of this study is to add to this growing body of knowledge by narrowing the focus to an examination of clinical concerns.

Today, many dramatherapists meet clients who have suffered sexual abuse; Chris Appolinari's chapter addresses some of the demands on a dramatherapist working with this client group and illustrates how dramatherapy can help the therapeutic process take place. Jocelyne James offers the reader the opportunity to examine ways of working with clients who have learning disabilities and presents some of the dramatherapy processes she employs to help this client group work through their particular problems.

Dramatherapy not only takes place in a hospital setting, but also within educational units, and Di Grimshaw explores some of the difficulties this might give rise to when attempting to develop a therapeutic relationship with disturbed children. For many people dramatherapy will be seen as a group process, but today, whether in private practice or in the clinic, 'one-to-one' work can be seen as the treatment of choice. In my chapter I present a ritual theatre model of individual dramatherapy and detail some of the issues of one-to-one dramatherapy with out-patients. Dramatherapists can also work as part of a psychotherapy team at a level that formal psychotherapy would call 'exploratory'. Judy Donovan details her approach, when working at this level of dramatherapy with a group of out-patients.

In contrast to depth approaches, many clients are supported in the community or within the hospital setting by attending 'supportive' dramatherapy groups. Lorraine Fox, in her chapter, examines one such approach, facilitating a group concerned with maintaining clients in the community. Madeline Anderson-Warren presents a similar level of intervention but in a contrasting way; her case histories of two 'therapeutic theatre' projects offer the dramatherapist an alternative rationale for a dramatherapy group.

Pete Holloway describes his work in an acute treatment unit. The work of the unit offers its clients an alternative to admission to hospital, but as in all acute work, the clients pass through the unit fairly quickly, and are in an acutely emotionally state. This chapter examines the issues of working within this area of psychiatry, where problem-solving and containment are paramount.

Depression, anxiety and panic attacks are clinical syndromes most dramatherapists are familiar with; Brenda Rawlinson in her chapter describes how she employs sandtrays and the enactment of dreams as ways of helping clients bring safely back into consciousness, unconscious material that may have been repressed and thus become the aetiology of depressive and neurotic psychopathology.

In recent years the number of clients presenting with eating disorders has increased. Ditty Dokter explores ways of working with this client group and details some of her approaches. The group is the drama! In her chapter, Katerina Couroucil-Robinson, describes how a dramatherapist can structure activities that allow the group dynamics to surface and be expressed through dramatherapy interventions. Jayne E. Liddy presents her own innovative model of the 'life cycle' and illustrates how she facilitates this model as a rationale for dramatherapy work with clients attending a day centre.

Finally, in her chapter, 'The Business', Lorraine Fox explores the clinical area from the needs of managers and describes how a dramatherapist might compile a business plan. This chapter will offer a model to any dramatherapist hoping to develop work in a hospital setting or within the private sector and is required to present a sound budget for their proposed service.

As dramatherapy as a profession approaches the millennium, I am continually aware of how young we are and what progress has taken place in such a short time. However, there is no room for complacency and there are still many steps to take and questions to ask about dramatherapy theory and practice. Training organisations are now beginning to offer 'master' programmes where studies of dramatherapy practice and the evaluation of that practice can be academically researched (University of Hertfordshire/Roehampton Institute). However, there also need to be other forms of research published. By this I mean practical studies which take place in the clinic, the studio, the community, the prison; work which grows from practice and the face-to-face encounter with clients. There is always a danger of excluding 'artistic' or practical study in favour of scientific studies. In this book the intention is to make a contribution to the area of practical study.

I would like to thank all those who have contributed to this book. Each chapter investigates dramatherapy with a different population and examines what takes place. But the reader will also notice certain omissions and for this I take full responsibility. Unfortunately, it is not possible to cover all the different areas in one book. My hope is that this book will offer a snap-shot of dramatherapy in the 1990s, and as a photograph can only focus with fine definition on a limited area; many more photographs are needed to do justice to the full panorama.

Finally, I must, on behalf of all the contributors, thank our clients. It is their painful and hopeful stories that fill out the clinical vignettes. Each author has taken care to maintain confidentiality by disguising the name and identity of the client, while at the same time presenting the necessary flavour of the clinical details for the purposes of this exposition. In certain chapters the clients too have been part of the writing process and to them I acknowledge our thanks.

Steve Mitchell, 1995
The Institute of Dramatherapy
Roehampton Institute, London

CHAPTER ONE

Dramatherapy and Personality Disorder
Echoes of Abuse

Chris Appolinari

Family Incest

Family incest's the game to play
Screw the kids and come out okay
Make them love you, make them cry
Then cover it up with a great big lie
Social workers, shrinks, the lot
Remember, remember the crib and the cot
Don't let parents fool you, don't be misled
Daughters often fill in for their mothers in bed

(Barlow 1979, unpublished poem)

I work in a once-famous psychiatric institution – sadly now declining into token community care. There are still three admissions wards, four small rehabilitation units and four small elderly units on site. We are at present building a regional secure unit on site. There are around 180 beds and, as the only dramatherapist, I tend to work throughout the in-patient service as well as in the community. Trying to work as a dramatherapist in a large psychiatric setting has proved to be difficult even although Arts therapists have been here since the early 1970s. At present we have two art therapists and four music therapists, one specifically for the elderly over 65. We are seen throughout the service as 'delicate little flowers' or 'all right until something goes wrong' and really 'we just don't know what it is like'. At the same time when a team needs a group facilitator for a staff group we are often their first port of call. As part of my attempt to show that I am involved in the day-to-day business of the hospital, I attend ward rounds and nursing handovers; generally spending time in the units.

During these visits several years ago I noticed how some patients were dismissed from the ward with the sense that it's 'just another PD [personality disorder], who's next?' My interest was aroused as these were patients who took part in much of the ward programme – they also absconded to the railway line, took overdoses, cut themselves, threatened to jump off buildings. They took up a lot of nursing time, 'they always let you down', or were generally thought of as a social problem, not a medical one. I have a belief that the overuse of medical solutions for people's difficult feelings leads us nowhere closer to a happier, more full person. These 'PDs' seemed to be of no great interest to our medical staff; anything 'as long as they don't kill themselves' was the main attitude from consultants whom I approached to see if I could work with their patients.

Before I proceed any further there are two issues that I wish to explain. First my use of the word 'we' when talking about the hospital: I work as I have said as a full-time dramatherapist employed by the local NHS Trust. I am very much part of the Trust and consequently work in conjunction with the rest of the staff, although as an arts therapist I am often seen, mistakenly, as being outside the establishment.

This occasionally comes up with patients. One example was when a patient I was seeing was being 'specialled' (where a patient is watched constantly by one or more members of nursing staff); once the patient was free of her 'specialler' and safe in the room she told me that she was going to run away and she knew I wouldn't tell. On informing her that she was very wrong on this her attitude changed. I do believe that I have a different view from others on many ideas in the hospital but I am part of it and on no account would I be allowed to be split.

I want also to explain my use of the term 'personality disorder'. I have no clear picture of what it means other than a badly psychologically damaged person, one whom I treat with the same respect I have for any other human being. I shall use the term when necessary as most people will be familiar with it.

I noticed that the majority of the personality-disordered patients were female. The prospect of a female therapy group with a male facilitator did not really appeal to me and working with someone else would also not be what I wanted. At this point I was vainly struggling to keep ward groups going, as were all the other arts therapists and group-orientated nurses, so to try to get a new one started was a daunting task.

With all this I decided against a group – individual work perhaps? At the end of an admission ward group a young woman approached and asked if I did individual sessions. I had been struck with her work in the group. She had painted a face then painted another two faces on top, I could see bits of all three faces on the paper. I told her I did do individual work, and if she wanted she could ask her primary nurse to make a referral to me (interesting that right away the institutional rules can get in the way!). When the referral came in I discussed it with my supervisor, at the end of which it was decided I would assess her for dramatherapy with a view to working with her.

My dramatherapy training was in groups; practically everything was done in the group. My job before my present position was as a day-centre organiser – again everything was done in the group. My belief in group work is total, so to be thinking about intensive individual work was scary. Of course I had the experience of being the patient in one-to-one therapy, but to reverse roles – well, I was not sure. My supervisor was a music therapist who had worked with individuals and groups for many years, so I did feel that with weekly supervision I would at least have a lifebelt. I hoped that the patient would have one too – me.

Throughout my psychiatric career, certain influences have helped me to understand and find my own way of working with people trying to recover from early damaging experiences. A full list of these influences is at the end of the chapter. At this point in my career (1991) I was heavily influenced by Alice Miller, Sheldon Kopp and especially by Irvin Yallom's *Love's Executioner and Other Tales of Psychotherapy*. My ex-supervisor Jane Puddy and my supervisor of the time Helen Miller were extremely important. More than anything I admired the honesty of these people and their ability to go on learning and teaching. I was taught that to be a therapist you have to be in your therapy and supervised and it is a rule that I totally adhere to. Without these two valuable tools I would never have been able to work with the patient group that I rapidly proceeded to become involved with. These individuals have found ways to manage their lives in reaction to a feeling of confusion within; they have used mutilation, alcohol, sex to block as well as to find out whether they are worth caring about. Without abuse/excitement they don't know of their own existence. Only with long, patient, caring, loving work can they rediscover what they started out as: pure innocent children sadly torn apart over years of abuse. Some will never rediscover; they are too badly damaged and too easily despised for people to stay with them in any therapeutic sense. This is something I have been able to assimilate into my working life and understand: that I can't work with everyone. Some therapists will of course be able to work with the severely damaged person.

I feel that the women I am working with are all long term in their search for themselves, if at all.

During my first meeting with Beryl I was fascinated by her story and her way of telling it; her long hair constantly over her face, her hands under her legs and her voice almost a monotone. She told me that since the age of 16 (she was now 26) she'd had an endless string of admissions to the hospital. This one, almost a year, was her longest and for the last six months she had been 'specialled'.

She frequently ran away, getting to the railway line and then stopping just before the tracks. Then she would be brought back to the ward where she would feel relieved and enjoy even more attention – albeit very negative: usually this consisted of medication and bed. Then the next day Beryl would be a model patient, taking part in things, being very helpful and apologetic. I asked her if the staff were angry towards her on these 'morning afters', and she said she couldn't really tell. I asked how she felt again; she said she couldn't really tell – 'everything is just all mixed up'. I was thinking then of what had gone on – what was going on – that jumbled her feelings so much. To end the session I asked how she was feeling now; again she was confused. I said that if she wanted to continue with the sessions one of my aims would be to look at what the confusion was about. After Beryl had left, saying she would be back next week, I found that I was feeling very confused, and also a little frustrated at the session. I also knew a little of what Beryl's confusion might be like – scary.

During my supervision sessions the confusion I was feeling was looked at, and a sense that I didn't know what to feel became apparent. If this was so for me then more than likely Beryl was the same – she didn't know what to feel. We looked at what this might be about but we ended supervision still really in the dark. During the weeks that followed, the sessions were more or less Beryl telling me what the hospital life was like for her; the most important facts for me were Beryl turning up as much as ten minutes early, and also trying to stretch the ending out. These early arrivals and the attempts to lengthen the session were never allowed. The tighter the boundaries were, the safer Beryl would be coming to the sessions. At the time I wasn't sure of my reasons, I just knew I had to maintain very strong boundaries. At this time Beryl was also writing to me and leaving the letters under my door. After the first letter, which I read not knowing her writing, I got Beryl to read them to me. The letters soon stopped as she found it very difficult to speak her words to me. I sensed that her feelings of indifference towards me were changing and that an engagement between us was happening. My sense was that Beryl was forming a sexual attraction for me.

I knew that if this was the case then some acknowledgement was needed as well as some distancing work. Beryl was becoming more flirtatious and giving me accounts of sexual encounters she saw on the ward.

Around this time I took on working with another in-patient whom Beryl had advised to be referred to me. This younger woman, Theresa, displayed very similar behaviour to Beryl although she also enjoyed drinking and taking amphetamines. As the weeks turned into months my work with these two women became twice-weekly, which gave me a much better chance to understand what was going on. Much of the work with Beryl was now centring around play. Some weeks previous she had asked if she could bring in her toy dog Toby, which she did, sitting it on her lap and occasionally stroking it. This led Beryl into play and she set up a hiding place/safe spot/den in the workroom. She used a table cloth over it reaching the floor. She had an electric light, toys, some water and Toby. She would go into her den about a third of the way through the session, and stay until the end. I was very much shut out of the playing and at times became bored. During supervision I wondered whether Beryl was also bored. At her next session I asked, as Beryl was preparing to go to her den, if I could play with her. At this she broke into tears, tears which lasted for a long time. When I tried to comfort her verbally she said, 'I wondered when... that's what my dad used to say...' Then back to tears. The next few weeks I was told her story, her with Toby on her lap at all times.

From the age of 7 to 16 (her first admission) her father had sexually abused her. Mother had worked evenings so only Beryl, her brother and her dad were in, and dad used this time to abuse her. She knew it must have been her fault as her mum and dad were both upstanding citizens, 'pillars of the local church', 'everyone likes them', and 'everyone knows I'm bad'.

Due to changes in the hospital set-up I had to move rooms again; the institution can decide something with no regard for what else is going on. This move set Beryl and the others back – lost was the safety, the security, the familiarity of the old room. During this time of change, Beryl started 'coming on' to me by stating what she would like me to do to her. One day she came in saying, 'Is today the day...?' – my confused look prompted her to finish, '...that you beat me and rape me'. I was quite stunned by this, and asked her if that would prove I loved her. Father always told her after his abuse of her that he loved her, she was a good girl and not to dare tell anyone or he wouldn't love her anymore. Beryl told me she needed to be punished for not keeping the secret and yes, if I did this I would prove I loved her. In supervision that week I spoke of how I was feeling. Beryl reminded me of an old girlfriend that I hadn't been at all fair with. I wanted to prove to Beryl that I did care about her. My supervisor thought I still had some work to do on the past relationship and also that I should try to get Beryl back to play, where it seemed she really had felt safe.

Around this time Beryl was put on a depot injection: Depixol, a low dosage on a weekly basis. She was already taking chlorpromazine and temazepam. I welcomed this not so much for its medicinal purposes but as a means for Beryl of weekly legitimate contact with medical staff. I had understood from our work together that Beryl needed excitement, something had to be happening, and also regular meetings with staff. I also felt that what was really beneficial to Beryl was me being there, when and where I said I would be. Tight boundaries, nothing fuzzy was what she really needed. I had a good relationship with her keyworker and consultant and together we agreed on a tight policy, although one that would allow Beryl space for development.

One curious aspect of the year's work I had so far done with Beryl and Theresa was that I was inundated with referrals for young personality-dis-ordered women. At this point I was working with four women and often I found it very difficult not to go along the same path – if Beryl was working well with play then why not the same for Theresa or Julia? Only by having an extra weekly supervision was I really able to keep each person separate in my mind and in the sessions.

Before play was reintroduced to the work with Beryl, she told me that shortly before her first admission she had tried telling her mother about her father's abuse. Beryl had brought this up because ever since she was 12 her mother and father had let her go out with a male friend of theirs every Sunday afternoon. This had soon turned into a sexual encounter with the friend having full sexual intercourse with Beryl not long before her 16th birthday. Her feelings of utter confusion grew too much and when her mother totally refused to hear her she overdosed and was admitted to hospital. That was the first of 25 admissions; 25 admissions in the space of 12 years, all of them very similar in her entry to the hospital and her behaviour during her stay.

These admissions were similar to those of the other three patients, although Beryl's was the longest list. All the patients whom I have met in my work who have been labelled or diagnosed 'personality disorder' have very similar admission histories. Some admissions last a matter of days, others a few weeks, others up to 18 months. Often the admissions are on a voluntary basis but within days or sometimes hours they are under a Section of the Mental Health Act. This is usually due to the patient's despair at not being understood or believed when they say they are distressed/depressed. What follows is some form of acting-out behaviour in the shape of overdose or mutilation. A terrified medic gets angry and uses the Mental Health Act to punish or maybe control or maybe reward the behaviour – this is also done to protect themselves. This of course gives the patient what they want – which is a hospital admission and relative safety from early discharge.

The information regarding the family friend and mother's refusal to believe Beryl added more to her pain and the belief that she was a bad person. I believe, however, that Beryl was glad of the space she had with me. In a subsequent session she told me of a dream she'd had.

> She is at the bottom of a well/chimney. Someone is at the top with a light letting down a rope to her. As she struggles up the person at the top pulls it away from her. She falls back – she can no longer see the light.

Am I going to pull the rope from her? Will I walk away? Beryl was unsure of this, she really doesn't know what to think, 'You still haven't tried to have sex with me, so maybe you can be of real help'.

My experiences of holding the boundaries so tight with Beryl helped me enormously with my other patients and in many ways my creativity was sparked more. I decided to give her some physical/transitional object to keep with her, which was a piece of rope from the toy basket. I asked Beryl to imagine that this rope was attached to me and that I was in a fixed position – unable to be pulled down into her pit but fixed and strong enough to help pull her up. I reminded her, although, that although I was pulling she had to climb or otherwise she would slip back down. The delight in Beryl's face at this piece of rope and my words was so genuine; for the first time I noticed that she was really quite a young person.

Beryl was living in a hostel in town at this point, a female hostel, and although she felt this was a safe place to live she found it slightly unreal. In a session she talked of this, and also of the relief of there not being men as this meant she didn't have to have sex. I queried this and she said that if men were nice to her, even by being polite, she felt she had to have sex with them. I asked if this was why she wondered why I didn't have sex with her although I was being nice to her. She agreed but said that now she felt she wouldn't know what to do sexually with me – this was a turning point. Beryl was beginning to see me as: a) a dramatherapist; b) a man; and c) a man she could trust without being abused. She seemed to be bringing more control to her life. She was occupying herself with voluntary work and attending a day-centre in town.

I decided to get Beryl back to playing and growing. When I suggested this she said yes, but that first she wanted me to see her as she saw herself.

She built a large object with chairs and cushions, and covered them all in some old blinds I had. She then built a very small structure with toys, balls and paints, telling me the large black object was how she saw herself, a dark shadowy monster when she first met me. She said nothing about the smaller creation, and then she pared down the large dark shape to something much smaller – still covered in black and still much larger than the other creation. Even after she had added to the smaller structure the dark object remained larger. She said, 'This is bad/evil me and this is happy me, good me'. I decided to concentrate on the good Beryl, asking her to tell me all about it. This proved a stilted exercise – she wasn't ready to talk about herself positively, not even with Toby beside her. As the session drew to a close she asked if she could leave both of her structures up and also could she leave Toby beside them. Unsure as I was about this, I agreed and these structures became the focus of Beryl's work for the next few weeks. I was unsure, as other patients used the room, whether the sight of such a large structure would disturb them. Also the cleaner might not like being unable to clean properly. The larger of the two structures was given a name, 'Billy'. Beryl unravelled each piece separately, saying what each one was – this was when she stole from the shop – lots of little things that had gone on in her childhood/adolescence. Then she said, as she picked up the largest of the chairs, 'This is me enjoying my dad in my bed'.

We examined this and what she had enjoyed and missed was her father's attention, his words of love. As we looked more at this, Beryl had more of an understanding that wanting the care, attention and love of her father was very natural and normal. This of course was a very sad time for Beryl, during which she had an admission, although this time she went about it in a healthier way, explaining to her consultant how she felt; unsafe and needing people around her as she came more to terms with herself.

This whole time had proved to be trying for me also, as I had a full-time job of which Beryl was only a small part in terms of time. I also found her admission beneficial as I was less a focal point for her. I had also been working in my own therapy and in supervision on my feelings surrounding Beryl and my one-time girlfriend. At times in the session I found myself struggling with my own feelings of wanting to make Beryl/girlfriend feel better and if sex was her method then I would oblige. Again this is where my supervisor's voice was on my shoulder guiding me, helping me stay firmly fixed on the here and now of Beryl. The actual supervision sessions were of immense value and my work in therapy proved to be very fruitful for me.

The length of admission on this occasion was slightly over a month, at the end of which I was feeling much clearer and stronger, as was Beryl; she decided to make a den for herself 'like the one I had before' – only it wasn't. Although similar in design, this den was much brighter, lots of toys, soft and hard, and it was easier to see. There was still a cloth hanging over it and in Beryl's first few weeks she kept the cover up, very inviting, almost lifting her skirt for me. I never commented on this. I never asked to play. I merely sat in the room being there. And when the cover came down after five sessions I felt a great sense of joy and from what I heard, Beryl was enjoying playing. Not long after this session I was asked to join her in play. I felt the space under the table a little bit confining and as I was wondering about this Beryl said we could use the big space, which is what we did. The play at first was very structured with lines of cars, men and animals; basically they moved up and down the space. Occasionally a bear would knock things down but then we would put them back up again.

Beryl was now living on her own in a shared house, still taking nightly medication, a daytime tranquilliser (low dosage) and weekly injection. She was also smoking heavily outside of sessions. She was turning up for every session, rarely late and phoning if she was going to be, always very polite. It felt as if there were definitely something in her make-up that was missing, apart from what we already knew. She seemed to be holding back, which could be due to the medication, but the low dosage and also the irregularity with which she took her tranquilliser made this idea a non-starter. During a session I produced some old postcards and, fanning them out, I asked her to pick one and try to make a story up about what she saw. As she looked at her choice her whole body screwed up tight into almost a foetal position and her tears flooded out. My immediate thought was to comfort her – the voice on my shoulder spoke otherwise. I listened and remained where I was – with the last ten minutes of the session rapidly approaching I tried to help Beryl to get herself back to a safe enough place for her to be able to leave the room and get herself home. There was no real escape for her and I ended the session as usual. I would be seeing her in two days time, so I knew I would have to trust in Beryl's new-found strengths.

On the Thursday Beryl unfolded what had been going on for her. The postcard, a picture of a mountain range and ski slope in black and white, had reminded her of her first school holiday. She was 14 when she and her brother went on this trip. She had a great time, enjoying being a teenager and no fear/excitement of her father coming into her room at night. Once home, her father came to her at night and this time instead of his usual 'gentleness' he beat her and then had sexual intercourse with her. This became the usual trend from then on until she managed through her overdose and consequent admissions to escape. Beryl never knew why it started but guessed it was because she had enjoyed herself and enjoying herself would make her a 'bad girl', and then her father wouldn't love her and give her his attention. The confusion in Beryl was intense now, as it had been when she was 14. Again she turned to sex and me, 'hadn't we better do it?'

Beryl was also wanting to go back to her family even if she had to sleep with her father again. At least she'd know someone loved her. Her loneliness was immense and very painful in years gone by. She had filled her loneliness with hospital admissions, lots of casual sexual affairs (mostly with married men), and with religion. Now she was trying to be with herself, trying new paths and finding the way difficult.

Some of my other patients were also trying different paths. The common links were their loneliness, sadness and their abuse from childhood onwards.

With Theresa the form of her abuse was neglect, consequently she grew up thinking no one would like her. Although a bright, intelligent woman she left school with no written qualifications. Then she discovered drink, drugs and hospital admissions. Theresa would use overdosing to get admission and followed a path that had been well-trodden by many others. Our work together over two-and-a-half years centred on her loneliness – being put out in the garden with a dog and a boat for company, her mother's ongoing depression and her father's constant affairs with young blond women. Theresa wanted so much to be liked by her father that she dyed her hair blond and tried to stay young and slim. She brought me dreams, always with a similar theme; being with a group of people, them turning against her and chasing her away, where she would meet a wall. Before she was over the wall she would be caught. She would then wake up or not remember what happened next. We looked at what might be over the wall, and if she climbed over would the landing be firm or marshy. I think over our time I was Theresa's solid ground and I stayed solid throughout, even when she sunk to the gutters where a broken jaw from the boot of a drunk gave her a chance to rest in hospital. Throughout our whole time she only turned up drunk once, and I let her sit in the room with a coffee until time was up.

That was over a year ago. She is now with a partner who cares about her. She sees me once a week and, as it always has been, our work is mostly talking therapy using metaphor and her dreams a lot. I imagine that our work will end soon. She has found that she is worthwhile – her parents had a problem with themselves, she was not a bad child. She is lovable and likeable – and becoming more so. Gone are her feelings of defending against early abandonment, no longer needing to attempt suicide to avoid being left, no longer needing sexual encounters to avoid her pain. A much more whole person has emerged; and, although still vulnerable, she is much more able to stay with her feelings without escaping to drink or drugs. Her self-esteem has had a restoration period; one which I believe she has come out of even stronger.

These last few pages of writing have been flowing past at quite a speed, and I realise that this was how the work has been over the past year. Both the patients and myself were rushing; there seemed to be no stopping-places. My worry was that I was missing some of what was being said. I think, however, that no matter what the speed, I would always miss something. In supervision, where the work was also speedy, we were able to slow our pace down, and this in turn helped me to slow down in the sessions. Slowing down with Beryl was essential for her to make sure she was assimilating what was going on for her – this was just as essential for me.

A great confusion had again arisen in Beryl regarding myself and her, the whole question of a sexual relationship. If we were to have sex then I would be able to see her for what she really was – a 'bad girl' – and as sex was always painful, this would reaffirm and confirm what she was. Some of the confusion was the fact that she felt that maybe because I was caring then sex would not be painful for her and I truly would be her saviour. We looked at what this was really about for her – she was scared I was going to discharge her, and if she could engage me another way, sexually, then maybe I wouldn't. Looking back over her sexual life, we used empty chairs to portray this. She went through a large number of men. There was no titillation in her actions – she had stopped trying to excite me. At no point in her life had Beryl felt happy with sex – it was all she knew men wanted from her and meeting me had thrown her. As she said, 'If it was sex, I'd know what to do'.

The work with the empty chairs continued until she left only two chairs. These were her father and her brother. No mention of her brother had come up during our work, and now finally here he was in the room. What transpired was that when he was 14 or 15 he had given Beryl, then 11, sweets and cash in return for sex. Beryl's rage, her sadness, her total hatred of her family came out during the next few sessions with the use of words, cushions and sticks. Still I resisted my urge to give her a hug. There seemed still to be danger lurking, yet I wanted to give her some physical reassurance. In supervision we looked at this deciding I was right not to, as Beryl could easily see this as a come-on, also a betrayal of the boundaries we had set up. She was still testing me. As the work with her father and brother came to its conclusion, Beryl was beginning to realise she wasn't to blame for her family, this realisation coming from deep within. Her sense of herself as a 'normal human being' was also beginning to push up to the surface. A different person was coming to the sessions, one who was now holding her head up, one who was able to look at the world from a realistic viewpoint. This was by no means a cured woman, but one who had told me her worst belief of herself, that she was evil, and had survived being listened to and understood. She had made a vital move away from her old position.

Beryl began her next session by asking if we could play catch-ball together, so sitting on seats we began throwing the ball to each other. Then other games began and a lot of our session time was taken up with play. She seemed very safe with playing and took the opportunity to explain some more about what had been happening to her when she wanted sex with me. I had always known that Beryl's feelings were different from the normal transference that happens in therapy – there was always more to her suggestions. She said during play that if we had sex then all her thoughts and feelings about herself would have been confirmed by me; as that hadn't happened she began to question that maybe it wasn't her fault after all. The work with empty chairs, the sharing with me of her brother's actions, had led her to acknowledge that she had been abused because the men in her life hadn't known any better. It wasn't her fault. I really felt she had started the healing process, although she had a fear that I would discharge her sooner rather than later. My view was that she would know when to stop therapy; she would take responsibility.

At the time of writing, I have been working with Beryl for nearly three years. Our work continues as her own belief in herself grows. Occasionally she will check out the firmness of the boundaries by turning up early or leaving messages to ring her back. Of course none of this is allowed and is discussed in the next session. Some days are easy for Beryl; others she feels trapped and unsure, losing her self-belief in her humanness. This is to be expected as no one can truly let such a horrific past just slip away as if it never happened. Also, if you've been behaving a certain way for all your life then change is often painful and the old ways look reassuring.

At the tail end of 1993 Beryl came to the session with some plastic bags full of bottles. She then proceeded to put them out in a circle before sitting down. The bottles contained chlorpromazine suspension – ones she had got on prescription over some years. I asked her to sit in the middle allowing whatever she thought or felt out towards the bottles. I was anticipating Beryl going round each one speaking to them as men – instead she looked at all 15 bottles telling them that for years they had been her way out when her pain was too much. Now it was time to say good-bye to them, no longer needing their help. When she was finished we took them to the pharmacy together for handing in. The dour-faced expression of the pharmacist nearly dulled our joy. However, this was short-lived; Beryl was so pleased with herself it was a delight to witness. She said she wanted to give up all her medication. She was still taking sleeping pills but, after taking them nightly for ten years, giving up would be no easy matter – the same for her smoking. I advised slowly, slowly, and this is what she is doing: gradually reducing both drugs. I think that if she had given up everything at once too great an emptiness would have developed and, like the majority of humankind, we all need something sometimes.

At present our sessions are once-weekly, a move Beryl instigated, not only in order to show herself she could but also to fit in with her college life. She has enrolled for an Access course with a view to completing a formal education. She has no outlandish plans. She still has bad 'wobbly' days where she feels alone and bored, although she can contain her feelings with much more ease now and she knows she has therapy once a week. I don't foresee more hospital admissions, although I think that when she decides, with medical staff, to come off her weekly injection we will all have to be very careful. Although Beryl won't feel a rejection as badly as she would have done, we must take care for us all to be fully involved in the discussion.

The work I am involved with is difficult. Often I have struggled with finding a dramatherapy-centred approach. I no longer struggle. I cannot always use dramatherapy – where I can, I do. I follow a belief in the therapeutic process, of a rebuilding of oneself – the same bricks and mortar just made stronger and more true.

Psychiatric hospitals are not in my opinion the place for abused people to come into. Boundaries in such places are, unavoidably, all over the place with so many different viewpoints around. Small family-type units which are safe and sound in boundary issues are what I would like to see. I think that homes such as these could give the injured abused person the safety to regrow and rebuild. I believe that my work has evolved around my very strict boundaries and a love of humankind as much as knowing what structure to put into sessions and where. Sometimes these structures work out, other times they don't. However, with tight boundaries the session remains safe for both the patient and myself. What is also needed is time. There are no short cuts here just as there are no short cuts in anything important. 'Don't walk before you can crawl.'

As the 1990s progress we are seeing a steady disintegration of our health, social and educational services. This will of course mean less care for everyone, and self-injurious people will be pushed even further back. Child abuse, whether emotional, physical or sexual, is not a high priority now, so I can only see these patients taking an even more distant back seat. Only when cycles of abuse are broken will we see a reduction and fading of this client group, and really I don't see this being recognised as a social priority at present.

List of Influences

Barlow, L. (1992–1994) Personal conversations.

Campbell, J. (1988) *The Hero With a Thousand Faces*. London: Paladin Grafton Books.

The Grateful Dead (1968) *Anthem of the Sun*. Warner Brothers.

Hesse, H. (1964) *Siddartha*. London: Picador.

Kopp, S. (1974) *If You Meet the Buddha on the Road, Kill Him*. London: Sheldon Press.

Laing, R.D. (1970) *Knots*. Harmondsworth: Penguin Books.

Miller, A. (1986) *Thou Shalt Not Be Aware, Society's Betrayal of the Child* (translated by Hildegarde and Hunter Hannum). London: Pluto Press.

Miller, H.O. (1988–1994) Personal conversations.

Nash, S. (1984–1994) Personal conversations.

Puddy, J. (1984–1991) Personal conversations.

Yalom, I. (1989) *Love's Executioner and Other Tales of Psychotherapy*. London: Bloomsbury.

CHAPTER TWO

Dramatherapy with People with Learning Disabilities

Jocelyne James

Introduction – The Dramatherapist

There are many contrasting theories, philosophies, techniques and approaches stemming from a variety of different sources developing in the field of dramatherapy today. The ongoing evolution of these is as mercurial as the creative process itself. It is my belief that each therapist can and perhaps inevitably must develop their own style, having been influenced and informed by their theoretical study, training, clinical practice, supervision, personal therapy and life experience. Each therapist will combine these differently and be drawn towards application with different client groups in varying contexts. If I may use the metaphor of snow, whilst we are all part of the same downpour of healing and change so necessary at this time, each one of us is also an individual flake, a unique constellation in our own right. In this chapter I am not concerned with promoting any particular methodology for use with this client group, but rather sharing a glimpse of my own understanding and experience of working therapeutically through drama and movement with adults with learning disabilities.

An Introduction to the Client Group and the Context of the Work

The term 'people with learning disabilities' refers to a large population of individuals who have a whole range of diverse and specific characteristics and special needs. These can range from conditions termed quite clearly as 'Downs Syndrome' or 'Autism' to others that can be less clear, complex and/or indefinable. It is an umbrella term used to label those historically described as the 'mentally handicapped', a title which many have suggested perhaps excluded the notion that they were people at all. This more recent description refers to a group of people whose rights and responsibilities are only just beginning to be recognised.

My experience has brought me into contact with this client group, providing weekly groups and individual sessions as a drama and movement therapist in the context of day-centres, adult education and training. I have been introduced to some of the most intelligent, insightful and wise individuals for whom the title has seemed unwearable. Others have demonstrated quite profound difficulties with mobility, sensory impairment, speech and communication. For the purpose of this chapter I am not concerned with diagnosis, perhaps also reflecting something generally about my approach in this context. This stems from the Humanistic tradition which prioritises the building of a relationship with a client over any analysis of them. In the words of one man I worked with who had refused to see a psychiatrist, but had been a little more receptive to the idea of a dramatherapist: 'I didn't want to go to the psychiatrist because I thought he was like a judge and would pass sentence... you know... "next please!"'

This client group has suffered many psychological and emotional consequences from potentially de-humanising labels and alienating institutional life. As the same client continues:

> The doctors treat you like a patient, not a person. They're five feet taller than me, looking down their noses... I have no control and no authority. There's nothing I can do about it. It's like having your arms and legs tied and not being able to move... I've just got to grin and bear it. It makes my blood boil.

These factors have undoubtedly had a serious impact on the potential and limitations, the abilities and so-called disabilities of a minority group who are only just starting to find their voice and locate their needs in society. As one young man commented, 'You could be another Einstein, but they won't accept that because you are handicapped.'

I would like to highlight the value of equal opportunities policies, normalisation philosophy, self-advocacy groups and community integration programmes, which among many factors continue to contribute to the development and evolution of all of our changing attitudes, values and beliefs. Such significant influences taking increasing effect in health, education and social services, bring with them new and fresh challenges. Some adults with learning disabilities are beginning to negotiate some degree of freedom, power and choice, perhaps for the first time in their lives.

The very big institutions which once housed large numbers of adults with learning disabilities have been closing down to allow people to move into smaller units; more independent-living community homes, a process involving the making and breaking of a great many affectional bonds. In conjunction with this many are also making the shift from being somewhat passive recipients of social service care and attention to becoming more active users of this, whether in residential or day-centre contexts. The effects of all this on the lives of individuals may range enormously, and have far-reaching implications, from being simply free to choose what they would like to eat or wear, or how to structure their time, to in other cases, considering decisions about where to live and with whom, having sexual and/or marital relationships, or going to work. This is a process of becoming fully participant in what it is to be a member of this society in this culture now.

Surprisingly enough the above mentioned may well be new experiences for some of this client group, and I consider creative and therapeutic work to be both necessary and integral in assisting with this adaptation, on all levels: physically, emotionally, psychologically, socially and spiritually. The dramatic form which has 'act'-ion at its centre is particularly appropriate for this purpose. One middle-aged man announced at the end of a dramatherapy group, almost as if realising for the first time: 'I am a human being!', continuing to say that he hadn't always felt treated like one, 'more like an animal...a child...a dog'. This is perhaps an extreme example that I have quoted, but nevertheless indicates the often high level of awareness demonstrated by the client group, contrasted to what might be considered as the tragic lack of it reflected in their historical treatment. He gave voice to what many adults with learning disabilities may not even have access to language to begin to say through words. I think it is impossible to evaluate the extent of some individuals' wounds and untold truths.

Treatment is a particularly operative word here when considering the context of therapy, and this begins, as R.D. Laing suggested, with the way you actually treat someone.

Direction of the Work

I have valued a close liaison with the institutions that my work has taken place within, among interdisciplinary teams. A good working alliance in this area can be a key to achieving therapeutic aims and objectives. In my experience I have at times needed to explain to day-centre staff or management specific ethical considerations related to therapeutic practice. For example, the psychological significance of time boundaries or, similarly, it was once necessary for me to help someone to understand why it was inappropriate for a particular client's attendance to the group to be part of a punishment/reward system in a behaviour modification programme. It is useful if there is a relationship between what happens in the therapeutic context and the cultural expectations of the client's environment. Therefore, to be congruous with the context of social change already described, I have found that the steady handing over of responsibility and power in the dramatherapy sessions, can be a useful and integral aspect of the group process.

In the early stages of a group, more direction and structure can be necessary for individuals who suffer from lack of confidence or ability to take initiative as well as a severely damaged creative self-image. This can be concerned with stimulating the group, encouraging communication, introducing them to the dramatic medium and waking up their creative resources, particularly the body, voice and imagination. Play can be a basic ingredient here as Ann Cattanach (1992) suggests: 'Social skills develop through playing together. The development of this work is through the developmental stages of play from embodiment play to projective play and symbolic play to role play' (p.11).

However, in the later life of the group I have found it increasingly valuable to promote the exploration of leadership qualities from within its members. This may involve being much less directive so as to enhance the developing initiative of individuals rather than encouraging dependency. I then become part of the resources of the group and am ultimately working towards my own redundancy. The words of Lao Tsu (1973) inspire my understanding of the element of emptiness useful in dramatic structures and in the group facilitator working towards this end:

> Thirty spokes share the wheel's hub;
> It is the centre hole that makes it useful.
> Shape clay into a vessel;
> It is the space within that makes it useful.
> Cut doors and windows for a room;
> It is the holes which make it useful.
> Therefore profit comes from what is there;
> Usefulness from what is not there.

Having worked for three-and-a-half years with one particular group, it was possible for me to depart from the 'scene' while they continued to go on working together independently, taking responsibility for both the form and content. This process perhaps reflected their journey towards autonomy in the wider world.

The 'Nature' of Relationship: Client–Therapist

Awareness of the transactional analysis model for understanding the human personality, relationships and communication first developed by Eric Berne, but very much evolved through his contemporaries, is valuable when working with this client group. The 'functional analysis of ego states' (Stewart and Joines 1987) can prove useful in a therapeutic context with a client group who can get caught up in their 'child ego state', as a consequence of the 'parental' model of institutional care they have received in the past. Historically, clients may have been addressed as if they were children in 'condescending' or 'patronising' ways and can therefore have grown familiar and accustomed to particularly 'parent–child' interactions.

I have found it is important in a therapeutic context at this time to engage with and strengthen the adult ego state which can be underdeveloped and I try never to forget the importance of reiterating permissions where freedom and choice are concerned with clients who can regularly forget that they have a right and responsibility to these.

Dramatherapy can make creative and therapeutic use of the regressive elements in play and drama as well as providing developmentally needed/reparative experiences through a reparenting element in the client–therapist relationship (Clarkson 1993). However, in considering the broader context of social change and the issue of 'age appropriateness' it seems important to avoid recapitulating a parent–child model of relationship care which might foster regression or prove to be disempowering.

Therefore I consider what Clarkson (1993) has described as the 'I–You' or the 'person to person' relationship to be of particular significance to my own therapeutic work in this field.

> The I–You relationship is characterised by the 'here-and-now' of the existential encounter between two people. It involves mutual participation in the process and recognition that each is changed by the other... The Self of the therapist becomes the instrument through which the healing evolves... its field is not object relations but subject relations. (p.32)

This is a model of authentic 'being with', recognising the equal adult status of both clients and therapist. Buber (1970) claimed that the therapist 'can only accomplish the task of regenerating the stunted growth of a person centre by entering as a partner into a person-to-person relationship, but never through the observation or investigation of an object'. Similarly Jung (1966) held as a central truth that the therapeutic relationship changes the therapist as well as the client. This form of therapeutic relationship is one of 'shared personhood. The two then become siblings in incomprehension, siblings in discovery, and siblings in the quest for wholeness' (Clarkson 1993). I have found it very valuable in practice with this client group to bring my own honest and natural responses to the role of therapist, and also to be aware of my own vulnerability, inhibitions and inabilities on all levels. In conclusion, 'what is therapeutic, when it is achieved, is "the moment of real meeting". This experience is transforming… because it is not what happened before (that is transference) but what has never happened before, a genuine experience of relationship in the here and now' (Clarkson 1993).

I have witnessed in some cases that particularly competent residential social workers, care assistants, day-centre staff and management make creative and therapeutic use of this form of relationship without necessarily realising it. There are undoubtedly some very special and natural healing relationships that exist outside of the consciously or specifically therapeutic context.

Theoretical and Philosophical Frameworks

My work combines influences from clinical, psychoanalytic, behavioural and humanistic traditions in psychology. I am committed to an integrative approach, which takes into account a multiplicity of perspectives. Therefore it is not possible to do justice to the range of theory and philosophy which has informed my practice here. However, for the purpose of this chapter I will focus more specifically on referencing those which I have considered to be particularly important in working with this client population. This will foreground the humanistic elements which I find particularly applicable in this context.

I resonate with what John Rowan (1992) defines as the 'integrative encounter' which unifies three strands to form a holistic model concerned with mind, body and spirit. These are the regressive, the existential and the transpersonal.

Regressive – concerned with revisiting past events from the individual's history from the personal unconscious and can involve re-experiencing and/or re-evaluating these in the light of the present to reach new levels of meaning, understanding or resolution. It may be important to revisit and attend to earlier wounds or crisis ('conflicts, confusions or deficits' – Clarkson) that have occurred during previous developmental stages. Working with and through the mediums of drama and movement can provide infinitely rich possibilities for developmental reparation. The art forms can operate literally through direct engagement or metaphorically through dramatic distancing and symbolic identification. They also provide access to pre-verbal realms of experience. Drama and movement can collapse the conventions of time and space to create powerful tools for healing and change in the present.

Existential – concerned with the significance of the here and now, aware that both remembering and planning are functions of the present and placing emphasis on the vividness of each passing moment. Sunderland (1992) suggests that:

> The very nature of artistic comment can intensify any human experience, and bring about a heightening of both sensory awareness and aesthetic sensitivity... the facilitation of such awareness can be central in promoting a richness, vitality and quality of life and in counteracting the often desensitising trend of present day technological society.

Like Keleman (1975), I recognise body awareness as the 'ground of our being' and place it at the centre, at the heart of my work. In my view, to work with the psyche without attending to the soma is, as it were, like trying to grow apples in the air, without root, without trunk, without branches. Therefore the emphasis on the physical aims at healing the splits between mind and body, constantly awakening into awareness of the present.

Transpersonal – concerned with deeper perspectives and the higher potentialities provided by spiritual insight and awareness. The dramatic arts can explore the imaginal realm, including the transcendent and archetypal dimensions of the collective unconscious. Drama can contain ritual and ceremony. As well as accessing positive affect and the potential for liberation through creativity, the dramatic medium can be a source of revelation and vision.

The influence of Jung is particularly prevalent in all my work and I continue to study and learn from him. Therefore what I consider to be the overall aim and purpose of the therapeutic process with this client group as with any other, would be that of individuation – 'A person becoming himself/herself, whole, indivisible and distinct from other people, although also in relation to these' (Samuels, Shorter and Plaut 1986). I am concerned with the fuller and fuller embodiment of each individual's unique potential and what Abraham Maslow has described as 'self-actualisation'.

I also relate very much and utilise the theory and philosophy of Gestalt therapy in which 'change is an inescapable product of contact... Through contact one does not have to try to change; change simply occurs' (Polster and Polster 1973). In the context of dramatherapy therefore it is through the process of contact and relationship with group participants, the therapist and the art form that healing and change become possible. I conceptualise the group context as an alchemical laboratory, and all the relationships therein, vessels of transformation.

Working with a client group who can sometimes suffer from profound and inherent problems in the areas of communication and relationship, my role as a therapist is to help facilitate the process of overcoming these difficulties and provide the necessary resources to enhance contact. The Innuits have an approach to sculpture whereby the role of the artist is to remove everything in the way of revealing the already present image contained within the uncarved block. There are parallels in the way I conceptualise my art form as a therapist. This is to assist in the removal of blocks to the healthy and natural growth and development of each group and its members. I find the Gestalt cycle an immensely useful map to assist in the diagnosis of interruptions to contact, change and creativity, and the dramatic form an infinitely rich resource through which to confront and overcome these.

Non-verbal Communication

In this area I have been particularly inspired by the work of the Sesame Institute, pioneered by Marian Lindkvist. Sesame established the first short course training in drama and movement in therapy at Guy's Hospital in 1964, and has been specialising in this field ever since. The Sesame Method is unique, focusing considerably on non-verbal experience and combining humanistic philosophy with depth psychology. It is a symbolic approach placing emphasis on the creative and expressive use of the imagination within the safety and containment of the art forms. The image Sesame associates itself with is a key, inspired by the notion of 'Open Sesame' – entering into oneself.

This work aims really to uncover the value of non-verbal communication through the use of music, movement and touch as integral aspects of the dramatic medium as well as art forms in their own right. The purpose of exploring and developing these creative vocabularies is obvious when working with clients who may find it difficult or impossible to make contact through spoken language. However, I have also experienced and witnessed the extraordinary benefits that these can have on those who are verbally articulate. Quality of contact can deepen profoundly when making relationships without words, and I have found that there is such a depth and range of human experience which cannot be spoken. Entering into the world of someone who does not speak can require the therapist to be fluent in the languages of music, movement and touch. To talk without words involves sensory awareness, emotional literacy and intuition, qualities that have perhaps been devalued in our particularly logocentric culture. Educating the 'thinking function' (Jung) tends to predominate in our school system where children are generally taught behind desks from the waist up, learning to identify almost entirely with their thought processes. Drama and movement remind us of our body language.

Therefore, finding words to describe this kind of work is difficult, as it is often neither cognitive, rational nor intellectual. I worked with one man for over a year on an individual basis who had no speech and was in his mid-30s. Within a very short space of time both his parents, whom he had lived at home with all his life, had died. Suddenly he found himself in the context of residential care as a consequence. Not surprisingly he became exceptionally withdrawn and depressed. He grew thin and contracted, refusing almost any form of contact with anyone. When I met him he seemed to me to be suffering from chronic grief and appeared to have built a wall up around him, partly due to lack of communicative resources, but also due to existential incomprehension of the circumstances. For the first few weeks our relationship was tentative. I sat close to him, speaking occasionally without ever quite knowing how much he understood. In such circumstances I always imagine that the client can understand, if not consciously then at least unconsciously. If he was willing to allow me, I just wanted to feel, to sense, to intuit my way into his internal landscape.

In these initial sessions I was acutely aware of his feelings of isolation and inability. Sometimes clients can tell you about what they are feeling by what Casement (1985) describes as 'communication by impact', whereby you find yourself experiencing their feelings quite directly. This is relevant when working with people who are non-verbal and I have found supervision extremely helpful in distinguishing between my feelings and the client's. I felt painfully alone, although we were both in the same room next to one another. In the loneliness of his grief he allowed me to hold his hand. His body was so tense, so agitated, like a tightly bound knot of elastic rubber bands. His eyes were glazed over and didn't meet mine. There was a prevailing sense of helplessness in the room.

It occurred to me that what this man needed was to be physically held. I moved behind him on the floor, resting against the wall. I created a kind of physical chair with my own body and he leant back against me. I rocked him gently, echoing the small sounds that he made. He began to cry, and I moved my body empathically to the sound of his tears.

Weeks passed in this way as when he arrived at our session all that he wanted to do was curl up in a ball and be held. I would play him what I experienced as sad and beautiful music and he would weep. An image I had of our relationship at this time was that he seemed like a pebble having been washed up on a beach from out of the ocean. Through touch I could give him the literal physical support, reassurance and containment he needed, where words were futile. Here he felt safe enough – on firm enough and dry enough ground – to begin to experience his feelings of profound loss, to mourn. Touch became the source of human contact and relationship through which he was able to regain some level of what Erikson (1977) described as 'basic trust' which had been shattered by the circumstances.

The tears he wept drained his body of tension and he began to let go, giving me the full weight of his body to hold. He relaxed and the knots of tension seemed to unravel, undo themselves in the process. This took time. It didn't all happen at once. In the consistency of my presence and the consenting environment he began to explore, to move, and I moved with him. I used my own body and voice to reflect, to mirror, to initiate and to respond to his, validating and valuing every inch of his self-expression. I brought rhythmic music with a vital pulse, encouraging him to respond to it by doing so myself. He let the music into his blood, and moved to it, giving shape and form to feelings through his body.

Later he began to make quite loud and free sounds with the movement. I joined him using the same pitch, the same intonation and attuning to the emotions I could hear in his voice. In response the sound grew and he began to make bigger and bigger noises until eventually he roared with feeling, he shouted loudly, and banged the drum hard with his hands, the ground hard with his feet. His frustration, rage and anguish were apparent. I told him he had a very real right to these angry feelings and that they were a natural part of the grieving process. I think he understood what I said more clearly when I too banged a drum alongside and joined his stamping affirmatively. Having creatively channelled so much 'destructive' energy, he grew tired and his mood changed. Again he wanted to curl up like a foetus or a kitten and be simply held.

In time, through exploring the many different expressive languages other than words, it was as if he began to breathe again. His life force, his energy, his 'Physis' returned – 'the natural curative force of Nature which facilitates the urge towards growth, self-experience and realisation' (Clarkson 1993). More than a year later when his eyes actually were meeting mine they were bright and alive, wide awake, looking right back at me. The therapy had 'held' him through this period of change and he was adjusting, recovering his confidence, his quality of life, and making new friends.

Working with touch can highlight ethical considerations. Issues concerned with boundaries and sexuality may need to be discussed in supervision. I have found that it is not always appropriate to work through this medium. Mitch Mitchelson (1993), in his description of Sesame, quotes from Shakespeare's *All's Well That Ends Well* 'I have seen a medicine that can breathe life into a stone'. I too have experienced this to be a powerful consequence of a therapeutic non-verbal relationship.

Another young man who had been attending a group for about two years asked if he could invite his sister for a visit. The group members gave their consent and so she came. That day, as the circumstances were unusual and the weather particularly good, I decided to move out of our ordinary room into a bright and sunny meadow close by. There we explored combining a simple trust exercise with the natural environment we were in. In pairs one person was blindfolded while the other, without talking, introduced them to the surroundings. Therefore one had the responsibility to guide and protect the other through touch while encouraging them to explore the smell, the feel, the sound and the sensation of the grass, flowers, stones, earth and trees, and so forth. Meanwhile the blindfolded partner was dependent, being without sight. This man paired up with his sister and she began the experiment in what seemed like a familiar role – that of looking after her younger 'handicapped' brother. Then they swapped roles and suddenly she was the one with the disability. She was vulnerable and had to trust her brother to take care of her, to be the authority. He demonstrated his reliability, leading her sensitively beneath the shade of a tree. I watched him take her hand and gently guide it over the bark, sharing and revealing to her its texture. He led her down on to her hands and knees, guiding her through the long grass, and stopping every now and then to explore. Once he picked a daisy and gently stroked her cheek with it. She smiled.

Having spent some time exploring in this way, all the blindfolds were removed and we came into a circle to talk together and reflect on shared experiences. She said that something rather amazing had happened which had opened up a whole new dimension to her relationship with her brother. She had met him in an entirely new and different light and something had significantly changed between them during that time.

The Oblique Approach

Sesame adopts what is often described as 'the oblique approach'. The rationale for this is that dramatic distancing can enable particularly vulnerable clients to work through psychological processes on a symbolic level where literal confrontation with material could meet with resistance or prove overwhelming. Jung's understanding of image, symbol and metaphor in psychology, and the language of myth, fairy-tale and dream, are crucial to this way of working. Campbell (1988) suggests, as Jung did, that the anatomy of the psyche is indeed mythic:

> Dream is the personalised myth, myth the depersonalised dream; both myth and dream are symbolic in the same general way of the dynamics of the psyche... it has always been the prime function of mythology and rite to supply the symbols that carry the human spirit forward.

Estés (1992) animates clearly the relationship between psychology and story telling, claiming that story is medicine and telling a healing art. She claims:

> In dealing with stories we are handling archetypal energy, which is a lot like electricity. It can animate and enlighten, but in the wrong place and at the wrong time, in the wrong amount, like any medicine, it can have no desired effect... archetype changes us.

Much inspired by Sesame, I am interested in developing this healing art form in the context of therapy, working with appropriate archetypal material in response to differing psychological needs. 'Only the bare bones of the story is what is needed' suggests Watts (1992) so that the group can embroider and enrich through their own interpretation. I may at times offer a particular story or myth for enactment if it seems that it could help a situation or circumstances. Similarly I might also mine those that are already present in the group or individual's consciousness to serve the same purpose. Clear ritualistic structures are necessary for the expression and containment of powerful archetypal energy.

I often work with the Greek myths which I have always had a particular affinity with; tales of gods, heroes and mortals including encounters with monsters, metamorphosis, true love, murderous hate, wild animals, tragic romance, envy, divine providence and retribution, aggression, sex, death and rebirth. This is the 'stuff of the unconscious' and the myth provides a dramatic form, a container for exploring such territory safely. The enactment builds bridges between the conscious and unconscious, the personal and transpersonal.

> The unconscious yields an endless and self-replenishing abundance of living creatures, a wealth beyond our fathoming... the only way to get

at them in practice is to try to attain a conscious attitude which allows the unconscious to cooperate instead of being driven into opposition.

(Jung 1966)

Through mythical enactment it becomes possible for clients who may not be able to speak through words to work in depth with the unconscious psyche. Improvised movement, free voice and percussive instruments, more expressive of the archaic nature of this material, are prioritised over the use of language. For example, a woman who usually seemed very introverted and without speech was inspired to play the role of an aggressive giant in a myth. She used large cymbals and expansive gestures to create its huge body and thunderous voice. Another somewhat armoured and 'tough' male, again without language, chose to play the role of a small wounded bird. He used a flute to play the sound of his broken wings. Later the bird cried while receiving some very tender care and attention in the process of mending his wings. This is an example of the regressive, existential and transpersonal interweave discussed earlier being made possible through the dramatic medium. In both these cases where words were unavailable it was through drama and movement that they were able to make safe inroads into previously unconscious or unrecognised aspects of themselves. There is much more to be written on this subject.

Joseph Campbell (1988) describes myth:

> It is the realm that we enter in sleep. We carry it within ourselves forever. All the ogres and secret helpers of our nursery are there, all the magic of childhood. And more important, all the life potentialities that we never managed to bring to adult realisation, those other portions of ourself are there; for such golden seeds do not die. If only a portion of that lost totality could be dredged up into the light of day, we should experience a marvellous expansion of our powers, a vivid renewal of life.

The Moving Imagination

My experience continually leads me to believe that given the appropriate conditions, relationships and resources, the imagination, once mobilised, will itself naturally provide the necessary symbols and metaphors for healing. What has been termed 'active imagination' by Jung and his contemporaries can therefore be a powerful tool. 'Fantasy images are both the raw materials and finished products of the psyche and they are the privileged mode of access to knowledge of the soul' (Hillman 1990). For people with learning disabilities who are maybe just beginning to discover their own 'author'-ity, the process of creating their own imaginary sequences and stories can be very valuable. Gersie (1992) has considered carefully the role of 'story making' in therapy.

Facing Change

In facilitating such work with this client group facing the sort of changes I have discussed previously, many of the images emerging from individuals and groups have been, not surprisingly, concerned with transformation. Just some of these that have been chosen for dramatisation have included: caterpillars, building a chrysalis and then re-emerging as butterflies; frogs that get kissed and change into princes; primal creatures breaking out of eggs; removing one set of clothes and leaving them behind to find new ones; and snakes shedding their skins. The enactment of archetypal images of transformation involving symbolic death and rebirth can provide a ritualistic form through which participants can come to terms with the process of change.

Facing the Challenge

Similarly another issue I have discussed which is of current significance for this group as a whole is that of overcoming the negative side-effects of living with a label that by definition assumes that 'you can't' or 'aren't able to'. This can be a tremendous hurdle to overcome. For example, in the words of one client who used the image of a ladder to articulate what he wanted to say:

> The ladder represents the stages of life. God is at the top and chooses some people to come up, and others he doesn't want he pushes back to the end of the queue. He knocks them off the ladder. It's like me. I've been pushed off so many times... I feel hurt, angry and frustrated... People say 'YOU CAN'T – END OF STORY'. But I keep trying to climb back on again.

One way in which I have approached this issue 'obliquely' is to set a task where the combined bodies of a group create a mountain while each group member individually climbs this. Therefore they find their own way up, down, over, under, around and through a physicalised obstacle course, accompanied by appropriately dramatic music. To meet this challenge can involve determination, will-power, courage, commitment and trust as well as a sense of humour. It is a symbolic heroic venture, parallel to the task of individuation.

Having used my own imagination to begin stimulating the group's, I might develop this by inviting them to think of their own heroic tasks or journeys. Again, just some of these that have been chosen by individuals and groups for dramatisation include: travelling across dangerous rope bridges while flames leap below; rowing from one side of a fast flowing river to the other; leaping across deep and vast chasms; knocking down and climbing over walls; breaking out of prisons; and fighting with dragons and/or evil creatures.

In one group I asked them to bring a piece of music that helped them think of facing up to challenges with the opportunity to share an interpretation through movement if they chose. I found their responses to this very moving. One man brought the Vangellis music 'Chariots of Fire' and provided his own very focused self-contained slow motion run for its duration. Another man came with the theme tune to the TV show *Gladiators*. He danced out many aspects of the strong, animalistic popular culture heroes from this.

In these examples clients have made use of symbolic and ritualistic structures, thereby exploring the themes of radical change and heroic accomplishment. Through the enactment and embodiment of their imagery we see people inventing their own rites of passage. As Dekker (1989) suggests 'Imagination used creatively is a dynamic medium. The capacity to image and embody moves consciousness into incarnation and where necessary into renewal'.

But what happens in the case of those individuals who may not feel able to make such 'heroic' journeys? To face that river, that wall or that mountain? It is so important that people do so in their own time, at their own pace, and in their own way, particularly so for a client group who may have been governed by controlling institutional rhythms in the past. Some may simply not be ready to attempt such transitions, while others perhaps can act out their heroism in the process of resistance. A client who decides not to participate in any group activity can be really strengthening their sense of self and ego identity in the process. This highlights the value of long-term therapeutic work in which people are simply given time.

Facing the Feelings of Inability

Some may need help to deal with introjects (Clarkson 1989). These can be internalised beliefs about their capability swallowed whole and never re-examined or investigated in terms of their relevance or applicability. For example one man when invited to participate in group activities would sometimes repeat out loud 'You can't do that, you're stupid!' It was as if this activated the replay button of an introjected voice he had heard in the past which was still controlling him in the present. Similarly a parent once said to me while I was working with her son that she couldn't understand why I did drama with him, because didn't I know he was mentally handicapped! It is hardly surprising that these men suffered from very low self-esteem concerning what they were capable of, and I would suggest that affirmative rituals to improve self-image and self-confidence can be a vital component of therapeutic work with this client group. I would often invite these men in particular to find postures and gestures, to invent physical sculpts and verbal statements which affirmed their competence and potency. In order to internalise new and different beliefs about themselves I have sometimes used such structures as a preface to creative risk taking. A particular favourite was raising arms, fists clenched, above the head to state clearly and simply that 'I can!'

Sometimes I will locate the 'introject' as a 'spoiling voice' and invite people to build characters based upon them. These may be realistic or can grow larger than life, become grotesque caricatures or monsters. Embodying the spoiling voice in this way can help to bring its inhibiting influence and destructive effects into conscious awareness. This allows the individual to externalise the otherwise unconscious power it may be having over them. Having done so they may choose to role-play a dialogue with it. They may want to kill it or find their own special way of disempowering, releasing or letting it go. Many a spoiling voice, once externalised and disidentified, has made an 'imaginative' exit via the window or door, being satisfactorily evicted and exorcised from the group.

One man wrote down and then read out all the names he had been called as a child, all the playground insults he remembered from the past. He said he had felt like 'bone china – easily broken-hearted... They hurt so much, the pain is still there.' I asked him 'What would you say to those people who called you names if they were here with us now?' He replied 'I'd say to the boys now "What makes you take the piss? – You could be like this too!"' He decided to tear up the paper with the names on it into little pieces and throw them in the bin. He wanted to relinquish the powerfully detrimental effect that they had had over him. He said 'I am angry and frustrated but the child inside must learn to forgive and forget. How else can you ever make a proper world where we can understand one another... I've got to look forward to a better world.'

A young man in his early 20s whom I worked with at length some years ago, both individually and in a group, found the weight of his so-called 'learning disability' overwhelming at times. He once said 'I feel all the odds are stacked against me.' I responded with an intervention in role by standing up and saying 'I am the odds and I am stacked against you, let's see if you can push your way through.' He rose to the challenge and with arms outstretched and palms facing pushed and shoved with all his might as I used my own strength and weight to resist. Eventually he began to gain some ground and slowly bit by bit he managed to shift me from one side of the room to the other. Here I was carrying the transference of his disability, and I didn't make it easy for him. Through the drama and movement he found the strength and will to stand up to these and determine his own way forward. This exercise was to inspire confidence in his capabilities, he told me later.

One image that I regularly refer to for myself which captures an aspect of the role of the therapist and function of the dramatherapy group is that of a splint, in place for a necessary period of time while a wound heals and the body regains strength. In this example we see the literal embodiment of this metaphor.

To consolidate this kinaesthetic experience I asked him to think of a visual image which encapsulated what he had done. He said he felt like 'a bull – standing firm'. I invited him to lie down, relax and breathe in this animal metaphor. From then on he would often refer back to this occasion claiming he needed to find his 'inner bull' in one situation or another.

Nowadays he is an extremely active representative for this client group involved in advocacy group work and talking on living with learning disabilities. Having read the chapter, given permission for publication, and chosen quite specifically to be named, I invited Gary Butler to speak for himself on the subject. He wanted very much to take this opportunity, and decided perhaps somewhat appropriately to write the end of the chapter himself.

> I found it very challenging to actually talk about my own feelings and emotions, and to have someone talk to me as if I was a human and not something that had been chucked away. It helped me to rebuild my confidence that had been destroyed. I am capable of things that people in the past have said I am not capable of. I draw on my experience of drama and movement therapy to help me out with problems and have a sense of power for myself. Once upon a time people with learning disabilities were shoved aside and its hard to face up to that truth and not sweep it under the carpet. I feel that now we are breaking down barriers and people are beginning to listen. It's like being put in a cell on your own and you have to find the key that unlocks the door to your freedom. The therapy was that key for me.

References

Buber, M. (1970) *I and Thou* (trans. Kaufmann). Edinburgh: T & T Clark.

Campbell, J. (1988) *The Hero With A Thousand Faces*. London: Palladin Books.

Casement, P (1985) *On Learning From the Patient*. London: Tavistock Publications.

Cattanach, A. (1992) *Drama For People With Special Needs*. London: A & C Black Publishers Ltd.

Clarkson, P. (1989) *Gestalt Counselling in Action*. London: Sage Publications.

Clarkson, P. (1993) *On Psychotherapy*. London: Whurr Publishers Ltd.

Dekker, K. (1989) 'Sesame'. Unpublished document.

Erikson, E. (1977) *Childhood and Society*. Hertfordshire: Paladin.

Estés, C.P. (1992) *Women Who Run With the Wolves*. New York: Ballantine Books.

Gersie, A. (1992) *Earth Tales: Storytelling in Times of Change*. London: Greenprint.

Gersie, A. and King, N. (1990) *Storymaking In Education and Therapy*. London: Jessica Kingsley Publishers.

Hillman, J. (1990) *The Essential James Hillman: A Blue Fire*. London: Routledge.

Joines, V. and Stewart, I. (1987) *T.A. Today*. Nottingham: Lifespace Publishing.

Jung, C.G. (1966) 'The psychology of the transference'. *Collected Works 16*. London: Routledge and Kegan Paul.

Keleman, S. (1975) *The Human Ground*. Berkeley, CA: Center Press.

Mitchelson, M. (1993) 'Sesame.' Unpublished article.

Plaut, F., Samuels, A. and Shorter, B. (1986) *A Critical Dictionary of Jungian Analysis*. London: Routledge and Kegan Paul.

Polster, E. and Polster, M. (1973) *Gestalt Therapy Integrated*. New York: Vintage Books.

Rowan, J. (1992) *Integrative and Eclectic Therapy: A Handbook*. Milton Keynes: Open University Press.

Sunderland, M. (1992) 'Integrative arts psychotherapy.' Unpublished diploma.

Tsu, L. (1973) *Tao Te Ching*. (English, J. and Feng, G. Trans.). Hampshire: Wildwood House.

Watts, P. (1992) 'Therapy in drama.' In S. Jennings (ed) *Dramatherapy: Therapy and Practice 2*. London: Routledge.

CHAPTER THREE

Dramatherapy and Out-patient Support Groups

Lorraine Fox

Introduction

This chapter will discuss the clinical approach dramatherapy has with an out-patient support group. This particular group is available for people who have mental health problems, having been referred from primary health care to the specialist services of a community mental health team, acute in-patient and/or acute day hospital.

As part of setting up an out-patient support group this chapter will examine the process involved in defining a need for the particular client group. The reader will also have the opportunity to view the procedure of setting standards of referral, assessment and discharge. There has also been an attempt at some form of evaluative process vital to the functioning of a dramatherapist in the present economic climate.

The model offered in this chapter involves three concepts, structure, process and outcome. The structure details the setting up of the group. The process involves the dramatherapeutic interventions used in the sessions and the outcome reflects the evaluative process essential to clinical practice.

Structure

This section relates to the process involved in determining that there was a need for an out-patient support group. Need was determined by a simple form being sent to GPs within the area to ascertain if they would use the service, should one become available. Inevitably a small return was expected. The same form was circulated to the acute in-patient and day hospital to determine whether these two units felt there was a need for a supportive group in the community. It is important to state that creating a need can provide a 'bolt-on' effect, that is, the provision and availability of a service not only determines, but can also create a need. However, further discussion with the agencies involved led to the setting up of a group, when and where this would be required further exploration.

As with any new venture, funding would be needed to establish where the group would be. Local facilities were explored to determine where would be most suitable, taking into account the 'stigma' attached to hospital settings. However, the location of the outpatient support group was to be placed in the community, within the availability of public transport and ideally, with the possibility of creche facilities. This process involved two procedures, the first to determine if funding could be sought and second was to begin the group in a shared community setting with creche facilities on site. As the reader is no doubt aware, the difficulties of using rooms funded by other authorities limits the availability of these services. The group began in the only available 'slot' in an afternoon.

Another problem encountered by setting up this group in the community was the inevitable difficulty of refreshments. An important part of the group process is the 'coming together' for a cup of tea or coffee. A ritual that people are very familiar with.

Standards

REFERRAL CRITERIA

Each area of the hospital unit has different methods of assessment. However, as part of a community mental health team and a multidisciplinary team, the referrals are first seen by two members of the team from different professions, having been referred to the service by a GP. This process, of course, did not include all attenders within the service. Some community psychiatric nurses and social workers became part of the team, bringing their caseload with them. However, the GPs, once notified of the out-patient support group, could refer to the service and one of the assessors would be either the co-worker or myself. Therefore, if a person was referred to the community mental health team, assessment would reveal what form of contact was required within the clinical multidisciplinary team weekly meeting.

If attendance was to be part of the care plan, it was then that an assessment for the group was carried out. A simple form was compiled which enabled both the workers and the person referred to feel 'at ease' yet provide information. Attendance at a new group, no matter what experience a person has had, can be quite difficult on occasions. There can be an argument for discussing the group with the client, rather than completing the form.

However, as clinical audit is becoming more important in clinical work, written evidence of patient contact is vital in the evaluative process.

If referral was received from other parts of the unit, this process highlighted the fact that the group was part of the person's package of care. The referral was then processed by the co-worker and myself to ascertain the person's own views as to their attendance at the group.

Assessment format

As an ongoing group the assessment format encompasses this aim and is not intended to be taken as the only form of assessment a dramatherapist would use.

Assessment Form

NAME: . . . . DATE: . . . .

ADDRESS: . . . . TEL. NO: . . . .

. . . .

DIAGNOSIS: . . . .

*RMO: . . . . GP: . . . .

MEDICATION: . . . .

Reason for attendance:

Experience of other groups:

Still attending? – if so what type of group:

Views of attending the community support group:

Are creche facilities needed?

Currently attending the hospital?

Expectations of attending the group:

Referring agent:

Form completed by:

Date:

(*registered medical officer – consultant psychiatrist or GP)

Informing GPs and referring agent

As part of the health service, cover is provided by a registered medical officer who is the consultant psychiatrist. It is imperative that the consultant psychiatrist is informed that a patient continued to attend, is absent from the group or is due to be discharged.

Often a GP and consultant psychiatrist will be used to their patients attending various groups offering different services. However, this situation has now been changed, particularly with fund-holding health practices. There is a need for medical records to provide charges for care provision by different health professionals.

A consultant psychiatrist who has regular contact with a patient needs to know what activities the person for whom they have responsibility for, is doing. It provides efficient feedback of what is happening in an individual's life and how the patient functions within the group setting, taking into account their mental health over a period of time. A consultant psychiatrist may have responsibility for quite a number of patients and it is in everyone's best interest that the communication channels are open and informative.

The GP and consultant psychiatrist need to know some or all of the following:

- whether the person is attending the group;
- relevant recent important information;
- rate of attendance and reasons for failure to attend;
- short formulation of presenting difficulties.

The following guidelines formulated by the co-worker and myself provide an effective communication between the support group and referrer.

Process of informing the referrer

This may be done:

- as the person is referred to the group;
- at first attendance;
- as an update in the first month and thereafter three monthly;
- if the individual fails to attend whether reason is given or not;
- upon discharge, including the reason for discharge.

An out-patient support group is viewed as an important mechanism in a package of care. The above criteria are functionally effective if all is well. However, it is important, should anything happen, that the RMO and GP be informed accordingly to provide support to the professional involved in the group.

Some examples of this may be the following:

- if a person is not as well they can be;
- if there are other factors such as illness/death in the family;
- if a person needs other services.

Discharge procedures

As with any ongoing group held over a certain period of time, the population of attenders changes for many reasons. Support may be seen as an ongoing process. Inevitably discharge is sought for many reasons, some of which are detailed below:

- the person fails to attend for personal reasons;
- the person's attendance is erratic and eventual discharge is sought after failure to attend because of failure to engage;
- attendance is not needed at this time by the person;
- the person is unable to attend due to return to work;
- the person wishes to attend other services within their area;
- the person does not wish to attend at this time.

The discharge policy for the group was defined following discussion with referring agents and other areas of the hospital.

Discharge policy

Out-patient support group

↓

Attendance ──────────────────────────→ ↑

↓

Failure to attend x 3   Letter to patient

↓   ↑

Letter to GP/consultant psychiatrist

↓

Failure to attend x 2 ───────────────────┘

↓

Discharge

↓

Lettter to consultant psychiatrist

↓

Letter to GP

↓

Complete discharge protocol

Statistics

This section will discuss the method of collecting statistics. The statistics, in this particular instance, relate to the numbers of people that have been referred to and attended the group. These numbers are collected and recorded on a weekly and monthly basis. These statistics are forwarded to medical records who in turn send data to the Information and Statistics Division annually. As well as the legal responsibility, collecting statistics provides important data for audit purposes and will provide valuable information in determining the skills available within the 'market place' for GPs to purchase.

Collecting statistics involves completing a simple form detailing *new* (N), *return* (R) and *total* (T). As a member of a community mental health team, a similar format is adopted specifically for group numbers. A section of this form detailing dramatherapy statistics is as follows:

DRAMATHERAPY

Out-Patient	N	R	T

The group form is detailed as follows:

DRAMATHERAPY GROUP

Type and Place	N	R	T

A new referral to the group is a new patient at first attendance thereafter a return. The results of this data will be discussed on page 46.

Process

This section will discuss the process and application of a particular dramatherapy model and developmental paradigm. As a dramatherapist, it is important to strive to work within a model as it provides 'safe' parameters for clinical work. Using the metaphor of a map, the model provides a guide on the journey of working with specific groups. A simplistic metaphor, but as I hope to point out, enabling safe practice.

As stated, in the first section of this chapter, this group began in a community centre using a room made available for two hours, one afternoon per week. There were creche facilities available on site. However, one of the difficulties encountered was the expectation that providing a room for the group would enable the professionals based in the building to refer to this group. This was not possible, due to the fact that RMO cover was provided by a consultant psychiatrist. It is also important to state that one of the standards set for this group involved the process of referral which had to be made by the GP to the psychiatric services.

The theatre model of dramatherapy offers the following criteria as defined by Meldrum: 'Thus a theatre model of dramatherapy would expect to have the following ingredients: an actor/client, or a group of actors/clients; a director/therapist; a set space; an agreed period of time and a common goal' (Jennings *et al.* 1994, p.22). The following criteria were met:

- a group of clients;
- co-worker and dramatherapist – director/therapist;
- community room – set space;
- two hours, one afternoon per week – time period;
- common goal/objective – out-patient support group for people with mental health problems having been referred to the psychiatric services.

The stage is set, actors in place and therapists waiting.

The group began with a structure of half hour arrival and refreshments, one hour work and half hour sharing. This was not exclusive to each session. As an out-patient support group, individual difficulties may be important. Pacing and timing of the group is obviously at the discretion of the co-worker and myself. An important factor in this decision-making process is the professional knowledge that the co-worker and myself have of the clients.

The group began with eight referrals. The range of problems and diagnoses was defined by coding for audit purposes. All members of the group were known to the services.

There were 28 sessions held in this particular venue until funding was obtained for a community room. The first ten weeks of beginning the group used a range of dramatherapeutic techniques which offered a safe and secure structure. I propose to highlight the first session as an example, rather than list what techniques were used.

First session

The aim of the session was to introduce each member of the group and realise what support means to individuals and the group.

Image work was shared with group members; a group sculpt was shared with group members; a group sculpt completed as a method of developing skills and creativity. Single words were encouraged, beginning the sharing and providing a common language for everyone. Individual's heard what others were saying and demonstrated their own view of support. As Jennings writes, 'The dramatherapy group is the empty stage which enables these images to be represented at different levels' (Jennings 1987, p.14). This session was a positive beginning due to the ease of sharing and method used in group therapy. The room was technically an empty stage, with the inevitable large easy chairs and coffee table that often form part of group rooms. However, the work began from an empty stage and an ensemble built.

As with any out-patient support group, not all attenders feel the same all of the time. One such occasion involved six group members.

Session 19

Upon arrival, there were lots of 'chatting' from four members who had obviously met while walking to the group. The community room was a good 20-minute walk from the town centre. Therefore, some 'sharing' had begun prior to arrival. Two other members arrived separately. A feeling of being 'left out' could be sensed. Refreshments and an up-date of the week using different space in the room, and a single word to represent feeling and events of the week. There appeared to be lots of excitement from the four who met on their way to the group. There were lots of 'things to say' and actions, but at no time did they include the two other people.

Members of the group were asked to find a partner and relate positive significant events at a certain stage of their life. Each person was given a few moments before sharing with their partners. They then changed partners and again shared the significant events they had just heard. A final change of partner completed the task of sharing with each group member. This process had enabled the two members who felt 'left out' to begin to relate to each other on an individual basis. Next, the group formed two groups of three, taking the essential elements of what they had heard and making an image (sculpt) which depicts their own and others they had heard. These images were then given a working title, a technique familiar to all dramatherapists.

There was sharing and lots of understood laughter. The two sculpts were then shown again, mirrored with the other group who related the working title with one added word and vice versa.

Finally, the task of creating one large sculpt from the two, with the notion of keeping the original image and attempting to add words used in the warm up. The group were encouraged to try different methods of determining what the title would eventually be. During the sharing everyone appeared to feel part of the group. A group member did, during part of the session, state how 'left out' she had felt at the beginning but added that she was 'ok' now. This disclosure enabled the four people to state that they had just met by chance.

REFLECTIONS

The dramatherapist has to work where the group want to begin. Thoughts of whether it would have been better to work with individual difficulties is a dilemma. However, as the group is supportive dramatherapy, it is important to work within the stated boundaries. Individuals in this group could have used 'feeling left out' as a starting point for the work. However, it is important to state that in supportive work the group process was important in this particular session.

Supportive work in this particular setting was far from ideal. At one point the referral rate had dropped so significantly that the co-worker and myself began evaluating the needs for this group.

A variety of techniques were used to determine the needs of the group members for supportive work. This was in a sense 'open-ended', depending largely on individual motivation and the realisation of other factors in the participants' lives. Therefore the model of dramatherapy which Jennings and Mitchell have discussed extensively is, I believe, applicable to this particular supportive out-patients group (Jennings 1992a; Mitchell 1990a, 1990b, 1994) This provides an opportunity to develop participants' creativity and generate the 'health and well-being' of the individual. As Gordon Wiseman states, 'I believe passionately that creativity allows us to explore our positive potential: it doesn't look for the bad areas within us and therefore label us, it looks for the positive areas and encourages those' (Jennings *et al.* 1994, p.168).

The members of the out-patient support group have had many different experiences due to their 'illness' and, by utilising the dramatherapeutic model and developmental paradigm, it allows the client to explore their own creativity which generates self-confidence and self-esteem. A 'bold' claim but important to an individual who feels that they have lost their confidence and self-esteem. As Grainger (1990) states, 'In the case of depression, someone who was sure about his or her relationship with other people is sure no longer, and hovers between hope and despair, striving to recapture the sense of belonging that they enjoyed before their image of themselves was shattered' (p.41).

Perhaps it is time for another vignette taken from the group's second year. The venue has now changed to a local community hall, a medium-sized room with movable comfortable chairs and tables. There is a working space and a sitting space. All group members approved of the change of venue. Public transport was available just outside, creche and local town facilities were a two-minute walk away. Less stigma was attached to the setting which was a well-used local resource. This room was available throughout the year, closing only for two weeks in summer and winter.

The group reformed with new members who felt apprehensive about the group. The reader may like to know that there was an information sheet given to anyone who had been referred to the group, providing details of where and when the group was held, including the time, contact person and telephone number.

The vignette will provide an example of what happens when new members join an existing group. What has often been discussed in the group is the fact that a new 'attender' will always describe walking in the door as the most 'frightening thing that they have ever done'. It is therefore important for the dramatherapist to recognise that a person arrives at the group feeling as although they have 'overcome' a difficult obstacle. The fears that may have become part of this involve the telling of one such story.

Session 44

The aim of the session was to enable new participants to feel part of the group.

The group was asked to remember a similar feeling that occurred when they were young. There was a tentative suggestion that it could be their first day at school; they were to share with the person next to them what it felt like when left by whoever had taken them there and how it felt meeting a new teacher or another significant person. Words such as stern, busy, feeling small, were disclosed. Each member then chose one word that was personally significant to them, for whatever reason.

They formed two small groups, four people in each group. A commonality exercise was introduced as often described by Mitchell (1990a, 1990b). Each person chooses one experience and shares with other members of the group. The group then present this non-verbally and sequentially – all four members doing the same action with each person's chosen experience. Presentations were shared and attempts were made to guess what the experiences were. There was shared laughter by the group members.

The group were then asked to remember stories that had a journey which involved a character facing some form of fear/anxiety. Members of the group provided examples of stories. The groups were given large pieces of paper and pens, and chose a small part of a particular story. The task was to choose images of what the character faced on their journey. The co-worker and myself were available if required to help group members. As Read Johnson suggests in his chapter, 'The dramatherapist "in role"': 'The sidecoach functions at the boundary of the playspace, every once in a while opening the door and making a suggestion' (Jennings 1992, p.115).

The suggestion is that, as sidecoach, the co-worker and myself were able to ensure that each member placed something on their journey. A story was compiled of each character's journey. Each group chose their story teller and related the character's journey in any style they wished, while the other group provided the audience.

The first group used simple rhythmic sound while the story was told and the second group chose to present their's non-verbally. The aspect of using simple movements in a somewhat spontaneous way is discussed in Grainger's (1990) book, 'What concerns us here is movement and gesture used expressively in ways that are spontaneous and expressive, owing more to feeling than to thought' (p.51).

The boundaries provided the 'safe experience' of sharing the presentation with the audience. Members of the group shared the feelings their characters had and compared them to their first experience of arriving at this group. The established members tended to reflect on their own memories of being a 'first-time attender', while enabling new members to feel less isolated. The sharing of this experience had enabled all members to feel that there was a sense of belonging to the group.

REFLECTIONS

The dramatherapist with supportive work often has to begin with the group process. This provides new and established group members with an opportunity to form some kind of relationship. The level of work has therefore to 'model' this. The structure had enabled the group to develop their own experiences in a positive manner, each person had been able to relate to the structure of the group and left feeling a part of it.

Session 55

This vignette is of a session which was particularly difficult, due to economic and environmental factors present at that time. Motivation was quite poor and the group were determined to avoid the aim of the session. It is therefore a problem that dramatherapists have in whether to 'move' or allow the group to sit where they are. It thus seemed appropriate to enable individuals to vocalise their opinion from the present position, that is, from where they were sitting. The atmosphere of the group appeared to reflect their lack of power as individuals to change the status quo in their lives. The aim of this group was then empowerment using their individual rights within the session. While participants were predominantly 'stuck' in to both the topic and their chairs, this change of tactic worked.

The group 'warm up' began with the 'passing of objects' to each other and then changing these to objects of power. The group then created these objects out of paper, and symbolised their use by remembering their favourite story, either read to them or by them to their own children. They used just a line of the story and shared the use the object had within the story. De-roling the objects was achieved by the end of the last person's story and the 'stuckness' they had arrived with felt less oppressive. The group did voice their own feelings they had brought to the group and each member placed this in a box and received something else. Group members offered their feelings of stuckness and hopelessness, etc. and gained feelings of hope and laughter back.

REFLECTIONS

The group, by using this form had been able to ventilate their feelings of how they felt. The co-worker and myself felt that it was important to allow the dramatic fiction to 'happen' while participants were sitting down. Empowerment is not easily gained but, if during the session they had begun to feel in 'control' by sitting in the chairs, then it was important.

In this final vignette, there are changes happening within the group. Some members have been working towards discharge and have begun to 'separate' from the group with the impending date looming closer. The group waited for members to arrive and the usual ritual of tea and coffee began. Events of the week pertaining to participants were discussed. Themes of change emerged in the group. This 'change' was obviously different for each individual person in the group which involved making decisions regarding the present and future problems.

The group began to discuss relevant titles and an accompanying tune. Words were changed to relate to their individual problems. Participants found a line that they felt was appropriate. This line was either from a well-known song or their own. Finding a voice for these dilemma's was not a problem, however, the solution proved to be more problematic. The group therefore started up a sequence of the stated line and the echo from the group members. Some 'shift' had begun.

In the sharing part of the session, members discussed particular problems in their lives and the reason why the line seemed appropriate to them. It would be impossible to say that a solution was available. However, an individual did say that hearing the problem had provided some semblance of order, and that often when something is voiced, the person who it is aimed at will hear an edited version for whatever reason.

Theoretical implications

This group provides an example of the basic principles as defined by Jennings, in that the distance that had been established on the journey of the individuals in the group had enabled exploration. The group had also experienced their own self and the other group members. Perhaps the most useful principle is that the metaphor for the journey had symbolised meaning which was demonstrated through their imagework and presentation (Jennings 1990, p.25).

The vignettes demonstrated the creative expressive model of dramatherapy. 'The model is intended to increase confidence and encourage people to be articulate' (Jennings 1990, p.29). This raises another important issue that, as previously stated, in dramatherapy, participants are able to work within their own skills and experience as group members. The range of examples shared with the reader demonstrates this with the fact that new and established members joined and departed the group.

The developmental paradigm has been presented in the vignettes. Embodiment, the first significant experience, was used in the memories that people had of attending an important event. This was shown to be evident in the fact that they had re-lived this experience by taking their own children to school. Projection was the image work on their journey to the group. Each person chose to be represented on their 'journey map' and the method of 'storytelling'. Role was highlighted in the fact that the individuals were able to present and represent their work to other members of the group.

The sharing that occurred in the group is, I feel, important. Many journeys to where the individual is at the present moment have been highlighted in the examples used here. Despite the fact that the group had established members, the approach also enabled new members to feel part of the journey of the group. As with supportive dramatherapy, group members were either newly ready to 'board', had been travelling for quite a while or were in fact ready to depart at the 'next station'.

Outcome

This section will discuss the types of evaluation used for this particular out-patient support group.

Evaluation

How can a dramatherapist prove that what they do works? This is not especially specific to dramatherapy but to all people working in health and social care settings. Any form of evaluation is open to interpretation. Perhaps it is more fruitful to ascertain the measures used in this clinical study in an attempt to determine the how far the group fulfilled its aims. The following methods were used:

- statistics;
- self-evaluation;
- group evaluation;
- therapist's evaluation;

We also considered what would have happened if this group had not existed.

Statistics

Due to the fact that the group was ongoing, the collection of statistics had to reflect this. Therefore a record of new referrals and attendances was collected for specific time periods.

This was presented in the following format:

Total attendance for first year	258
Average weekly attendance	5.5

This information would be recorded in an annual report for management proving that the service is financially cost effective.

Other details such as the financial cost of the hall hire and refreshments were detailed. The expense of having two members of staff was offset by the fact that they could see more people during two hours of groupwork than they would have seen within the two-hour period in individual work. This is one form of evaluation that appears to be somewhat difficult. However, as most organisations now realise the number of people sitting at, say, a performance is vitally important for the economic stability of the company.

Self-evaluation

Questionnaires designed for specific use with this group were circulated near the end of the financial year. The easiest form of evaluation to complete is the yes/no or 'tick' type. The evaluation form detailed here used both methods. The various headings related to:

- introduction to the group;

- length of attendance;
- content of the group.

An example of the evaluation form is detailed below:

Evaluation form

Were you given enough information about the group?   YES/NO

How long was it before you felt part of the group?

less than 1 month   3–6 months   6–12 months over   1 year

How long have you been coming:

less than 1 month   3–6 months   6–12 months over   1 year

Has this group helped you?   YES/NO

In what way?

What improvements would you like to see?

The form was completed anonymously. The rate of form completion was quite good.

Group evaluation form

This form used similar information detailed above but was completed within the sessions approximately every three months or just prior to new referrals attending the group. Details were again recorded in a report format.

Facilitator's evaluation

The co-worker and myself met on average every three months. As clinicians from different professions it was important to determine that the aims and objectives of the group were discussed. This meeting also had the aim of determining whether the needs of service users were being met and in line with the supportive mechanism of the group. It is important to add that this meeting was for business purposes only and did not preclude supervision which was regularly maintained.

Overall, it was felt that the group was effective in determining the needs of the organisation and service users. As an example, two group members had not been re-admitted into the hospital throughout their attendance. I realise that these are 'bold' claims but nevertheless this is important data. The service proved to be cost effective to the needs of the organisation. However, it is important to realise that while the group ran for two hours every week, the staff time required was approximately one session for clinical and administrative work. While the number of actual attenders was sometimes quite low, there was never any occasion when no one arrived at the group.

This method of evaluation determined that the needs of the individual group members were being met while keeping to the boundaries of supportive work. The fact that this 'work' did not at any time 'interfere' with any other profession involved with the group members was viewed positively. It was definitely viewed as an 'adjunct' to other services available within the multidisciplinary team, which as a dramatherapist, I feel proves without doubt the unique approach that dramatherapy as a specialist service has to offer.

Conclusion

This chapter has discussed the dramatherapist's role with an out-patient support group, detailing the structure, process and outcome.

The structure discussed the setting up of the group and informing the reader of the standards required and the procedure for ensuring an efficient communication network for all professions within the primary healthcare service and multidisciplinary teams based in hospital and out-patient settings.

The process offered vignettes and comparative evidence of a dramatherapy model with this particular form of supportive work.

The outcome suggested one evaluative process which determined that this group functioned effectively from the attenders', therapists' and organisational perspective.

I hope that the reader has found some of this model helpful. I have, on purpose, placed emphasis on the structure and outcome parts of this chapter. This is due to the fact that a dramatherapist is quite capable of doing dramatherapy. The problem that is often highlighted involves having an understandable structure that anyone can understand and proving that what is done is effective. I therefore hope that the contents of this chapter are helpful to the dramatherapist who is about to embark on their own journey in their clinical work.

References

Grainger, R. (1990) *Drama and Healing: The Roots of Drama Therapy.* London: Jessica Kingsley Publishers.

Jennings, S. (1987) 'Dramatherapy in groups.' In S. Jennings (ed) *Dramatherapy Theory and Practice for Teachers and Clinicians.* London: Routledge.

Jennings, S. (1990) *Dramatherapy with Families, Groups and Individuals: Waiting in the Wings.* London: Jessica Kingsley Publishers.

Jennings, S. (ed) (1992a) *Dramatherapy Theory and Practice 2.* London: Routledge.

Jennings, S. (1992b) 'The nature and scope of dramatherapy: Theatre of healing.' In M. Cox (ed) *Shakespeare Comes to Broadmoor. 'The Actors are come Hither'.* London: Jessica Kingsley Publishers.

Jennings, S., Cattanach, A., Mitchell, S., Chesner, A. and Meldrum, B. (1994) *The Handbook of Dramatherapy.* London: Routledge.

Meldrum, B. (1993) 'A theatrical model of dramatherapy.' *Dramatherapy 14, 2,* 10–1.

Mitchell, S. (1990a) 'The theatre of Peter Brook as a model for dramatherapy.' *Dramatherapy 13, 1.*

Mitchell, S. (1990b) Dramatherapy Northwest Workshop.

Mitchell, S. (1994) 'The theatre of self-expression: a "therapeutic theatre" model of dramatherapy.' In S. Jennings, A. Cattanach, S. Mitchell, A. Chesner and B. Meldrum (1994) *A Handbook of Dramatherapy.* London: Routledge.

Wiseman, G. (1994) Interview with S. Jennings, 'What is dramatherapy? Interviews with pioneers and practitioners.' In S. Jennings, A. Cattanach, S. Mitchell, A. Chesner and B. Meldrum (1994) *The Handbook of Dramatherapy.* London: Routledge.

CHAPTER FOUR

Dramatherapy with Children in an Educational Unit
The More You Look, The More You See

Di Grimshaw

Risks

To laugh is to risk appearing the fool
To weep is to risk appearing sentimental
To reach out for another is to risk involvement
To expose feelings is to risk exposing your true self
To love is to risk not being loved in return
To live is to risk dying
To hope is to risk failure
But risk must be taken
Because the greatest hazard in life is to risk nothing.

The person who risks nothing, does nothing, has nothing and is nothing

They say avoid suffering and sorrow
But they cannot learn, feel, change, grow or live.

Chained by their certitudes they are a slave, they have forfeited their freedom.

Only a person who risks is free.

(Anon)

Introduction

This chapter is a theoretical and practical exploration of the use of dramatherapy with children and young people who experience and are recognised as having emotional and behavioural difficulties.

The children, aged between 8 and 14 attend a small educational unit. Organisation of the unit includes class sizes of no more than six students, a staffing ratio of 1:3, use of behaviour charts, and the employment of a dramatherapist: all factors believed to contribute to a positive learning experience for these children, enhancing motivation, not only in the area of academic learning, but also in the many aspects of emotional and behavioural (re) learning.

My theoretical orientation has evolved principally from the theories of Melanie Klein, Donald Winnicott and Sue Jennings; together with the perspectives and beliefs of Alice Miller. My dramatherapy practice is also greatly influenced by the client-centred approach advocated by Carl Rogers, as the nature and content of the therapeutic process is ultimately determined by the individual child and his perceived needs.

Clinical vignettes of dramatherapy sessions with two young people are shared with the reader to illustrate how the developmental process of drama interweaves with the object relations model allowing the therapist a theoretical understanding of the child's 'inner' world, and thus the opportunity to facilitate the child's self-healing process. It follows that for the therapist to truly believe that the child in therapy has the ability to meet the needs of his own 'inner' child, she must first recognise the needs of her own 'inner' child. (Generally the masculine gender has been used throughout this chapter with reference to the child to avoid confusion with the female dramatherapist and with the mother.) A child plays more easily when the other person is able and free to be playful (Winnicott 1993). The focus of this chapter, however, is not the therapist's own process (Grimshaw, 1994), but rather on an exploration of the nature and value of dramatherapy with this particular client group.

Specific clinical considerations will be discussed and how these may be dealt with practically by the dramatherapist in an educational setting.

The chapter concludes by reflecting upon the relationship between therapy and the special educational provision made for these young people, whilst proposing a number of ways in which the child's emotional difficulties may be acknowledged and addressed in the wider educational context.

Behind the Mask of a Label

Children and young people identified as having emotional and behavioural difficulties are not generally looked upon compassionately or sympathetically by society. Their behaviour is often anti-social and unacceptable. Within many people, feelings of helplessness and hopelessness are aroused, frequently shown in anger, a need to control, a wish or urge to punish or to avenge. Frustration and stress experienced by teachers while trying to cope with these children is recognised in the Elton Report (Department of Education and Science 1989). A simple definition of the term, emotional and behavioural difficulties tells us *how* certain children behave (and that this behaviour is understood to be problematic), but it does not tell us *why* children behave in this way. We may know for example that a child is a non-school attender, or withdrawn, unable to concentrate, is disruptive or aggressive, yet the reason for, or cause of this behaviour evades us. Exploring the cause of the behaviour is not a means of excusing it. On the contrary, it is my belief that only by exploring and acknowledging the roots of a behavioural problem within a therapeutic context, can real and sustainable change take place.

I believe that all behaviour occurs for a reason. If behaviour is not understood then a person may be declared 'mad' or 'bad'. If that individual is a child or young person whose behaviour leads him into criminal activity, he may then be labelled as 'delinquent'.

I want to emphasise that not all young people experiencing emotional and behavioural difficulties will resort to criminal activities. However, a great many will. (In contrast, some children and young people will identify with the 'victim' role, experiencing themselves as passive and powerless, unable to make any positive changes in their lives.) I am concerned with the prevalent attitude in society which seems to be much less indulgent of young people. This growing intolerance has been reflected in the courts' increasing reluctance to accept that a child under the age of 14 may be ignorant of the difference between right and wrong. A law which has stood since Victorian times requiring the prosecution to prove that any child defendant under 14 knew what he was doing was 'seriously wrong' has recently been abolished by the High Court (Rhead 1994). This will almost certainly result in more children being put through the judicial system. Consider this in relation to the politically 'fashionable' attitude whereby workers are deemed 'do-gooders' for permitting and encouraging pleasurable or fulfilling experiences for these young people, and it becomes increasingly apparent that society on the whole is not concerned with understanding anti-social or criminal behaviour, only with punishing the perpetrator.

The issues are not simple enough to allow society to feel comfortable with this 'solution'. It is facile to believe that it is possible to isolate young people from mainstream society, label them as 'evil' or 'bad', punish them for their misdemeanours, and then possible for the same young people to subsequently integrate into society as 'reformed characters'.

It is precisely this 'splitting off' from society, this use of group labels in place of individual human beings, which further magnifies the internal or inner splits already experienced by these children. Rather too conveniently it also allows 'society' to abrogate any responsibility it may have towards these children and young people and their often pitiful circumstances.

It is interesting to note the etymological origin of 'delinquent'. The term is derived from the word 'relic' which itself means 'something left behind' or, 'something left undone'. I believe the dramatherapist's role is to enable the child to pick up those scattered pieces of himself, and to allow that child the space and time to explore and evaluate the pieces; to do what he needs to do in the process of healing himself.

The therapist's role is a specific one, and unless it is part of a wider culture where children and their needs are valued and respected, it can easily be rendered largely ineffectual. Positive behavioural changes thus need wider acknowledgement and validation, together with a societal responsibility in meeting a child's emotional, physical and educational needs.

Object Relations and Drama

The theory of object relations defined by Melanie Klein (1932) has as its core the belief that the human psyche and personality are determined, in part, by the interactions or relationships an individual experiences in the external world. These relationships take place, with others or parts of others defined as 'objects'. It is the relationship with the object and the individual's self-image in relation to the object which is internalised. That is, the psychic world mirrors these external object relationships.

The infant is seen to possess 'potentials' (Mahrer 1978) or an infinite 'repertoire of roles' (Landy 1986) or as being in a state of 'anlagen – that which will become' (Estés 1992).

The complex dramatic process of 'becoming' begins when the infant, having embodied enough of the 'object' (mother) to allow itself to *separate from* the mother, thereby creates the potential for a relationship *with* the mother.

Klein (1932) proposed that the infant's first experience of relational objects are the 'good' and 'bad' breasts, part objects of the mother (usually the infant's primary carer).

The dramatic nature of object relations lends itself perfectly to the metaphor of a theatrical stage. Once the potential for relationships has been created, the stage is set for the principal actor or 'protagonist', the child himself, to step out. He enters the 'potential space' (Winnicott 1971) with a mixture of eagerness, anxiety and expectation. He has internalised or embodied enough of the 'object' to believe and trust that he is not alone; and it is this trust which allows him to enter the space. Winnicott's 'potential space' is the place of play; the universal facilitator in the process of 'becoming' the self.

The protagonist is a sentient being, and is therefore vulnerable to many extreme sensations, some immensely comforting and pleasurable, some which threaten to destroy the shell-like fragility of the unevolved 'I', and all other sensations in between. He cannot tolerate or make sense of these sensations on his own. There has to be another on to whom he can project these seemingly contradictory states, thus relieving himself of the threat of annihilation. In order to contain these feeling states safely it is necessary for the protagonist to create two others, the first to hold the 'good' feelings (the good breast), the second to hold the 'bad' feelings.

If the mother herself is able to tolerate these feelings of 'good' and 'bad' within the protagonist's relationships with her, he comes to understand that the two others, the contradictory breasts both belong to the same object, the mother. This process of toleration is internalised and mirrored in the protagonist's inner world, giving rise to ambivalence. This is a creative acknowledgement in the drama of 'becoming' because it suggests choice and possibility.

I referred earlier to Winnicott's 'potential space' as the place of play. Winnicott (1971) believed that the self may only be discovered through the creativity of the individual and that the ability to create comes through play and play only.

What is it that the self creates in order to 'play' in the 'potential space' with another? Landy (1986), believing the self to possess an infinite repertoire of potential roles, proposes that through the process of role playing, the self is brought into relationship with another role, the embodiment of particular thoughts, feelings and behaviours, acts as a mediator between self and other. Thus the role in relation to the other is internalised or 'taken' into the psyche.

Implicit in the process of role taking is the phenomenon of identification, whereby the infant sees himself not only *doing* like the mother (sounds, gestures) but also *being* like the mother.

The mutual processes of role playing and role taking develop the self, and the evolving self will subsequently influence the nature of future role playing and role taking, role taking and role playing, and so it goes on. The self, considered to be greater than the sum of all roles realised in the individual's experience, is forever changing, however subtly, as the repertoire alters.

The term 'good-enough' (Winnicott 1971) most often used in relation to the primary object, the mother, is a means of communicating a sufficiently healthy relationship which sets the stage for the unfolding dramas to take place. The term suggests that the object relation need not be *all good*, nor could it possibly be *all good*, for how could something be considered good if there is no *bad* against which to measure it? Alternatively, if the mother object relation is deemed not good enough, that is, the inner mother is experienced as largely persecutory, indifferent or overprotective, then future relationships based on this primary one will be similarly perceived.

The creativity, or dramatic dialogue, lies between the 'good' and 'bad', without which there would be no potential for empathy or connection with the self and others. It may be suggested that the aim of dramatherapy is to facilitate this creativity through play and drama enabling healthy acknowledgement of both sides or poles.

Play is, by definition, a risk, for it exists in the interface between inner and outer realities; between the subjective and that which is objectively perceived.

The developmental play model (Jennings 1990) encompasses embodiment play, projective play and role play. Through the process of engaging his senses, the infant is able to relate to the environment and the objects he encounters therein. He is also beginning to develop an awareness of his impact upon the outside world. He realises that by making particular sounds and movements he can effect another's response. When he has embodied enough of the other (or others) it is safe for him to entrust these with his feelings and to imbue them with his meanings and interpretations.

Early embodiment play is a particularly sensitive phase in the developmental process, and without *enough* embodiment play a child will find genuine engagement in projective play or role play acutely threatening. This is illustrated in Winnicott's account of a young girl who suffered from frequent fits; causing her, understandably, to live in a constant state of anxiety. He discovered that she appeared unable to enjoy play (Winnicott 1971). Several sessions into the work, he noticed the child's intense fascination with her toes. Unlike the toys she momentarily engaged with, her toes could not be discarded. This, he observed, gave her great satisfaction. The fits (for which no obvious medical cause could be found) subsequently ceased. The girl's mother described her as a 'different child'. The significant discovery of toes took place whilst sitting on Winnicott's knee. The child was being physically held by another.

It is only when one encounters a child who is unable to engage fully in embodiment play that the fragile nature of play and creativity is understood. It is the therapist's task to bring the child into a state of 'being able to play'.

When a child's sense of self is sufficiently formed within, only then is he able to project outwardly, giving meaning to the objects he encounters. He is ready to engage in projective play.

Winnicott's 'transitional object' is an example of the developmental relationship between embodiment and projective play. The shift of emphasis from the good-enough breast to a thumb allows the child to separate from the mother and discover the same sense of security and comfort from his own body. Later, an inanimate object, such as a blanket or soft toy may be imbued with these same feelings. The toy, often given a name by the child, takes on a symbolic quality, 'as if' it were the mother, or part of the mother.

Stories, and fairy stories in particular, are a form of projective play. The fairy story is a metaphor for the basic human predicaments and inner conflicts a child will undoubtedly encounter throughout his life. The inner conflicts between good and bad are externalised through archetypal characters, and brought into relation to one another. A satisfactory resolution to the conflict reassures the child that hope is possible and life has meaning. Bettelheim (1976), whose exploration into the importance of fairy-tales is widely acknowledged, believed that the most important (and the most difficult) task is to help a child discover a meaning to life. Bettelheim, also a therapist to children with emotional difficulties, recognised the innate quality of fairy-tales by which the child is given the opportunity to form a sympathetic understanding of the aims and motives of the characters involved and thereby draw sense and meaning into his own existence and his place in the world.

Through the processes of projection and identification a child is able to take on a role in relation to another, and play out that role with the other (or with another 'other' who resembles or represents the original other in some way).

The range and quality of roles a child is able to develop and his readiness to experiment with new roles will greatly depend upon the role models he has encountered, and whether his own creativity has been allowed to flourish. Creativity in this sense is taken to mean the approach of the individual to the outside world.

If a child understands the world as a rejecting and meaningless place his capacity to relate in a meaningful way will be severely limited. His need to find meaning, fundamental to myriad potential roles, is hidden away. As a consequence, the roles better suited to surviving in a hostile world are brought to the fore. This misrepresentation of the self, or false self (Winnicott 1965), serves as both protector and jailer to the true self. It defends against the exposure of unmet needs, whilst perpetuating the belief through the roles it has taken that the world really is without meaning. The risk is not deemed worth taking.

Taking the Risk

A referral was made for individual dramatherapy for 14-year-old Jake, following yet another and more vicious incident of bullying. Staff believed Jake to be involved in the incident although his style of bullying was by proxy, wherein he would incite other boys into bullying smaller, vulnerable children. When confronted by staff, Jake would withdraw. This was perceived by the staff to be an act of defiance and showed an inability to accept any responsibility for himself and his actions.

The increasing frustration of the staff led them into a sense of hopelessness, which Jake understood as rejection. The staff had no means of penetrating the wall that Jake had built up around himself.

I wondered what it was that Jake saw in the vulnerable children he despised so much, and could tolerate so little, that he needed to destroy them? Or rather, to have them destroyed?

Was there also the hope that the vulnerable child would somehow overcome the bully, and win the conflict? In reality this hope never seemed to come to fruition.

Jake's mother left his father when Jake was seven. This loss in Jake's life, staff believed, had never been acknowledged. Jake resisted any invitation to communicate his feelings, although staff acknowledged these invitations usually came about after further confrontations, with both Jake and staff member still in crisis. It is not possible for a child to communicate freely his vulnerability when he considers himself to be under threat.

The one person Jake seemed to be emotionally attached to in any meaningful way was his father, who had kept in regular contact since Jake's admission into care at eight years old. Jake visited his father most weekends. Staff felt that Jake idealised his father, noting how Jake responded aggressively to any derogatory, or seemingly derogatory statement made about him.

A meeting was arranged with Jake's father, seeking his permission for Jake to enter into dramatherapy, should Jake himself agree. During this meeting his father expressed the thought that Jake would agree, explaining that Jake was a creative child and enjoyed writing stories. He did, however, comment on my being female and indicated that this could be problematical in the therapeutic setting.

Jake did agree to meet me; I felt sure his father's permission had something to do with that.

One of the comments written on Jake's referral mentioned his lack of eye contact, and questioned whether this could be improved. My sense was that his eye contact would only develop if he believed the risk of meeting someone else's eyes was worth taking. To focus directly on developing his eye contact would serve no other purpose than to add to his anxiety. In our first meeting I witnessed this small, lost-looking child looking anywhere other than at me.

Jake told me in a small, unsteady voice that his father had spoken about drama sessions. I explained that drama was not only 'acting' (he smiled slightly at this), it could also mean telling stories and drawing. 'I write my own stories', he told me. His father apparently knew about the stories, but Jake, explained that he didn't share *everything*; his father had 'enough to worry about'.

Jake applied himself to recreating these stories, in pictures and words with the precision and care of a draughtsman – head bowed and pencil held so tightly his knuckle turned white. I sat on the other side of an invisible, impervious screen.

All these early stories, had, as a main character, a fantasy creature, covered in brightly coloured fur and without arms. This creature, Dusty, lived alone in a mansion, his mother had 'passed away', his father had left home. Two other characters, the Jester and a seahorse called Holly appeared frequently in the stories and their influence dictated the outcome for Dusty each time, whatever the situation. The Jester, a roguish, mischievous individual, whose sole intention seemed to be to lead Dusty into dangerous or criminal activities, whilst Holly would attempt to protect Dusty and keep him out of trouble.

I first encountered Dusty in the process of building a time-machine and desperately in need of new parts. The Jester appears and suggests stealing a car together. Dusty is 'in two minds', he knows that it would not be right but a car would provide all the parts necessary. Holly tries to help Dusty resist the temptation, but fails. The car is stolen, Dusty is caught and sent to prison whilst the Jester manages to escape.

Released from prison the following week, Dusty would again be subjected to further conflict, and always the Jester seemed to win, leaving Dusty bewildered, hurt and usually in trouble.

In Jake's eighth tale, Dusty's father appears for the first time and has a surprise for his son. He has sold the mansion (and with it the unfinished time-machine) and bought a small cottage for them both to live in. I learnt at this point that Dusty's mother 'passed away' when he was seven. His father's advice was to forget her. Dusty is devastated at losing his precious time-machine and decides to strangle himself. Holly, however, is able to stop him. She assures him that he *still* has a lot to live for. The Jester is nowhere to be seen. I ask Jake what the Jester might do in this situation, 'probably just watch'.

In the following and final story, Dusty finds a girlfriend like himself, furry and armless, and they marry (much to the Jester's annoyance). Dusty's father attends the celebrations in a wheelchair as he is dying. Although Dusty did not manage to finish his time-machine, he achieved his other task; to be the 'complete opposite' of his father. The Jester is finally imprisoned, and Dusty remains in contact with Holly.

Jake's perseverance with the Dusty stories suggests his own need to stay with the conflict until he was able to find a satisfactory resolution. Erikson (1950) notes how a child will recreate in play a traumatic experience again and again in an attempt to master it. This recreation of a conflict situation was also a reality in Jake's outside world. The conflicts Jake experienced in his relationships with others had contributed to his being statemented as having emotional and behavioural difficulties in the first instance.

Through the stories, Jake allows the dramatherapist the opportunity for greater understanding of *his* perception of himself in relationship to the world; Jake's object relationships.

Dusty, the stories' main character, has a mission to build a time-machine. He is parentless, his mother 'passed away' when he was seven. In the outside world Jake has regular contact with his father, yet the story tells of Dusty being abandoned by his father, to live alone in a rambling, empty mansion.

When completed, the time-machine would transport Dusty back into the past or forwards into the future. What was it that Dusty needed from the past? What did he want from the future? Whatever his wishes they are thwarted by his returning father. Although the father's intention to be with his son again appears admirable, he knowingly or inadvertently causes the loss of the time-machine. The father's denial of Dusty's feelings in relation to his mother ('forget her') is a further indication that the machine was intended to revisit the past.

In reality, Jake could not express to his father his feelings in relation to the loss of his mother. He had witnessed as a seven-year-old his father's own distress and anger at her leaving. Jake internalised the father who could not, must not see this child's grief. In relationship to the inner father who needed protection was a small, bewildered child unable to show his pain. Nor could Jake allow himself to acknowledge the anger he had towards his father, after all, his father *let* his mother leave. With mother gone, Jake only had his father. How could he be angry with him? He might leave also, and then Jake would have no one. Jake could not tolerate anyone else being angry with, or disapproving of his father either, thus, in his outer world as in his inner, Jake's role in relation to his father was as protector. When Dusty's father sells the mansion and the time-machine, Dusty expresses no anger towards him. Instead the anger and despair are turned in on himself; he decides there is nothing worth living for.

In Dusty's darkest hour, he finds he is not alone. Holly, the seahorse, appears and Dusty is able to hear her for the first time. Previously, Holly had never been able to overpower the destructive forces of the Jester. Holly is able to reassure Dusty that despite the loss of the time-machine, he *still* has much to live for. The Jester, had he been 'present' would not have made any attempt to stop Dusty.

The characters of Holly and the Jester, according to object relations theory, are roles that Jake has internalised within his psyche.

The Jester, clearly a powerful 'shadow' lures Dusty into dangerous and criminal activities, whilst Holly looks on helplessly, yet *she is always present*. These two roles are always in conflict with one another. Although the Jester is not a positive influence on Dusty, he fools Dusty into believing the activities are necessary in order to build the time-machine. The Jester is a bully, achieving power through his humiliation and exploitation of Dusty. The time-machine is never completed, and one wonders if it *ever* would be if the Jester had anything to do with it.

The Jester part of Jake, scornful and hateful, too threatening to keep inside needed to be projected out on to others. Jake's intolerance of other children's vulnerabilities (that resonated with his own) and his need to gain power, legitimately or otherwise, culminated in the vicious bullying of these children. As with the Jester character, Jake learned how to incite others to commit the acts on his behalf.

Finally, the Jester is thwarted by Dusty as he overrides his advice and marries his girlfriend.

The stories ceased when Jake was able to create a number of satisfactory resolutions. Jake had reached a point of 'satiation' (Gersie 1987). Dusty is able to give up the hope of ever having a time-machine (the possibility of changing the past); he manages to imprison the Jester (a powerful role which has helped Jake survive, yet needs proper containment); and, of course, Dusty discovers that there is someone else *like him*. (Again, in object relations terms this would imply the discovery or creation of an inner ally.) The role of Holly is maintained. Dusty also achieves his other task; to be the 'complete opposite' of his father (this task was not apparent until the penultimate story). The father attends Dusty's marriage in a wheelchair. He is an invalid (he is *invalid*, he can no longer affect Dusty), and he is dying. To be the complete opposite of his father, Dusty would be, by definition, *living*, able to separate from his father and create a new life for himself with another.

It may seem surprising that qualities such as understanding, protection, empathy and love (generally regarded as positive attributes), were encompassed within the female role in Jake's stories. Was it possible that Jake had, in his early life, experienced enough good mothering to internalise some of these qualities? Where had Jake experienced these qualities?

To the outside world, Jake appeared to mistrust all females. He needed to protect against exposing his unmet needs; after all, life had taught him that women abandon you. He had learnt to deny his need for female love. Jake projected a sense of indifference towards women. This was supported in the session by his comments in relation to his mother, 'I don't care about her, because she doesn't care about me'. Jake had learnt to reject through his experience of being rejected.

Jake's need for love, protection and understanding from a 'mother' had not disappeared. These needs continued to exist within his inner world, and through his creativity he could acknowledge their presence in the outside world. The role of Holly, the protector, existed for Jake long before he came to dramatherapy. Now she could be witnessed by another; the dramatherapist. Jung (1964) believed that a child's use of imaginative expression in the presence of a therapist may enable him to release intense unconscious symbols at a critically emotional time.

As the dramatherapy progressed Jake discovered my stone collection, and seemed drawn towards one stone in particular. The blue tiger eye nestling in an array of rose quartz, citrine, turquoise and aventurine caught his attention and caused him momentarily to hold his breath. The stone reminded him of a toggle from a blue duffle-coat he once wore. The coat belonged to a hurt and lonely seven-year-old.

The stone allowed Jake to engage in a sensory experience, which, like embodiment play accesses unconscious 'bodily held' sensory memories. (What did his release of breath also release from his body?) Like George in the psychodrama group (Holmes 1992), Jake made a sensory connection between the stone and his duffle-coat, which in turn emotionally connected him to his mother, his relationship with his mother and his understanding of himself within that relationship. For the first time in his sessions, Jake sobbed as he recalled his memories, 'she didn't want me'. Through the symbolic association of the stone Jake could finally express the feelings of desperation and rejection he had suffered throughout the years, a time during which such expression had been repressed in order to survive.

It is not the task of the therapist to *become* mother in relationship to the child or to become a *better* mother than the child's own mother. The dramatherapist may have a personal or universal urge to mother a child such as Jake. Although the dramatherapist herself will possess qualities of under-standing, empathy, and dare I say, love, for a child, it is not her role to be mother. There is a subtle difference which may best be illustrated by examining the feelings evoked in the dramatherapist at this moment in the session.

As I witnessed Jake's pain, a powerful urge to hold and comfort him threatened to overwhelm me. In resisting this feeling, I began to experience a rejection myself. I was certain that what I was feeling was *my* need to stop his pain. I had to acknowledge that Jake's pain could not magically be taken away. The task of the dramatherapist is to be *with* the child in his pain and to trust him to find his own resolutions.

The 'tiger eye' session was Jake's first engagement in sensory, embodiment play. Whereas the stories allowed Jake a mental connection, the stone allowed a bodily connection.

In the following session (having explored the subject in supervision) I shared my dilemma, to hug or not to hug, from the previous week. Jake immediately responded with 'no one ever hugs me but my dad'. In addition, I shared why I had not acted on my urge. This, I believe, served two purposes; first, explicitly communicating to the child that the reason for being there was to explore *his* needs, and second, showing an ability to hold on to, to tolerate, conflicting needs.

Jake's catharsis, witnessed within the therapeutic setting, was an impor-tant step but not, as is often mistakenly believed, the final one.

A number of sessions passed where Jake chose to talk only of present-day events, how he planned to spend his weekends, what he had been doing in school and the like. His eye contact was now fleeting, perhaps once or twice during an hourly session.

When he did catch my eye, I sensed that he was not only *looking*, he was also *seeing*. He made no reference to his mother.

With the summer holidays fast approaching I wondered if Jake was retreating once more behind his protective wall.

He arrived at his next session, thoughtful and quiet. After our usual greeting his eyes remained fixed on me for what seemed an astonishing length of time. Finally, he broke the gaze, but not the silence. Then he asked if I had brought my stones. He took the blue tiger eye, deliberately and carefully, in his hands.

He stared at it, and turned it over again and again using his fingers. He began to tell the story. I strained to hear his small, shaky voice.

> I was outside, wearing my duffle-coat. By myself. I could hear my mum and dad rowing in the house. That's why I was outside, I'd run out. Just grabbed my coat. Usually it warmed me but today I'm cold. My hands are cold (he is still turning the stone). My mum shouts me inside. She's crying and she yells at me for not fastening my toggles. She holds out a glass of orange juice. I'm fastening my toggles, but my fingers are burning cold. She shouts something and I look up. She throws the orange in my face. It stings my eyes. She's all blurry. I hear my dad scream and I run away upstairs. I sit on the stairs. Cold, sticky, wet. They're screaming at each other now. Banging. Smashing. No one knows I'm here.

I ask Jake if he will 'be' the seven-year-old on the stairs. He hesitates but moves towards another chair. He is still holding the stone.

> 'I can hear them. My mum is crying. It goes all quiet and I don't know what's happening.'

'What are you feeling, Jake?'

> 'No one knows I'm here. Then the door slams. I *know* it's my mum. I want to tell her not to go, I don't mind about the orange juice. My dad's crying. I can hear him. He slams the kitchen door. I just sit there, holding my toggle thinking, 'if I can keep hold of it, she'll come back'.

After a moment of silent recognition, I ask him if he is able to come out of the scene and stand by me.

If you were watching this child sobbing on the stairs, what would you do Jake?

(Will you be like the Jester, or like Holly, I wondered.) He chooses to sit down next to the seven-year-old, and tells this child that things will be alright for him, and that he *still* has a lot to live for. His gaze never leaves the child by his side.

Finally, I ask if there is anything he could give to the child, to comfort him in his suffering. Jake gives the child a friendship bracelet, carefully tying in around the tiny wrist.

Jake becomes the seven-year-old again and I ask him what he is feeling now that he has heard those special words and received the bracelet.

'I know I'm alright. She won't come back now, but I know I'm alright.'

Jake's journey continues in dramatherapy. No doubt he will revisit this child at other times, having found him again. He will always miss his mother but crucially, he has now given himself permission to miss her.

One of the therapeutic aims in the work with Jake was to help him to better understand himself and his relationships with others. Jake's stories were both representations of his inner world and the means by which his inner world could be communicated to another. However, the communication stayed in metaphorical form, and only became explicit when it was safe to do this. Jake was then able to express some of the grief and pain he had repressed in relation to his mother, and her loss.

With some, particularly younger children, as in the case of Sammy, gaining insight is not necessarily a focus of the therapy. At times, the role of the therapist is *to be there* and to witness the expression of the child's repressed or denied feelings.

Sammy

Eight-year-old Sammy was referred for individual dramatherapy two years after her mother's suicide. Although Sammy was a rather introverted child, the teaching staff were increasingly concerned by the general lack of interest she showed in school. The change in Sammy had been gradual, a slow withdrawal into her own world. In the playground she could often be found standing alone, seemingly indifferent both to the weather and her classmates alike. When Sammy spoke, which was usually only in response to a question, her voice was soft and almost inaudible.

Sammy appeared most withdrawn during activities such as drama, music and PE. The physical and emotional freedom offered by these subjects caused Sammy much anxiety almost as if the noise and excitement threatened to overwhelm her.

My first encounter with Sammy was as observer in the weekly drama group. I noticed how this child, on entering the room, physically froze, her back against the wall, her eyes staring with bewilderment as she watched her five classmates rolling and tumbling over one another in play. Sammy was terrified. She muttered something about telling them to stop, and only when the group were settled could she risk joining it. Sammy sat slightly removed from the circle, resisting her neighbours' well-meaning attempts to bring her in closer. She recoiled from their repeated requests to hold hands.

The circumstances surrounding her mother's death were far from straightforward. Sammy's mother had suffered from prolonged periods of depression for most of her adult life which eventually culminated in her committing suicide shortly after Sammy's sixth birthday.

Sammy was admitted into local authority care a year after the death, at her father's request. He felt he could no longer take care of his daughter, particularly with his demanding work schedule and thought that she would be better taken care of by professional carers. He confessed to his feelings of awkwardness and embarrassment when Sammy spoke of, or asked about, her mother.

Sammy was gradually being introduced to her prospective foster parents, who sensitively understood the process could not be hurried.

There had been concern that Sammy may be autistic; her behaviour certainly suggested this at times. However, the teaching staff who had known Sammy prior to her mother's death were of the opinion that her present emotional state was a direct consequence of her bereavement.

The initial dramatherapy sessions were spent trying to establish the basis for a therapeutic relationship. This was not easy, and at times I wondered if this child would ever feel safe enough to risk making a connection with someone else. It was an effort to resist urging Sammy into some kind of encounter with me, and instead simply to be in the space with her.

I began to witness her presence, occasionally expressing some of my thoughts aloud, 'I wonder what Sammy would find in that box? She doesn't seem too sure. No, she's moving away. Perhaps another day she'll take a look.'

I noticed that she was listening to me, sometimes seeming to test my observation skills by making small deliberate gestures – lifting one foot a little off the floor, sticking the tip of her tongue out, wrinkling her nose. Sammy, the child everyone believed could not play, *was* playing. When the gesture was commented on she would smile in acknowledgement. At other times, I sensed the comments were an irritation to her, this often led to Sammy turning her back and curling up on a cushion. We would spend the remainder of the session in silence.

Sammy entered the room a little early one day and found me admiring a new monkey glove puppet. She paused fleetingly to glance at the puppet, then turned to remove her coat. We greeted one another in our usual way. She sat on a cushion a little away from me. The closest she had ever positioned herself. I continued to stroke the monkey, describing its softness and its thick, 'squidgy' tail. Sammy asked where it came from, and we had our first conversation about jungles and tall trees. Sammy proudly announced that she knew monkeys ate bananas, and bananas were her favourite food. She especially liked banana milkshake. She smiled when I asked if monkeys drank milkshake.

With the puppet still on, I laid my hand down beside me on the cushion. Sammy remarked that 'she', the monkey, must be feeling sad to want to lie this way. I looked at the monkey. She did indeed seem sad.

'Are you crying?' I asked the monkey.

'No, she's not', replied Sammy moving her cushion still closer. She stretched out her hand and began stroking the monkey's head, re-peating the words, 'she's not crying'.

'Even when you're very sad, monkey, you still don't cry?' I asked.

'No.'

'Would you like to cry, monkey?'

'She mustn't cry.'

'Where do all her tears go?'

'Down here' (Sammy pointed to her abdomen).

'She swallows them then?'

'Hmmm' (still stroking the monkey).

'They don't taste very nice, though, do they monkey?' (I shook the monkey's head slightly and noticed Sammy's silent tears.)

'I think you're crying a little now, aren't you monkey? We'll stay here with you whilst you cry. Sammy's crying with you. I think she may be feeling sad too.'

It was almost time for the session to end. I explained to the monkey that we would need to go soon, but we would meet again. The monkey gave Sammy a gentle pat and thanked her for allowing her to cry.

We said goodbye to the monkey and laid her in a box. Sammy hesitated then on her tiptoes she gently lifted the puppet out again, kissed it, then laid it down again. She whispered 'goodbye' and 'see you next time'.

The monkey became a key figure in Sammy's subsequent sessions.

Sometimes she was not feeling *too* sad, and on these occasions monkey might meet another character, often Badger who told the monkey fairy-tales. The monkey seemed particularly fond of two fairy-tales, Hansel and Gretel and Cinderella.

Sammy had formed an immediate identification with the monkey puppet, particularly when the monkey curled up on a cushion. At this point something resonated for Sammy. She recognised the monkey's sadness and responded by taking on a caring, comforting role. Sammy's understanding and empathy for the monkey informed me that the scenario was not unfamiliar to her.

In terms of developmental play Sammy moved freely through the spectrum of play. She was able to engage in embodiment play as she stroked and physically cared for the monkey. This developed into projective play as Sammy imbued the glove puppet with her own feelings and meaning. She then entered into a role play scenario, with the monkey in the role of someone who is sad and Sammy as a carer to the monkey.

Sammy allowed herself to take a risk by entering the 'potential space' (Winnicott 1971) and creating the possibility of a relationship between herself and the monkey.

I, too, had established the beginnings of an empathetic relationship with the monkey which was further developed as Sammy shared more background into the role. Thus, indirectly Sammy was also creating a 'potential space' between us. And of course, it was my hand inside the glove puppet.

From an object relations perspective, Sammy, through a process of embodiment, identified with the puppet and was able to project her *own* sad feelings on to the puppet. In Winnicott's terms, Sammy created a transitional object as the puppet came to represent qualities belonging to her mother and to the relationship with her mother.

The developmental play model and object relations theory offer the therapist conceptual frameworks which hopefully will serve to further the child's own natural healing process. However, during this particular session it did not seem necessary to know whether the monkey represented Sammy, her mother, or someone else, or why she may be sad. Having her sadness witnessed was all that seemed necessary at the time.

Child and Dramatherapist in the Wider System

It is not uncommon for a child to be considered for dramatherapy whilst in a state of crisis. This inevitably means there is often a temptation to override or short cut the referral procedure, particularly if professionals/carers have over-identified with the child's chaos or if their own relationship with the child is causing *dis-ease* to those professionals.

The referral process is the starting point for further therapeutic work and should be protected from such influences using the following means. Permission must be given by the parent or guardian before a child can be seen by a therapist. It is imperative that the child's feelings about or thoughts towards therapy are respected. Ideally, the child will be involved in the composition and content of the referral form. This assumes that the child is able to communicate some of his difficulties with someone other than the dramatherapist.

The dramatherapist must resist the role of 'rescuer' either to the child or others. Responsibility for a child's treatment recovery, or rehabilitation cannot be solely laid at the dramatherapist's door. The dramatherapist is part of a wider system which might include a social worker or probation officer, and will most certainly include parents/carers and teachers. She cannot avoid being a part of this system, nor should she.

How the dramatherapist negotiates her role within an educational setting will depend on the expectations of the team she is part of, but will hinge ultimately on the therapist's own understanding of her role in relation to meeting the child's emotional needs.

When considering a referral, the dramatherapist takes time to reflect on the following areas – what support systems already exist for the child? Who is referring the child? (the teacher, parent, social worker). How does the child understand or acknowledge his difficulties? Is the child able to make a connection between his behaviour and his emotional state? How does the child believe the therapy may benefit him? How do significant others (parents, teachers, carers) understand the child's difficulties and the purpose of therapy? What would be regarded as a successful outcome to the therapy, and by whom?

Often a dramatherapist is asked whether it would be appropriate and beneficial for any child in difficulty to receive dramatherapy. The dramatherapist working within an educational setting may be able, in as few as three hourly sessions, to make a clinical assessment/judgement which will ascertain whether a child is responsive to therapy, or whether the child is likely to respond to therapy in the near future. The therapist's role within the system may mean she is also able to predict *how* the changes a child feels ready to make in his life may be received by others; whether or not these changes will be encouraged, confirmed, validated or resisted.

The dramatherapist based within an educational unit may be required to liaise with other professionals in the child's life, in order that the changes a child is able to make tentatively within the therapy are validated by those others. For example, Jake was consulted on his behaviour programme devised and adopted by the teaching and support staff in the unit.

A multiprofessional approach to meeting the child's emotional, behavioural and educational needs is particularly important when the dramatherapist is working with a child whose behaviour is deemed to be aggressive or disruptive. The ability of the team to work together in order to meet the child's differing needs is also a valuable experience as adults are able to demonstrate to the child skills of cooperation and communication.

Conclusion

In this chapter, I have endeavoured to present an exploration of dramatherapy in an educational unit for children and young people recognised as having emotional and behavioural difficulties. Using clinical vignettes of work with two children I have illustrated how the developmental process of drama interweaves with the object relations model allowing the dramatherapist a theoretical understanding of the child's inner world.

As a dramatherapist who understands the child's inner world from an object relations perspective it follows that the child's outer world will also be of concern to the therapist. It has not been possible within the context of this chapter to explore more fully the child's relationships in the outer world.

In order for the child in difficulty to implement the tentative changes

he has begun to make in therapy, it is necessary for others to acknowledge and validate these changes in the outside world. This is a statement not only to the child's immediate others to ponder on, but also a society which seems increasingly unable to meet a child's emotional, physical, social and educational needs.

References

Ayto, J. (1990) *Dictionary of Word Origins*. London: Bloomsbury.

Bannister, A. (1992) *From Hearing to Healing*. London: NSPCC Longmans.

Bettelheim, B. (1976) *The Uses of Enchantment*. London: Thames and Hudson.

Department of Education and Science (1989) *The Elton Report*. London: HMSO.

Erikson, E. (1950) *Childhood and Society*. New York: Norton.

Estés, C.P. (1992) *Women Who Run With the Wolves*. London: Rider.

Gersie, A. (1987) 'Dramatherapy and play.' In S. Jennings (ed) *Dramatherapy Theory and Practice for Teachers and Clinicians*. London: Croom Helm.

Grimshaw, D. (1994) 'Shall I be mother?' In S. Jennings (ed) *Dramatherapy with Children and Adolescents*. London: Routledge.

Holmes, P. (1992) *The Inner World Outside: Object Relations and Psychodrama*. London: Routledge.

Jennings, S. (1990) *Dramatherapy with Families, Groups and Individuals: Waiting in the Wings*. London: Jessica Kingsley Publishers.

Jung, C. (1964) *Man and His Symbols*. Garden City, NY: Doubleday.

Klein, M. (1932) *The Psycho-Analysis of Children*. (Revised Edition.) London: Hogarth Press and The Institute of Psychoanalysis.

Lahad, M. (1992) 'Story-making in assessment model for coping with stress: six-piece story-making and BASIC Ph.' In S. Jennings (ed) *Dramatherapy Theory and Practice 2*. London: Routledge.

Landy, R. (1986) *Dramatherapy Concepts and Practices*. Springfield, Il: Charles C. Thomas.

Mahrer, A.L. (1978) *Experiencing: A Humanistic Theory of Psychology and Psychiatry*. New York: Brunner/Mazel.

Miller, A. (1987) *For Your Own Good*. London: Virago.

Rhead, A. (1994) 'Age of innocence.' *Community Care 18*, 11–17.

Rowan, J. (1983) *The Reality Game*. London: Routledge.

Winnicott, D. (1964) *The Child, the Family and the Outside World*. Harmondsworth: Penguin.

Winnicott, D. (1965) *The Family and Individual Development*. London: Routledge.

Winnicott, D. (1971) *Playing and Reality*. London: Tavistock Publications.

Winnicott, D. (1993) *Talking to Parents*. Cambridge, Ma: Alison Wesley.

CHAPTER FIVE

The Ritual of Individual Dramatherapy

Steve Mitchell

> The Challenge for the experienced clinician is to remember that the process of helping people is a constant act of discovery.
>
> (Emunah 1994, p.25)

I am presenting here a ritual theatre model of dramatherapy which I call *the theatre of self-expression*. The work I describe is the result of working for six years in adult psychiatry with individual clients and I must acknowledge how much I have learnt from them in developing this form of dramatherapy.

Model of Healing

My approach to dramatherapy comes essentially from theories of theatre and from both eastern philosophy and modern-day western psychology. The important influences have been Brook's and Grotowski's research from the theatre, Maslow's, Rogers' and Kelly's work in humanistic psychology, and the teachings of Gurdjieff from eastern philosophy. In more recent years I have been influenced by the work of Rebillot (1994). He states that in ancient Greece the theatre was a central aspect of healing, as was the hospital, the temple and the gymnasium, a patient would be asked to witness a performance as part of their treatment:

> Certain plays that dealt with a psychological reflection of the illness would be prescribed as part of a person's healing. In the plays the person saw the mortal human being in confrontation with the eternal archetypes. The Greek audience so identified with the actor that they could experience through him the healing power of the conflict, crisis and transformation of the hero. (p.18)

But now, simply going to the theatre does not have the power of healing it once did:

In order to recover the therapeutic magic of the theatre, we must enter the theatre of our own soul and become the leading actor in our own cosmic drama, allowing the eternity of the mythological structure to penetrate the chronology of everyday life... In the ritual drama format, the individual becomes an actor and experiences these relationships directly.' (p.19)

We learn from Rebillot's work the importance of theatre as a part of healing as it gives the client the security to embark on a mystery, towards health. By employing myth or given stories, the client contacts what Joseph Campbell has called the 'monomyth', a pattern similar to Jung's archetypes. But first the client needs to be initiated into the form, into the ritual space and the the use of theatre processes which will be employed to contact the 'essential self'. The therapeutic process becomes a 'ritual', an active preparation. If the ritual in its composition and enactment radiates into the very being of the client, it will inspire the client to make the change in daily life.

Why Individual Dramatherapy?

There is first the question as to whether dramatherapy can or should be employed as an individual therapy? I personally believe that individual dramatherapy is an acceptable option for dramatherapists to practise and on certain occasions the only form of dramatherapy appropriate for a particular client.

The reason that individual work would be indicated as the treatment of choice includes those clients who are too damaged to be exposed to the 'rough and tumble' of group dynamics or find disclosing problems in a group too overwhelming. Clients who have been sexually, physically or emotionally abused often have an issue with trust and confidentiality; a group experience may hold for them the potential to be abused again. There are also clients who are referred to work on issues concerning sexual problems, where a group could become hostile rather than supportive to a client when the issue becomes known. If you are working in a small community clients can be afraid that people they know may be in the group. There are also those who are well known in a community, famous people, or people in the caring professions who would find the idea of sharing their problems in a group setting untenable. For these reasons the clinical team would appropriately view individual dramatherapy over a dramatherapy group as the better form of intervention.

The Ritual of Individual Dramatherapy

In this next section I will detail the ritual structure of the 'form' of individual dramatherapy I practise. It is a structure that has seven stages:

Stage one: assessment

I will see a client who has been referred to me for five sessions during which time my concern is to see whether a therapeutic alliance can be developed and to introduce slowly dramatherapy procedures. I will tell the client that I see my work as a collaboration in their process, that dramatherapy is a practical therapy and that during the following assessment sessions I will be introducing some of the ways I work. This will give them the opportunity to see if my form of work is useful to their needs and whether my style as a therapist is one with which they can feel free to explore their problems. This is also their assessment. The only practical structure I employ in the first session is to introduce the client to how we will work in the space. I therefore explain that sessions begin in the *first area* on the seats we are presently occupying. Here in future we will discuss any 'business' such as apologies for future absences or holidays. It will also be a time to reflect on the previous session. After this we will move into the *studio area* where the practical part of the session will take place. At the end of each session, we will return to the chairs, once more to reflect on what has taken place before closing the work.

To practise using the space I will ask the client to move into the designated studio area and to choose a cushion or chair to sit on, to look around the space from this position, to notice colours, to comment on whether they like or dislike the space and if this space reminds the client of any other location. I will then ask them to close their eyes and take them through a sensory exercise which concentrates on how s/he feels now, then to open their eyes and make contact with the room again. I then ask the client what brings them to this meeting. When there is ten minutes left, it is time to put away their cushion or chair – they do this – and we return to the first first area. Here the client reflects on the session and shares any feelings it has brought up. This first session closes with my asking the client whether he or she will return the following week.

In the second session I facilitate an exercise called the *life map*. I ask the client, once we have moved into the studio area to draw on a piece of A3 paper a map of the important incidents in their life. I caution the client that this is only the second time we have met, to be careful not to disclose any material that at this stage that might be uncomfortable for them, but maybe to indicate through a private symbol a period in their lives on the map, that may have some future important relevance if we agree to engage in therapy. I will give the client ten minutes to draw the map and the remainder of the session will involve the client telling me their life story using the map as their prompt sheet. I ask clients to tell their story in the third person; this offers both a form of containment for potentially emotive material and subtly introduces the first step towards dramatic distance.

Once this has been completed we return to the first area where the client looks at their map, their journey through life, to see if there are any major themes. I talk about how problems in adult life can sometimes have their origins at a younger age, when the *younger self* can only understand what's happening by relating what feelings are experienced to the world of stories. This younger self sometimes needs to be given the opportunity to express itself, or to use the *adult self* to help it communicate what has been withheld. This withheld material sometimes surfaces by attracting us to particular stories. What hidden story or mythic legend, piece of literature, children's story, play, TV drama or film does the client relate to? Sometimes the parallel is very clear: 'Yes, it's *Odysseus*', 'It's like Hansel and Gretel'. On other occasions the image is not so clear and the client needs time to think about it during the week. I help, by suggesting they seek a story either from childhood or from adult life they are attracted to in some way. Why there is this attraction may not be clear; that doesn't matter. They can simply allow the process to take place. At the close of this session I once more ask them if they will return for their third session the following week and with this the session closes.

In the third session, if the client has identified a story, the process of dramatisation begins. If the client is unable to identify an established story, the session will be given over to creating an original story. For this I employ Lahad's Six-Piece Story-Making as the structure for a client to create a story (for details of this procedure see Lahad 1992). If the client has a story, the process moves to the next stage.

Stage two: dramatisation of the first story
We move into the studio area. The client is asked to place a cushion or chair to represent a neutral position; this will be where the client sits while out-of-character. I will place two upright chairs in front of their neutral position, each chair facing the other. One chair will become the 'character seat', the other chair will be the 'interviewer's chair'.

Before the client begins to explore any character, I teach a ritual of entering and 'stepping out of character'. While the client talks about the character, the plot, action, or reflects on the process, this is all done from the 'neutral position'. When the client moves from this seat to the character seat the process begins. The client sits in the character seat. I ask them to close their eyes, to find a zero position, a posture that does not embody their everyday personality but one which offers the potentiality of new physical possibilities and, from this zero posture, to allow their body to change shape into the posture of the character. A similar process is employed at the end of embodying any character. The client closes their eyes, finds a sculpt of the character, breathes into this sculpt. As the breath is exhaled, the body lets go of the energy and physical shape of the character and returns to the zero position and from this posture to their own everyday posture. The client opens their eyes and returns to their neutral seat to complete the ritual. In the early sessions I ask the client to observe this ritual until it is internalised or the client has developed another process of engaging and disengaging with a character which is unique to their needs.

When this ritual has been learnt I ask the client to pick one of the characters from their story. What quality of personality does this character have? If the client could choose a well-known person, actor, film star or politician to represent this character who would they choose? I ask the client to imagine how their character might sit in the character seat. The client becomes a director and directs me, as their actor, into a sculpt of the character.

The next phase involves using the ritual of entering and letting go of characters, to experience the energy of their character by making their own sculpt. I guide the client through the zero position into a sculpt which will depict the essential nature of this character. At this time I suggest to the client that they keep their eyes closed, as it helps in individual work to decrease inhibitions and focus on the interior experience of the character. I also limit the time of being in character to short moments, so as not to flood the client with dramatic inhibition. Therefore quite quickly the client moves through the ritual process of taking a character and letting it go, returning to the neutral position and reflecting on how it felt.

Before we start this process of developing characters I will tell the client that I am not teaching him or her to act. I am not too interested in the outward presentation of any character, but much more interested in helping the client experience the dynamic of a character from inside. The physical posture is an aid to this process because it helps to generate the interior experience. For example, we all have our own particular dynamic related to who we are: who we are is the sum total of our genetic inheritance and biographical history. This shapes how each person holds their body, but it is not the only shape possible. If we work on the body, let's say diet, we can physically change our shape. If on the other hand we work on an emotional block, as we reduce the emotional tension, the physical 'holding' in the musculature will soften and our posture will change. By starting with an imagined posture of a character, the client begins to contact other energies which are available to them. Sometimes these 'energies' are positive affirmative characteristics the client employs in everyday life. At other times the client may touch an energy his or her 'ego ideal' has suppressed or repressed because during their development certain characteristics were not allowed.

It is unlikely the client will move into this territory while they learn the process of work. Normally, a client, will pick a positive character to make early experiments with the process. Only when the client has an overview of the form, and the alliance between the therapist and client has deepened, will the client begin to choose characters which challenge the psychic status quo. However, this is not always the case, as some clients are in a hurry, but soon these clients trip over themselves, because their unconscious processes stop them even in the dramatic metaphor from experiencing a particular aspect of themselves.

Once the client has experienced the posture of the character, we begin to examine the character's background. I ask the client to think about their character during the week: in their story, what has happened to this person, what are their likes and dislikes, hobbies, friends and enemies? In next week's session we will be developing the process to discover more about the biographical history of this character, or maybe there is another character to whom the first character wishes to express themself. The time of this session will almost be up and it will be time to move from the studio area back to the first area. Once more I will ask the client to close their eyes and reflect on the session. To open their eyes and share with me any feelings it has given rise to. I will also share with the client any impressions I have of their work and once more ask the client if he or she will return for the next assessment session. On this note the session will close.

The fourth session may involve the client interviewing their character to discover the character's background or the client developing another character and taking the first steps in improvising between the two characters. The final assessment session is concerned with business, setting up a contract for a specific period of dramatherapy, or closing if the client or therapist feels it is not suitable to continue. If this is the case, the client may need to be referred on to another therapist.

Stage three: exploring the play

In this phase, the process develops *the first story* with the client exploring characters that interact with one another. The dramatherapist will also, where necessary, act as the substitute character the client wishes to engage in an improvisation. The scene will be explored in such a way to enable the client, within the dramatic metaphor, to examine the issues for which he or she is in therapy. An important part of investigating the play is to focus on the 'dramatic conflict' and this may arise from the 'sub-text'. The result of this may mean discovering the need to develop a new story or to adapt the first story to meet a new agenda. At this stage of therapy, the first three to six months, I continue to build the therapeutic alliance, thus setting the scene for the client to risk deeper disclosures.

Stage four: the search for ritual

In this section I shall describe a number of different ritual processes the dramatherapist can employ:

THRESHOLD RITUALS

These are rituals which are devised by the dramatherapist and client either in the opening or closing moments of a session. The client enters the session and takes their seat in the first area, and a threshold ritual takes place each time the client moves from their seat into the work area. On most occasions the threshold ritual is no more than crossing into the space, on other occasions the ritual is more elaborate.

A client may be working thematically on a particular drama but when they arrive s/he may feel emotionally overwhelmed by a life event which may be a side issue to the 'through-line' of their therapy. The session may begin by giving the client time to share their feelings about the current issue, but this may not suffice. At this moment the dramatherapist needs to structure a ritual that will allow the client to express whatever feelings are present so that they are then ready to cross the 'threshold' and continue their therapeutic work, which may incorporate into it the feelings the client brings into the session or otherwise. The threshold ritual is a structure that has an organic evolution. There are no prescribed techniques, except to ask the client to focus into their body: 'What physical shape does this feeling have – let's embody it'. From here I move into intensifying the sculpt or developing any impulse, any dynamic into an action or movement form, and adding voice. The important principle is the client takes the 'here and now' feeling and finds a three-dimensional dynamic, a bodily form, to ventilate or acknowledge the feelings that belong to it. Some clients want to dance, others to drum out their feelings; for others simply making a sculpt and using their breath fulfils their need to be ready to cross the threshold.

Once the client has arrived in the studio area the process of the session will commence and continue until the final 15 minutes. Once more a threshold ritual will take place as the client closes with the experiential work and returns over the threshold to the first area. On many occasions this ritual will simply involve the client in making a statement that 'phrases' where the session has taken their feelings and 'striking the set'. This acts as both a de-roling of everything that has been employed in the dramatic space and a further grounding, stepping out of character, exercise for the client.

On certain occasions the closing threshold ritual may take on a more elaborate form, the following clinical example may demonstrate how this operates:

Kirstie

In her drama she had been playing an ego-character that she rarely inhabited in daily life, in a scene where she lost her temper and 'trashed' the room. Kirstie, was sensitive and rarely assertive or dared to show aggressive feelings towards anyone. Her way of expressing anger was passive in the manner of a little girl. In this session she had explored in character parts of herself that she rarely showed and at the end of the drama stood proudly, assertively, full of smiles among the cushions she had employed as 'props' as she had 'trashed' her character's room.

In this case the threshold ritual evolved in the following way: two empty chairs were employed as character seats to depict the positive and negative qualities of the character. I asked her to sit on each chair in turn and define these qualities and to close by sitting in the chair that depicted the positive qualities and invited her to hold on to these qualities as she crossed the threshold to the first area. She chose to take them with her out of the session.

TRANSITIONAL RITUALS

On certain occasions a threshold ritual is inappropriate, such as if a client is engaged with a life crisis such as the death of a significant person. The dramatherapist needs to allow the client to be with their feelings, to offer transition rituals that help to express, hold and contain the client as painful feelings are processed. At such times the thematic work needs to be put on 'hold' until the client has completed their process of transition. During a time of crisis, such as facing the loss of a loved one, I will offer a client additional sessions and be with them in a way they indicate.

TRANSFORMATION RITUALS IN CHARACTER

A client having set up their drama begins to explore a character but discovers difficulty in fully expressing the quality or attitude of that person. I would begin helping the client to explore the problems of inhabiting this character in much the same way that a theatre director might work with an actor. What is the difficulty for the client and how can this be overcome? Once the problem of embodying the character had been identified, I would suggest to the client a number of theatre exercises to help them work towards overcoming the problem. If for example the client is playing a powerful character but has difficulty in contacting that part of the self to use it to furnish the character, I might explore ways of physically elevating the client in the powerful character by raising them off the ground, such as standing on a table, until the required feelings were manifest. If a client has taken an angry character and is finding it difficult to allow aggressive feelings to be expressed, an experiment might be to begin by doing the scene in the manner of a Punch and Judy scene, where through the style of Commedia dell' Arte, fun can be had with shadow feelings. Often experimenting with a scene in different theatre styles can help a client move towards expressing emotions that otherwise would be unacceptable to their ego-ideal.

Charles

This client was working with his dramatisation of Hansel and Gretel and had no problem with the witch, but in a scene between Hansel and Gretel where their father abandoned them in the forest, Charles had great difficulty in expressing the sadness he wanted Hansel to feel. I suggested a number of experiments, two of which were with theatrical styles: the first was using Victorian melodrama, the second Greek tragedy using masks. The first experiment led to the second. The first was fun, very physically expressive, and by employing exaggerated actions began to allow Charles to contact feelings. The Greek tragedy working with masks enabled the him within, what Jennings calls 'the epic metaphor', to discover the accompanying feeling.

There are many drama exercises and improvisations around a particular character or scene that can be employed to help a client transform a difficulty of getting into character – see Boal (1992) Williams (1988) and Spolin (1963) as examples of how theatre exercises can be employed as rituals of transformation in character.

RITUALS OF TRANSFORMATION

There is a growing myth that the theatre model of dramatherapy always takes place using dramatic distance. In this ritual theatre model this is not the case: what is important is that the client is given the space to design the rituals that are appropriate to their issue. The only consideration that would demand I 'veto' a proposal would be if a client wanted to include in their ritual an action that would break the agreed ground rules. Therefore if a client wants to explore an issue directly then I will collaborate in designing a ritual that will meet their needs.

Jason

This client had been working with scenes from Shakespeare's *King Lear*. He had invented a scene involving the character of Edmund directly confronting his father Gloucester. The scene had been improvised and selected lines had been employed to create a 'collage' that expressed the feelings he wanted to work on. The scene was rehearsed and a number of rituals in character took place, but still Jason felt 'uncompleted'. He then asked to work on his step-father directly, outside the metaphor. The ritual that was designed had the following structure:

> *Scene One*: using empty chairs, Jason's younger self confronted his step-father. The step-father spoke the 'negative messages' Jason gave him. In this scene Jason experienced the feelings that had brought him into therapy.

> *Scene Two*: the same scene, but this time Jason took the role of his adult self who entered the scene to support his younger self. As the adult self, Jason was able to express his unfinished, unspoken feelings to the empty chair representing his step-father. (At Jason's request I substituted the role of step-father, stating the negative messages of scene one, and Jason responded to them.) In this scene Jason was able to argue against the injunctions he had internalised from his step-father, and released himself from their hold.

> *Scene Three*: Jason addressed the characters of his drama, before crossing a threshold that would mark the possibility for him to be sexual with women rather than suppressing these sensations. After he had said his goodbyes and stated his resolve, Jason

came across the threshold and was greeted by me as a man who could be sexual.

In processing this *ritual of transformation* with Jason he told me that although doing the Lear scenes was a useful preparation, he needed to do the ritual. I often find this is the case with many clients. Working through dramatic distance alone is not enough; they feel a personal need to move what has been explored in the dramatic domain into the world of the everyday. The *ritual of transformation* offers a client the process of doing this if this bridge between the dramatic world and everyday reality needs to take place.

TRANSFORMATION RITUALS TAKING PLACE OUTSIDE THE SESSION

On certain occasions a client will want to use a dramatherapy session to plan a ritual that is performed outside the therapeutic space, when you are not present. For example, some clients feel inhibited expressing themselves loudly in the dramatherapy studio, because of soundproof problems and the proximity of other people. In this case the client may plan with you to go to a remote location and shout or express angry feelings. One client who was coming to terms with his father's death and wanted to speak to him, to express all that had been unsaid, didn't want to do it symbolically in the studio. Instead he planned a ritual journey that took him to the Lake District where his father's ashes had been laid to rest. I asked him what he would like to do there and he said to bury the negative feeling he carried towards his father. I told him how the native American Indians would dig a hole in the ground and speak all their negative thoughts into it and then once more cover the hole up and build a cairn of stones above it to honour the feelings below it. My client chose to speak to a particular rock he found on the mountain side, to write down these feelings, burn them and bury the ashes. Another client, who had suffered religious abuse during his childhood, after two years of therapy planned to take all the objects he associated with his illness down to the sea shore. The ritual would take place through the night. There he was intending to burn them on the sand and wait for the dawn tide to come in and wash these ritual objects away. As he planned these events in the session, I noticed how engaged he was with the idea of it and took him through a guided fantasy that enacted what he had planned. In the end this turned out to be enough and there was no need to enact the ritual.

When a client wishes to perform a ritual outside of the therapeutic space, my major concern is that of safety in terms that the place chosen is secure from intrusion by other people. Also my concern is that the action of the ritual will not damage the environment or be harmful to my client or anyone else. This includes not only physical harm but psychological harm. I suggest that the client makes sure to allow plenty of time to set up their ritual space, to perform the action of their ritual and to have time after the ritual to earth any uncomfortable feelings that might have arisen before re-entering the everyday world.

One of the most influential books I have read concerning the use of rituals outside a session is by Tracy Hansen called *Seven for a Secret* (1991). Hansen was sexually abused in childhood and in adult life addressed these issues by creating a number of rituals for herself. The only help she had was from a priest with whom she would share the rituals she planned or discuss with him what had taken place, or what emotional material had yet to be worked through. The contact with the priest helped to contain and be witness to Hansen's journey of coming to terms with abuse.

Stage five: ritual enactment

In this section I intend to give a clinical example to illustrate 'ritual process' that has taken place in individual dramatherapy:

Sue – a ritual through voice work

I had been working with Sue for about 18 months and during this time many issues related to childhood had been approached but not fully dealt with. Sue had a deep mis-trust of men that dated back to her father leaving the family home after a number of affairs. Now in her 30s, Sue found herself having a number of relationships with men, enacting her anger out towards her father through sexual sadomasochism games with her partners who more often than not left her. Sue was stuck and not only used an intellectual defense to stay at the impasse but re-enacted her mis-trust of men with me, a male therapist. In fact it was only on an occasion when she told me of a particularly wretched experience she had endured as a child that moved me to quite genuine tears – that I chose to show her – that she later told me she began to trust me. It was just after the above incident that again the therapeutic process became stuck in terms of contacting feelings that Sue stated she wanted to feel. Yet she wasn't certain about what, although she had been discussing her anxiety towards an exam she would be shortly facing; Sue was now a mature student.

There are times in the dramatherapy process when being at an impasse, stuck, is healthy, and the most important therapeutic procedure is to stay there, thus allowing the client to experience fully the impasse, until she begins to surface the issues that give rise to it. In my work with Sue this had often been my approach but time and again this form of no intervention had gone nowhere. On this particular occasion, as we sat facing each other and Sue was rationalising her sense of depression towards her course work, the idea of working with voice floated into my consciousness. The idea quite surprised me as this had not been part of my work with Sue, but it had emerged from my subconscious in response to 'being present' to what my client was saying. Over the years I have come to trust these intuitions more and more, or what Alida Gersie once referred to as 'informed intuition'. The sum result was that I suggested we work with the voice to see if she could access the feelings that were potentially present but at the same time absent. She agreed.

For the next two sessions, I worked as a voice coach, teaching some basic voice exercises, before developing this to employing a particular voice exercise from the Grotowski Laboratory Theatre that I intended using as the base of a 'voice ritual'. The exercise (used by Zygmunt Molik) involves employing a physical posture as a starting point for the energy of the psyche to be expressed through a process of vocalisation he calls 'singing'. Once Sue had learnt the theatre exercise we then employed it as the form of the ritual process.

I asked Sue to enter the space set aside for the ritual and to begin to focus on whatever feelings were present for her, to use some paper and art materials to make shapes to give some definition to her feelings. When she was clear what the feeling was (she chose 'defensiveness'), I asked her to find a physical posture to reflect this feeling. She curled up on the floor in a position similar to a foetal position. I asked her to focus on her breath and to start the vocalisation, as in the voice exercise, to keep the tonality going, to allow the body to support the sound by changing its position to keep the resonance of the sound in the body while at the same time externalising and sharing the sounds with the external world.

Sue found a sound and began to allow it to evolve. As the sound grew in texture she changed her body position. Slowly she began to rise from the foetal position to a kneeling position. Here the sound too changed to a sound of wailing. Her gestures supported this; with the sounds came tears. She cried. For what seemed a long time I waited allowing her to be with her process. When she had recovered I placed a blanket around her shoulders and suggested she imagine the blanket represented comfort from someone important to her. She clasped the blanket to her and physically lowered herself from a kneeling position to simply sitting on the floor. Throughout the process she had her eyes closed. Again I waited. After a while she opened her eyes and to close the ritual I asked her if she would like to share with me what had taken place. She told me that she was grieving for her mother and as she spoke, once more she cried. If she had chosen not to share her process with me I would have accepted that: sometimes to find words immediately after an intense experiential experience takes you away from the feelings you are with, or because of this words are unavailable. I also believe clients have the right not to tell their therapists everything and if they choose to keep silent I need to curb my natural curiosity to know all. However, should I feel that to keep quiet would in some way be damaging, I will explore ways of sharing their process. In most cases, as with Sue, after a ritual which has been emotive I usually find that the client has a need to share what has taken place as a way of re-entering the everyday world.

Stage six: termination

After working with a client for a considerable length of time it is important that termination of therapy is approached carefully. A client needs to be given advance notice that a long-term contract will be coming to an end and not suddenly surprised with the information. In my one-to-one work I always have a set duration that is part of the contract of therapy; initially this may be for three to six months. It is agreed to work on a weekly basis for this period of time and then at the designated time have a review. If it should be decided to continue therapy a new period of time is stated, again with a review, but should the decision be to terminate therapy, the review session will be followed with four further sessions to close the therapeutic process.

The contents of these four sessions will first review the progress of dramatherapy and detail what practical steps of change have and will be made in the client's life. Second, the client and dramatherapist need to close their relationship. In both cases I would usually employ empty chair work as the structure to work these separation issues through. For example, to structure the review of the dramatherapeutic work I will ask the client to place an empty chair in the centre of the studio space to represent them. Then, choosing items from the space, to place around the chair all the significant people or issues the client has worked with during the course of therapy. Once the circle has been created the client then sits on the empty chair in the centre and addresses each person, stating in a simple statement in what way the relationship has changed and what practical step the client will make towards that person outside the therapeutic space. This is a closing ritual to emphasise the work already undertaken, not to re-open work that hasn't previously been completed before the review.

In the second of the four closing sessions the focus changes from the work to separating from the process of dramatherapy. Once more I would employ the use of empty chairs to explore with the client both their resentments and appreciations concerning the dramatherapy, at this stage, not the dramatherapist. I place two empty chairs before the client, one is for resentments, the other is for appreciations. The rule is that if they make a statement in one chair, it is required that the client also makes a statement from the other chair.

In the penultimate session the same structure is employed but this time the focus is the relationship with the dramatherapist. For this exercise I employ three empty chairs; I place one in the space to represent the dramatherapist, facing this chair two others, one for resentments, the other for appreciations. On this occasion the client is asked to clear or make all resentments to the dramatherapist's chair before moving on to appreciations. In so doing, any negative feelings can be fully stated and owned by the client and heard by the therapist without mixing them up with feelings that may be positive towards the dramatherapist. For separation between client and dramatherapist to take place in a constructive and integrated way both sides of the coin need to be fully expressed. If they are confused in some way, the client may remain in a more dependant position towards their therapist. By being explicit about both the resentments and appreciations, this allows the client to respect the fact that the therapist is human and may make mistakes as well as respecting the dramatherapist's collaboration in the therapeutic work.

The final session is given over to a closing ceremony. I ask the client to bring to the session some talisman they would like to have that would carry for them in an important way the essence of their therapeutic work. In the session we will create a ceremony that allows the client to receive their object that is to be a future 'instrument of power' now therapy is completed. This ceremony is described in more detail in my chapter 'The Dramatherapy Venture Project' (Jennings et al. 1994). The following clinical vignette may help to illustrate how this operates in individual dramatherapy.

Jayne

This client chose as her talisman a pair of ear-rings that could also be worn as an 'instrument of power' when dealing with relationships of a sexual nature that prior to therapy had placed her in a powerless position, copying old patterns in her archaic relationship with a father who had physically abused her. In designing the ceremony I ask Jayne to consider how and where she would like to receive the talisman, with what words, if any needed to be said, either by her or by the giver (myself). Jayne wanted to enact the ceremony outside, as nature was important to her. Fortunately outside the dramatherapy studio were the hospital gardens and it was a hot summer's day. Outside Jayne chose a location between two trees and knelt on the ground. She wanted me to move to her and put each ear-ring through her ears, and as I did to tell her of the significance these ear-rings would have for her. Once this was done she then made her own vocal dedication as a way of anointing the ear-rings with their symbolic purpose. The ceremony closed with us returning to the dramatherapy studio and saying our goodbyes to celebrate the termination of therapy.

Terminating long-term contracts

A client you assess for dramatherapy may begin with a short contract of three months and when that time has been completed may contract for a more extended period. I normally extend the contract for no longer than a further nine months; at that time a further review takes place, after the client has been in therapy for a year. For some severely abused clients, whether physically, sexually or emotionally, a year of therapy may only be beginning to allow the therapeutic alliance to be truly formed and at least another year of therapy will be indicated to make a start on working-through the issues that brought the client to therapy.

I have not found it unusual for clients to require at least two years of individual dramatherapy, for some, three or four years. This raises an even greater importance on the preparation for terminating the dramatherapy sessions as the attachments for both client and dramatherapist will be greater. For any client who has been in therapy for over two years I give at least six months notice that dramatherapy will terminate on a given date. Such a date gives focus to the final period of therapy and I intensify this by moving the client towards a *closing ritual* that concludes their therapeutic work.

THE CLOSING RITUAL

This is a final piece of work done by a client who has been in therapy for over two years and is working towards terminating dramatherapy. The closing ritual is a structure devised in collaboration with the dramatherapist and will consist of a specific piece of work. The ritual is a planned event and worked towards as the climax of the client's therapeutic work. The client has the choice as to whether the ritual process employs dramatic distance or whether it addresses issues directly. The usual choice at this stage of dramatherapy is to explore an issue without dramatic distance, but to employ the security of ritual as the container for any feelings that need to be expressed.

Sarah

As Sarah approached the termination of dramatherapy she wanted to express feelings of aggression towards a father who had abused her, in a direct way and not using dramatic metaphors. It was as although the various dramas and scenes she had previously enacted had brought her to the point where she needed to stand up as her now adult self and ritualistically protect a younger self that was still open to abusive relationships. Sarah was quite clear what she wanted to do; she wanted symbolically to be aggressive towards her father and this would entail not only violent actions but loud and abusive language. Unfortunately where we worked sound-proofing was a problem; it was therefore arranged to meet in a more remote venue on the hospital site. This also involved a number of important professional procedures, such as alerting my manager, and gaining permission to work with a female client in a more remote location on my own. Sarah also found it took her time truly to get into her feelings and asked if she could have more than an hour to do her ritual. I agreed to this for a one-off session and it was agreed that on the day of the ritual we would work for three hours.

As part of the preparation for the ritual it was decided that four sessions would take place in the new venue; the first session would be focused towards becoming accustomed to the new space; the second session would rehearse the structures that the ritual would employ; the third session would be the enactment of the closing ritual and the fourth session a debriefing before returning to the dramatherapy studio. Carol had read a book I had lent her called *No One is to Blame* by Bob Hoffman (1988) that describes his 'Quadrinity Process' where the client moves through a structure where a parent figure is prosecuted. During the action of 'prosecution' the client releases on to cushions any feelings of anger, aggression, rage or violence that have been felt towards the parental figure. Sarah, having resisted any such work during the two-and-a-half years in dramatherapy chose this as the skeletal form for her ritual. In her ritual Sarah began by defining the role of her father and her younger self. I was asked to substitute Father and given specific statements to speak. The ritual process began with Sarah in the role of the younger self, re-experiencing the wounds in the form of the negative statements from her father. At this point, an ego character, which Sarah called her protector, entered the action and supported the wounded younger self by physically expressing her anger by hitting cushions representing her father. The ritual took two-and-a-half hours to complete before Sarah felt the anger she had ventilated towards the figure of her father had reached a point of catharsis. It should be observed that up to this point in her dramatherapy Sarah had suppressed anger and the work she managed in her closing ritual was due to the realisation that if she was to gain from therapy she was responsible for making it happen. In her ritual she did make it happen and this opened a door to her feelings that she had previously kept closed.

Advantages and Disadvantages of Individual Dramatherapy

In this final section I want to look at some of the advantages and disadvantages of one-to-one dramatherapy in terms of clinical practice. In many respects the answer to these questions depends upon what point of view you are taking, that of the client, the dramatherapist or the manager.

From the client's perspective individual work has many advantages. Like with many psychotherapies, a client can feel safer, that they are having more attention and don't necessarily have to cope with difficult transactions (from group members). On the other hand, a client may feel one-to-one dramatherapy is too intense because there is no one else there. The gender of the dramatherapist may mitigate against dramatherapy due to the issues a client might wish to explore. The client might also find dramatising material in front of only one person too intimidating, however carefully this is facilitated.

The issue observed from the role of dramatherapist can include both the gender issues as well as the difficulty of the client working practically in front of one witness – the dramatherapist. Added to this is that individual work lacks the resources that a group culture carries with it. For example in groups one of the curative measures cited by Yalom is getting relief from knowing others may have similar problems. In individual work this doesn't happen unless the dramatherapist chooses to disclose personal issues. Second, the human resources that are available to the client to cast his or her dramas or help with ritual processes are not present in one-to-one dramatherapy. It therefore requires the dramatherapist to take a more active part in the 'substitute' roles and unless this is structured carefully, so the client is aware when the dramatherapist is being a character and when they are being the dramatherapist, confusions can be possible. On the other hand, individual dramatherapy makes it possible for those clients who are too damaged or too concerned about the pressures of group work, to benefit from dramatherapy. I have also found that clients who take up individual dramatherapy tend to work at greater depth once the therapeutic alliance has formed. This may be because the security of one-to-one enables more risks to take place.

The advantages and disadvantages from a manager's perspective may be concerned with other issues, although managers may have concerns to do with ethical considerations such as working individually with someone of the opposite sex or members of the same sex where sexual transferences are possible. In fact every time a dramatherapist works individually, the risk of 'accusation against the dramatherapist' is heightened much more than when working in groups. A manager, therefore, will want to be sure that the dramatherapist has taken all the necessary precautions and behaves in a professional manner. Managers also have to play the numbers game and will need to be sure that there is a need for an hour of a dramatherapist's time to be spent with one person when it could be spent with six or seven others within a group context. Managers will also be concerned with the turn-over in terms of long-term contracts and will want a balance between group work, short- and long-term contracts. However, to date, I have found managers understanding when explaining the arguments I have already outlined in this chapter why individual dramatherapy is the treatment of choice.

In my view there is an important place for individual dramatherapy both in the health service and for dramatherapists who are practising within the private sector. I have tried in this chapter to present a particular form of structuring one-to-one dramatherapy when working with the ritual theatre model *the theatre of self-expression* and to illustrate with clinical examples the way it operates in practice. This format has evolved over a long time and is still developing and shouldn't be viewed as set in stone. As I meet with every new client who participates in this approach, the form evolves, and the ritual of individual dramatherapy continues to be discovered.

References

Boal, A. (1992) *Games for Actors and Non-actors.* London: Routledge.

Brook, P. (1993) *There Are No Secrets.* London: Methuen.

Emunah, R. (1994) *Acting For Real.* New York: Brunner/Mazel Publishers.

Hansen, T. (1991) *Seven for a Secret.* London: Triangle SPCK.

Hoffman, B. (1988) *No One Is To Blame.* Oakland, CA: Recycling Books.

Jennings, S., Cattanach, A., Mitchell, S., Chesner, A. and Meldrum, B. (1994) *A Handbook of Dramatherapy.* London: Routledge.

Kelly, G. (1955) *The Psychology of Personal Constructs* Vol 1 and 2. New York: Norton.

Kumiega, J. (1987) *The Theatre of Grotowski*. London: Methuen.

Lahad, M. (1992) 'Storymaking in assessment method for coping with stress: six piece storymaking and Basic Ph.' In S. Jennings *Dramatherapy Theory and Practice 2*. London: Routledge.

Maslow, A. (1971) *The Farther Reaches of Human Nature*. Harmondsworth: Penguin Books.

Miller, A. (1990) *Banished Knowledge*. London: Virago Press.

Mitchell, S. (1990) 'The theatre of Peter Brook.' *Dramatherapy Journal*, Winter 1990, 13.

Mitchell, S. (1992) 'Therapeutic theatre.' In S. Jennings (ed) *Dramatherapy Theory and Practice 2*. London: Routledge.

Mitchell, S. (1994) 'The theatre of self-expression.' In S. Jennings *et al. The Handbook of Dramatherapy*. London: Routledge.

Rebillot, P. (1993) *The Call To Adventure*. London: Harper Collins.

Roth, G. (1989) *Maps To Ecstasy*. San Raphael, CA: New World Library

Spolin, V. (1963) *Improvisation for the Theatre*. North Western University Press.

Williams, D. (1988) *Brook: A Theatrical Casebook*. London: Methuen.

CHAPTER SIX

Exploratory-level Dramatherapy within a Psychotherapy Setting

Judy Donovan

Introduction

I am grateful to the many clients whose stories, thoughts and feelings inform this account of my work in a Health Trust psychotherapy and counselling unit, where for one afternoon a week I facilitate a two-hour exploratory-level dramatherapy group. Each of these clients' lives is unique, and so each session is new and surprising. Yet, over time, patterns emerge. In this chapter I use an extended account of a single dramatherapy session to illustrate some of these patterns and how the dramatherapist might respond to them. In her task of responding accurately and creatively to the messages of her clients, the dramatherapist will benefit from a working understanding of how the self develops, how groups develop, and a conceptual basis for working with whole-group process. I suggest that the sessional material described might be construed as a condensation of processes involving the formation of self and identity, and that within the dramatherapy group some of the experiences of seeing and being seen that affect the core self in relationship to itself and others are made particularly visible. The relevance of this to the dramatherapist as director and witness is addressed throughout.

Like Meldrum (1993), I note the relatively scant attention given by dramatherapy literature to theories of the development of self: I look to the work of Winnicott (1982) for a renewed appreciation of 'good-enough' mirroring in the emergent play space between mother and infant, to Erikson (1959) for an understanding of psycho-social developmental stages in the formation of self, to Kohut's (1972) respect for healthy narcissism. Mollen and Parry provide a useful overview of narcissistic disturbance and 'the fragile self' (1984, p.137), and Kaufman's (1993) work on the genesis of shame and the breaking of the interpersonal bridge provides a conceptual basis for reparative work in the presence of narcissistic injury. The group focal conflict model (Whitaker and Lieberman 1964) provides a useful frame for exploring whole-group process. John Berger's work enriches my understanding of the process of seeing (1975).

The Dramatherapy Group

In the unit where I work, prospective clients are assessed on their ability both to contain and to work with presenting problems, their ability to establish relationships within a group, and their commitment to change. (Individuals who have experienced recurrent psychotic episodes are not considered as prospective clients.) Most commonly, clients' stated problems of historical abuse (emotional, sexual and physical), depression, eating disorders and personality difficulties are reflected in social and emotional difficulties within current relationships. These current issues become the primary focus for work in the psychotherapy unit.

Each client meets once a week with a key worker, is a member of a small psychotherapy group which meets four times a week and participates in all large-group activities, including the dramatherapy group. The average number of clients attending full time (four days a week) is approximately 14, and the average length of stay is 14 weeks. The unit is staffed by psychiatric nurses and one occupational therapist, most of them with specialised counselling and/or psychotherapy training, and supported by two psychiatrists (one with special responsibility for psychotherapy) and one dramatherapist.

In addition to myself as facilitator, two members of staff attend the dramatherapy group and, very often, two student nurses on long-term placement. The group is previewed by those members of staff who will be present in the group, and reviewed immediately following the session with the entire staff team. It meets in three 12-week blocks over the year: the following session is week three in a block of 12 sessions.

> People came into the room in twos and threes, settling into the circle of chairs. Tom and Lucy exchanged glances and giggled. Someone else giggled at the giggling. Matt pulled his chair back slightly and then leaned forward, his gaze on the floor. Several others looked tense. There was little eye contact. The group felt fragmented.
>
> At 1.30pm the dramatherapy group began. The immediate silence felt heavy and when I gazed around the circle few eyes met mine. I felt shut out, but not by their solidarity: I sensed their separateness from one another as well as from me. I was unprepared for this beginning and searched for clues to meaning that might reduce my own rising

tension. I quickly scanned our last session together: was there something I hadn't noticed, but that the group had carried throughout the week? Or, as was often the case, had something from the morning's small psychotherapy groups entered, in oblique fashion, the large dramatherapy group? Perhaps, given the giggles and glances, something had happened in the lunch hour? Was it something to do with the new member? I assessed the session plan I always brought and often did not use: today I would not use it. I brought myself back to the moment; if the group was in retreat, I was in momentary flight.

I initiated the opening we always used when newcomers joined the group: introductions and an open invitation to the others to tell Mary something about the dramatherapy group. It was a useful ritual of meeting and incorporation and often helped existing members to notice the group in a new way. For me, it was a time to notice not only what was said, but how. From this formalised beginning often came the group's work for the next two hours.

Today my invitation was met by continued silence: the energy for withholding what would have been normally shared rippled its way around the group. Finally Jonathan gave a brief and very factual account of things we had done in the recent past – stories, improvisations, sculpting. Tess, speaking more spontaneously and referring to her own experience, said that the group often surprised her with its unexpected turns. Not without irony, I inwardly agreed.

During the introductions I glanced at one of the members of staff present in the group. She looked perplexed, but she was leaning forward and her eyes were alive and attentive. I felt my own curiosity returning and allowed myself to wonder aloud about the group's energy for what felt like secrets. Several people looked up, engaged. Over the next couple of minutes there was a gradual buzz of interest that, as we talked, turned into active curiosity. What is a secret? What is its opposite? What happens when it's revealed? I worried briefly that my intervention had carried them away from more difficult, central issues within the group. But I also felt sensibly cautious: how might we work with this curiosity without evoking premature revelation of 'secret' material?

It would be interesting to read an account of these first few minutes from the point of view of Ellen, Matt, Mary or Tess – or any of the 16 people in the group that afternoon. Each would no doubt be different, as each responded to what could be seen and heard in term's of their own internal images, beliefs and imaginings. As it is, the group is described through my eyes and coloured by my thoughts and feelings. On the basis of those thoughts and feelings, I act. Each act involves choices – sometimes between two things, but most often from a range of options that are as baffling as they are rich. It is useful, I think, to reflect on what informs the first and often crucial choices we make as facilitators in a session of this kind.

As much as possible, I provide structures that are responsive to the here-and-now dynamics of the group, and my 'plan' arises from the work of the previous week and my anticipation of the group's next developmental task. The four working days between sessions, however, often influence the dramatherapy group in ways I can't anticipate: they may have travelled further than I could have imagined, backtracked on their journey, taken a detour or become stuck. The choice to abandon a prepared plan and think anew is not unusual; but without it I am confronted by the anxiety-making business of remaining a faithful witness to what I may not understand: Sue Jenning's advice to 'stay with the chaos and allow the meaning to emerge' (Jennings 1987, p.15) is wise but difficult to follow.

There are, however, ways of reflecting on what I see that I find helpful in the overall presence of not knowing. In the psychotherapy unit where I work, many clients are dealing with the long-term effects of childhood abuse and emotional neglect manifesting themselves in present relationship problems, difficulties in negotiating life transitions – particularly those involving loss – problems of self-esteem, eating disorders and self-harming behaviour. In the dramatherapy group clients may or may not address these issues directly, but within the here-and-now dynamics of the group old scenarios are constantly recreated. The dramatherapist interested in whole-group process might make the imaginative leap that, at any given point in the life of a group, the interplay between these individual scenarios and group-level processes constitutes a kind of play, often invisible but experienced as tension.

This notion of group tension is at the core of the group focal conflict model developed by Whitaker and Lieberman, and I often find it a particularly helpful frame for moments like the one just described. In its simplest form, the theory suggests that, on the level of the group-as-a-whole, members experience both a here-and-now shared wish (disturbing motive) and a fear of its consequences (reactive motive). The group's energy is constantly devoted to finding a shared solution to its present conflict between desire and fear: enabling solutions (which partially minimise the fear but primarily gratify the wish) allow the group to develop and mature; restrictive solutions (which primarily appease fear) work against healthy development. The felt group tension is the conflict between desire and fear and, often, between two or more competing solutions (Whitaker and Lieberman 1964).

What can be 'seen' is the solution. For example, a group wishing to express its anger towards its leader but fearing the leader will retaliate or collapse, may find a suitable scape-goat in another group member. The group solution acknowledges both desire and fear, but in this example focuses primarily on appeasing fear.

The dramatherapist responds to this kind of seeing in ways quite different to the psychoanalytically trained group therapist. She may invite group members to discover the shape, texture and driving power of that tension through embodiment, or she may initiate sculpting or maskwork. She makes, to use Keith Johnstone's term, a dramatherapy 'offer' that may be 'accepted' or 'blocked' by group members (Johnstone 1990, p.97).

Making a dramatherapy offer is an invitation to play. In my experience, using a speculative frame such as the one I describe can help the dramatherapist to make an offer that is more likely to be imaginatively recognised and accepted: if the group is vexed over the best way to build a house, I have found to my chagrin that offering a cricket bat is unlikely to be of use, even if last week the cricket match was crucial!

A theoretical frame, used in a way that can expand rather than limit possibilities, affords a place to be in relation to what we see: curiosity in such a place often offers the optimum balance between engagement and detachment.

In this case the offer was accepted. As group members talked, there was much to notice in the tension inherent in secrets that could inform the work to follow: grasping and withholding vs letting go and sharing; the fear of exposure and the impulse to show/tell; control/lack of control/autonomy; visibility/invisibility; safety and risk. The dramatherapist might muse over the safe, secret hideaways of childhood, the embodiment of holding on and letting go; the multitude of games concerned with secrets.

> We were entering a work phase. We thought about stories with secrets and soon settled on enacting and exploring two scenes from *The Emperor's New Clothes* – the first, our version of the Emperor's visit to the tailor; and the second the parade, when out of the crowd comes the astonished cry of the little boy: 'Mummy, look, the Emperor isn't wearing any clothes!'

My working hypothesis is that the group holds, at the beginning of every session, the stories that might explore the key tensions that the group must resolve in order to move forward. I don't mean that *The Emperor's New Clothes* is there in its exact form, but that it contains the narrative elements which match the group tension. In the manner of Winnicott's transitional object (Winnicott 1982), it is there to be found and used to explore creatively the interplay between inner and outer realities present in the group at the time. The story is not visible because there is no vantage point from which it can be recognised and imaginatively witnessed: no created space to shed light on it. Gersie links notions of play space to those of distance and seeing: 'In the act of imagining we create a separation between our current, actual situation and one that we imagine as an alternative... As long as we are identified with an experience we cannot see it nor can we illuminate it. Distance is needed' (Gersie and King 1990, p.36). Given this premise, I often choose to engage curiosity, not revelation. I invite people to notice, not to disclose.

The group's heightened energy for speculating on the business of secrets might be described both as engagement and a willingness to take a step back in order to see. From this vantage point it was possible to 'discover' the story that effected a transition from the beginning to the working middle section of the session.

A colleague once told me that when he feels especially 'at sea' with a client, he sometimes allows himself quickly to scan Erikson's stages of psycho-social development to help him become more alert to the stage-appropriate task his client might be engaging. I find his advice as useful in working with groups as with individuals, in relation to both the long-term development of the group and the recapitulation of developmental phases that may characterise an individual session. Such a scan might have been useful in this group.

Erikson's description of the first stage of psycho-social development, basic trust versus basic mistrust (Erikson 1959), highlights the social dimension of primary narcissism: the infant must have sufficient faith in the 'good-enoughness' of his environment before he can move on to the second developmental phase characterised by autonomy versus shame and doubt. In this phase, when the child is supported and affirmed in his attempts to 'stand on his own two feet' he experiences 'self-control without loss of self-esteem'. When he is exposed ('visible and not ready to be visible') and made to feel small in the eyes of others and himself, he experiences shame (Erikson 1959, pp.68–69).

In this session I might have reminded myself of the issues and tasks likely to present themselves when a group feels sufficiently safe to begin its journey towards autonomy: restrictive parental messages and attitudes, repressed negative feelings and disowned parts of self re-emerge as group members work at the task of establishing psychological control over their lives. The desire for independent exploration and choices calls up the spectres of exposure and shame: the experience of control over 'secret' material is, in this phase, crucial to a developing sense of healthy autonomy. How group members experience being seen confirms old patterns or provides the basis for learning to see themselves in new ways.

Such considerations are not meant to pin down our clients or to provide answers for the bewildered therapist; but they can help frame questions. How can I best assist the group in creating the kind of play space where they can both enter and observe their own emerging drama? What level of dramatic distancing may be required for individuals to experience repressed or disowned parts of themselves without shame? How do I best witness a group experimenting with 'standing on its own two feet'? How can I best hold this group as it works towards becoming its own authentic witness?

> The visit to the tailor's shop involved the Emperor, the tailor, and a mirror who reflected back to the Emperor his deluded grandiosity. We set up the scene very quickly and enthusiasm for the task seemed to spread throughout the group. There was high energy for having a go at playing the tailor, developed by the first player as obsequious, cunning, witty and imaginative – a true trickster who, like a master fiddler, made the Emperor dance a pretty jig: each time the tailor presented the Emperor with a more sumptuous garment she used the same scarf described differently. She was aided and abetted by a joker mirror who exaggerated every gesture of the Emperor's vain ogling and beamed back with comic approval at the Malvolvio-like flaunting. The roles were played with comic artistry and the audience was delighted: the Emperor was meticulously set up for a group banana skin. I, too, was delighted by the inventiveness of the players and the response of the audience. I was also wondering whether we might be in comic flight from our starting point an hour earlier; whether I, like the Emperor, was being led a merry dance. Where had this mass of energy come from?

The decision to depart from the original story and replace one of the trickster tailors with a mirror accounts in part for the shift from secrets and the consequent emphasis on language to something much more about reflections and how we are seen by others and ourselves. The group also both enters the enactment and becomes its own audience: it experiences itself watching itself. And, most obviously, the content of the story itself invites this new emphasis. Yet there is an energy for working with reflection not fully accounted for by these structural shifts. That energy is, I think, the narrative drive of the group itself as it plays with the business of seeing within the frame of the story and its possible meaning within the group.

As dramatherapists we recognise this kind of 'serious play' when we see it; but I find it a much more difficult business to describe. My attempts to do so have led me to construe much of this session as a kind of condensation of processes involving the self and identity, making visible some of the experiences of seeing and being seen that affect the core self, in relationship to itself and others. In the dramatherapy session these processes are modulated through dramatic distance and an understanding of them might usefully inform a range of directorial decisions and interventions.

In the first enactment the space between character and actor is deliberately sustained by the actors themselves through comic distancing. There is obvious delight in playing with the Emperor, teasing and tantalising him towards his inevitable fate. Both actors and characters play with notions of seeing, reflection and illusion and, by urging one another on, play with one another in a way that is both cooperative between actors and one-upmanship between characters. In Johnstone's terms, they are engaged in the creative process of offering, accepting and yielding (Johnstone 1990).

This is what most delights the audience. One could speculate that it is a needful warm-up into a space where spontaneous and creative engagement becomes possible. There is also, it seems to me, a component of much needed adult mastery over potentially overwhelming material. Landy describes this as an intrapsychic need to create internal 'distance from one's own feelings, thoughts and physical self-image' (Landy 1983, p.175). Meldrum's description of dramatic distance as both protecting and revealing the vulnerable self (Meldrum 1994) brings the process even closer to the tensions inherent in Erikson's second stage of development and, perhaps, to the business of this group.

The creative one-upmanship also expresses itself in a kind of flamboyant and healthy 'showing off,' thriving on having the fullness of itself reflected back through audience approval and delight. (The most exaggerated of the wiley tailors was played by a serious young woman whose usual pattern was to care about others and give way in the presence of someone else's need, which she presumed greater than her own.)

In so speculating I am working with the tangle of threads that reveal themselves in the simplest of dramatherapy dictums: 'This larking about is serious business.' In thinking about how the self develops and the relationship of that development to the dramatherapy space, one might postulate an interplay between a playfulness which is about mastery and one which is reparative of a much earlier and broken interpersonal bridge. In this scene the task of mastery goes on between actor and character and is maintained by comic distance. Reparation is located between performer and audience.

In reference to the latter, I am reminded of Winnicott's sense of the healing play space as belonging historically to the potential space between mother (mother-figure) and infant and the inter-personal bridge established through the baby's reflection back of him/herself through the mother's gaze. Winnicott (1982) links this historical process to seeing, and I suggest that his formulation is a useful way of reflecting on the processes of seeing and being seen within the dramatherapy group:

> When I look I am seen, so I exist.
> I can now afford to look and see.
> I now look creatively and what I apperceive I also perceive.
> In fact I take care not to see what is not there to be seen (unless I am tired). (p.134)

Kohut (1972) describes this first and essential experience of illusion ('When I look I am seen, so I exist') as infantile narcissism and he, like Winnicott, stresses the need for gradual disillusionment; for it is this primary narcissism which becomes slowly transformed into a healthy, bouyant and mature sense of self. Two of the transitional phases in this process are the 'grandiose self' and the 'idealised parent' (Mollon and Parry 1984, p.139). It is through the 'admiring response to his or her exuberant showing off' and the pleasure of 'feeling merged or linked with an idealised other' (Mollon and Parry 1984, p.139) that primitive grandiosity becomes transformed and gradually internalised into a coherent sense of self that can be susceptible to reality testing.

When this 'mirroring' is inadequate, archaic narcissistic structures cannot be fully integrated into the emerging self: the adult may be unrealistically dependent upon the mirroring approval of others; archaic grandiosity may survive as split-off false pride, impermeable to reality testing and ineffectually defending a 'fragile self' (Mollon and Parry 1984, p.137).

When I recently read over my description of the *Emperor's New Clothes* session (written shortly after it took place), I was amused and a little startled – not by my observations of delight on the part of the group and myself as we watched the enactment of this first scene – but by my almost besotted prose, broken only at the end by a passing suspicion that I was 'being led a merry dance'. For all intents and purposes, the account of an admiring mum astonished by the feats of her exuberant two-year-old!

Speculating more broadly about this, I suggest that individual and group re-enactments of the historical and developmental processes described by Winnicott and Kohut are often particularly visible in a dramatherapy group: the activity going on between performer and audience may mirror historical processes in the development of self. (This will include times when the only audience/witness to whole-group performance is the dramatherapist and times when individual members can perform both functions at once.) The group moves from a good-enough reflection of itself – which is the basis of trust – through acceptance and approval of phase-appropriate grandiosity, to creative apperception and reality-testing, towards becoming its own witness. The work in this movement is both about mastery and reparation, and the latter is partially accomplished and revealed through shifts in the relationship between performer/performance and audience. If this is so, an awareness of phase-appropriate work can inform the dramatherapist as witness as well as the dramatherapist as director.

> In the second scene an excited crowd lined the street through which the Emperor walked, like a smug peacock. When the 'ooh's and ah's' were punctured by the clear cry of the little boy – 'Look, Mummy, the Emperor isn't wearing any clothes!' – there was a gasp from the crowd which was also the group. Action stopped, and we replayed the same scene three or four more times: the queue to speak out clearly was long.

> When we sat down to talk about what we had done, the desire to speak replaced the energy for silent withholding so high at the beginning of the session: 'It was great fun to be the tailor.' 'When I was the little boy waiting to speak, I was amazed at how scared I was – my heart was really beating fast.' 'I was surprised at how real it was to be the little boy.' 'I felt I was really in the crowd.'

> No one mentioned the Emperor until Tess spoke: 'When I was the Emperor, and the little boy called out, I knew I was naked. It was terrible. I felt so exposed and ashamed.' Although less audible, there was an inhalation of breath not unlike the crowd's gasp following the

child's speaking out in the street scene. The character who had served the group so well as comic dupe became the focus of empathic attention as members felt what he felt. As the group's reflections deepened they came, through the Emperor, nearer to themselves. Some spoke of their fears that his experience could be theirs – nakedness, exposure and shame when the 'truth' became known; nowhere to go; a sense of self stripped away. At the same time, the child's cry engaged them: unlike the duplicitous mirror, the child's words were an accurate reflection of what he saw.

In the second enactment the group-cum-audience enter the scene as the crowd. Out of that crowd a small boy speaks out what he sees and everyone else knows: the Emperor is naked. The crowd gasps. This gasp is not wholly in-role nor wholly from the internal worlds of the actors. It is both at the same time. The group experiences something of the Emperor's story as both the same as and different to their own. The gasp is part recognition experienced as feeling. In terms of dramatic distance, the group appears to have moved from under-distance to over-distance to a point between where creative engagement and recognition can happen. This is the third phase of Winnicott's process: 'I now look creatively and what I apperceive I also perceive' (Winnicott 1982, p.134).

What follows is a desire to stand in the little boy's shoes and speak his words. The little boy completes Winnicott's historical/developmental process: 'I take care not to see what is not there to be seen (unless I am tired)' (1982, p.134). For purposes of examining the processes involved, let us separate the story of the Emperor from the group story.

We can imagine the Emperor on parade, where being seen is turned into the torture of exposure, the experience of public nakedness and paralyzing shame. Translators of the tale show a remarkable diversity in tackling the vexing business of how the Emperor reacted and how he escaped from the gaze of his subjects,[1] and we don't know how he lived thereafter. But we

---

1   Brenda Apsley's version of Hans Christian Anderson's tale (Cliveden Press 1990) goes for insight: 'The emperor realised that they were right. He felt very foolish, and vowed that never again would he pretend to see what was not there.' Haugaard's translation (Victor Gollancz 1974) goes for inflation of the grandiose self: 'The emperor shivered, for he was certain that they were right; but he thought, "I must bear it until the procession is over.")' And he walked even more proudly...' Finally, an anonymous writer (Nelson and Sons 1965) opts for a kind of stiff-upper-lip dignity: 'The Emperor heard the whispers and realised that what they said were true. ".But", he said to himself, "I have started on this procession and I must finish it." So he walked on, straight and dignified, under his silk canopy, and the pages walked solemnly behind him, carrying the train which did not exist.'

can imagine his feelings of humiliation and shame and experience them as unspeakable.

We might also speculate that the Emperor's nightmarish experience was present in the group from the very beginning of the session, in the form of deeply held fears of exposure, fears that one might be both 'visible and not ready to be visible' (Erikson 1959, pp.68–69). In other words, the internal tensions and narrative drive of *The Emperor's New Clothes* existed within the interplay of group and individual dynamics without the dramatic distance that would enable them to be seen and entered into as story.

In work with clients who have experienced abusive, neglectful or emotionally inadequate early relationships, an understanding of the genesis, magnification and internalisation of shame can illuminate the here-and-now group dynamics that play out internalised shame scenarios. Kaufman's (1993) affect theory stresses the interplay between affect, scene and language in shame-based syndromes and affords a useful clinical perspective to the dramatherapist working through enactment and the medium of dramatic distance. It suggests that when shame becomes internalised, external and often wordless shaming scenes are stored as visual imagery, bathed in shame affect. Preverbal shame scenes are modified and made available to cognition through the later addition of language. Somewhat paradoxically, it is the feeling of interest or enjoyment in particular areas that correspond to internalised scripted scenes that activates shame.

Shame is experienced as an injury to self. Kaufman (1993) describes its interpersonal origins in the 'breaking [of] the interpersonal bridge' (p.34): the rupture which occurs when 'fundamental expectations of a significant other... are suddenly exposed as wrong or are thwarted' (p.35). The shamed person experiences acute and sudden exposure, seeing himself as he perceives others to see him: 'phenomenologically, to feel shame is to feel seen, acutely diminished' (p.29). It ranges from the self-consciousness of slight embarrassment to deep narcissistic wounding, but all experiences of shame involve the excruitiating and often paralyzing sense of the self watching the self, momentarily or for long periods of time. When we feel deeply shamed, we experience ourselves as bad, as flawed in the core of self. Shaming may be followed by acute distress, or narcissistic rage, as archaic grandiosity attempts to protect a disturbed and vulnerable self from further exposure.

We all experience shame and immediate reparation can restore the interpersonal bridge and minimise the shaming effect; but when shame becomes internalised, the self attacks itself: an external agent is no longer necessary. 'Shame feels like a wound made from the inside' (Kaufman 1993, p.24). The shame-bound individual in a group may feel disturbingly transparent and fearful of further exposure simply because he is in the presence of others.

When the group in the session described comes together to talk about what they've done and Tess shares her own feelings that come from playing the part of the exposed Emperor, she is in a sense doing within the group what the little boy does in the crowd. The inhalation of breath is audible, as some members recognise the experience of shame and exposure as partly their own, but in a way that does not overwhelm them. They also begin to develop a language for describing and thus holding their experience, and in this way the group-cum-audience-cum-crowd moves closer to becoming its own authentic witness.

In his classic text on the subject of seeing, Berger (1975) describes the historical relationship between seeing and language thus: 'Seeing comes before words... It is seeing which establishes our place in the surrounding world; we explain that world with words, but words can never undo the fact that we are surrounded by it. The relation between what we see and what we know is never settled' (p.7). We might look at this unsettled relationship as it develops through the beginning, middle and end of this session. Some of this looking is observable, some speculative.

'To look is an act of choice. As a result of this act, what we see is brought within our reach' (Berger 1975, p.8). One might further imagine that choosing not to look creates at least a partial illusion of not being seen – that it is possible to protect oneself against the experience of exposing a naked and vulnerable self. I say 'naked' because that is the usual word; but in his discussion of the female nude in painting Berger makes an interesting distinction between nudity and nakedness. 'To be naked is to be oneself. To be nude is to be seen naked by others and yet not recognised for oneself... Nakedness reveals itself. Nudity is placed on display' (p.54).

The tension felt in the first few minutes of the dramatherapy group might be usefully construed thus: the longing to be experienced as fully seen – to have oneself 'held' in another's gaze in a way that affirms one's existence – along with the simultaneous fear of being seen but not recognised. The fear is to be exposed as wanting, bad or small, to experience being dropped rather than held.

Tess, who spoke of her experience as Emperor, also spoke out at the beginning of the session when she said the group often surprised her.

'To be taken by surprise', as was the Emperor, poses a very different relationship between self and other, and the consequent rebounding effect on self, than does 'taking myself by surprise,' as experienced by the member playing the little boy and by the members who responded with inhaled breath to Tess's description of her feelings as Emperor. Winnicott's exploration of the corrective play space is concerned with the latter: 'the significant moment is that at which the child surprises himself or herself' (Winnicott 1982, p.59). In an off-guard moment, in the safety of a defined play space and in the presence of a good-enough witness, the child experiences himself or herself in a new way, opening the possibility for a new relationship with self.

These intra- and interpersonal processes involved in surprise suggest a relationship between the nature of transformation and reparation in the dramatherapy play space and Winnicott's historical processes phenomenologically rooted in seeing and being seen. In the right moment, in the right space, at an optimum point of dramatic distance, the self sees the self in a way that can lead to recognition and acceptance of disowned parts of self. The dramatherapist – in working with scene, affect, language and dramatic distance – uses the materials and processes involved in the development of self and the genesis and internalisation of shame for purposes of healing and transformation.

> As we pondered this business of reflections, I suggested that we might find a different way of exploring it in another story, *The Ugly Duckling*. Some knew it well, a couple had never heard it; so together we briefly told the tale of the ugly duckling's journey towards discovering his true identity as a swan. The session would soon end, so I chose to focus on one passage, told at the time from memory but recorded here from *Women who Run with the Wolves* (Estés 1992):

> Paddling on the pond were three swans, the same beautiful creatures he had seen the autumn before; those that so caused his heart to ache. He felt pulled to join them. What if they act as though they like me, and then just as I join them, they fly away laughing? thought the duckling. But he glided down and landed on the pond, his heart beating hard.

> As soon as they saw him, the swans began to swim towards him. No doubt I am about to meet my end, thought the duckling, but if I am to be killed, then rather by these beautiful creatures than by hunters, farm wives, or long winters. And he bowed his head to await the blows.

> But, la! In the reflection in the water he saw a swan in full dress: snowy plumage, sloe eyes, and all. The ugly duckling did not at first recognise himself, for he looked just like those he had admired from afar... it turned out that he was one of them after all... And for the first time,

his own kind came near him and touched him gently and lovingly with their wing tips. (pp.170–171)

The quietness in the last couple of minutes in the session felt reflective and there was an increase in easy eye contact throughout the group. John, however, spoke loudly and clearly: 'It's alright, that, if you really are a swan, but what about if all you find out is that you're an ugly duckling?' The response from Rachel was equally clear: 'I think being a swan is really only being fully yourself.' The session ended.

I offered the story of *The Ugly Duckling* near the end of the session. Except for the brief exchange noted, there was little interplay between group and story and no real basis for speculating on how it was heard. It was a tempting gift to give, for the story is both a fairy-tale and a creative account of how the self develops through processes of seeing and being seen. It is, in one sense, a fairy-tale answer to the Emperor's excruciating predicament. However, I would have been wise to resist the temptation. John's question, which carries both disquiet and defiance, was a timely reminder that gifts which are answers to barely articulated problems are unlikely to be experienced as useful. The business of the group is exploration: the business of the dramatherapist is to facilitate and witness that process. Answers, such as the one proffered by Rachel, emerge from the stories which are the fabric of the group itself.

As witness, the dramatherapist sees, holds and reflects back what – in the beginning and in the end – belongs to her clients. As director she uses what she knows to give it form; through the modulation of dramatic distance she creates a range of possibilities for experiencing it and reflecting upon it.

This essentially 'I–Thou' relationship, as I have tried to show in this chapter, is usefully informed by key areas of theoretical understanding. In reference to shame, an awareness of its deadening effects on an individual's capacity for creative engagement can practically influence decisions about dramatic structures, dramatic distance and needs around safety and risk. I have been made more alert to the potential dangers of reactivating shame within a dramatherapy session and respectful of the power and responsibilities in my role as witness. The sinews of 'creative looking' (Winnicott 1982, p.134) are the beginnings of bridges between people.

Finally a brief caveat: it is an unsettled and unsettling business, this relationship between what we see, what we know and what we are. And it is essential that it remains so. This kind of looking is at the basis of creative engagement with our clients and what they bring to the dramatherapy space. We recognise in the shapes and colours of client experience our own shape and colour. When we process experience, the frames we use change what we see as well as help us to make useful sense of it. So it is good both to have a range of frames and to be capable of entering, at least for a while, the experience unframed.

Conclusion

This chapter identifies three primary theoretical needs for the dramatherapist facilitating an exploratory level dramatherapy group within a psychotherapy setting: a model for reflecting on whole-group process, an understanding of how the self develops, and a working knowledge of the genesis and internalisation of shame and its effects upon intra-psychic structures. The relevance of this to dramatherapist as witness and director is explored through clinical material that highlights some of the experiences of seeing and being seen that affect the core self, both in terms of Winnicott's historical/developmental processes and the psychopathology of shame. I suggest a relationship between these core processes and the nature of the dramatherapy play space and use the notion of 'surprise' to explore this relationship in reparative and transformational drama.

References

Berger, J. (1975) *Ways of Seeing.* Harmondsworth: Penguin Books (first published 1972).

Erikson, E. (1959) 'Identity and the life cycle.' *Psychological Issues (Monograph 1), 1,* 1.

Estés, C.P. (1992) *Women who Run with the Wolves.* New York: Ballantine Books.

Gersie, A. and King, N. (1990) *Storymaking in Education and Therapy.* London: Jessica Kingsley Publishers.

Jennings, S. (ed) (1987) *Dramatherapy Theory and Practice for Teachers and Clinicians.* London: Croom Helm.

Johnstone, K. (1990) *Impro: Improvisation and the Theatre.* London: Methuen Drama. (first published 1979).

Kaufman, G. (1993) *The Psychology of Shame.* London: Routledge (first published 1989).

Kohut, H. (1972) 'Thoughts on narcissism and narcissistic rage.' *Psychoanalytic Study of the Child 27,* 360–400.

Landy, R. (1983) 'The use of distancing in dramatherapy.' *The Arts in Psychotherapy 10,* 175–185.

Meldrum, B. (1993) 'A theatrical model of dramatherapy.' *The Journal of the British Association for Dramatherapists 14,* 10–13.

Meldrum, B. (1994) 'A kinship with monsters: aesthetic distance and text.' *The Journal of the British Association for Dramatherapists 16*, 8–11.

Mollon, P. and Parry, G. (1984) 'The fragile self: Narcissistic disturbance and the protective function of depression.' *British Journal of Medical Psychology 57*, 137–145.

Whitaker, D.S. and Liebermann, M.A. (1964) *Psychotherapy through the Group Process.* London and New York: Tavistock and Atherton Press.

Winnicott, D.W. (1982) *Playing and Reality.* Harmondswoth: Penguin Books (first published 1971).

CHAPTER SEVEN

Therapeutic Theatre

Madeline Andersen-Warren

Introduction

This chapter is concerned with an examination and description of a hospital-based dramatherapy group which includes performance as an essential component. Performance and a 'sharing of work in progress' with people outside the group is often stated to be contra-indicated in dramatherapy practice. However, my intention is to illustrate that, for some clients, this can be a valuable and confirming experience while remaining within the confines of therapy, as distinct from the therapeutic value that can be obtained from community theatre projects and other forms of communal theatre/drama.

The client group involved in this therapeutic theatre group were all people who had received long-term mental health care and experienced varying degrees of institutionalisation.

Dependency on systems of health care had, in many cases, created a mode of behaviours which sabotaged attempts to provide structured plans of care. This had led to a 'revolving door' syndrome where frequent admissions to hospital were followed by periods of attendance in day hospitals and, in some cases, by residential care.

The majority of the group had a range of diagnoses but most had been prescribed some form of antipsychotic medication.

The History of the Group

The formation of the group

The group was initially formed in 1986 as a result of a collaboration between a community theatre group Proper Job Theatre Projects, the writer and nursing staff.

Nurses from wards and day-care areas had expressed concern about a number of clients who were not involved in any consistent way, within diversional and therapeutic activities, and/or were so disruptive that they could not be contained within the existing milieu.

Getting the group together

Against this background 16 clients were interviewed in an informal manner and the nature of the proposed drama project was explained to them. This was to be an evening activity and has, in fact, remained so, being held from 6.30–8.30 on Thursday evenings, outside the normal daily programme. No formal assessment procedures were set up for the pilot scheme, evaluation depended on verbal and written reports from the participants.

Where it begins

Ten clients arrived the first evening. We had a high client/staff ratio as there were two theatre workers, the dramatherapist and two nurses. The setting for the group was – and still is – a large multipurpose room with a cork floor, some comfortable armchairs and also some stacking chairs. This provides a light and airy working space and is ideal for the drama and theatre games with which things began slowly. During the first weeks, group members showed more interest in the tea trolley than in the activity and also frequently left the room for 10- to 15-minute intervals. However, these absences decreased as the group, led by theatre workers and dramatherapist, became more and more involved in the action.

The group comes to life

Very slowly, over the 24 weeks, a unique relationship between staff and clients began to build.

At the time I recorded in my notes the possibility that 'outside' and 'outsiders' were becoming 'inside' and 'insiders'.

The group was being held outside the usual plan of activities, and people from outside the hospital were facilitating a group of people who had come together specifically because of their role as outsiders in other groups. The fact that the people from outside were themselves actors, that is, people who practise a craft which historically has been viewed as outside the scheme of society produced a bonding within the group. There was a sense of flexible group cohesion.

The structure of the drama allowed members to flow in and out of the activities which were coordinated in small groups. Each involved a staff member, overseen by a main facilitator.

Drama is created

Eventually the group constructed improvisations around the theme of 'the midnight hour' until a piece of theatre that contained conflict, unity, destruction and reconstruction, good and evil, distress and resolution emerged. This was recorded by video and group members suggested that we should show this to an invited audience.

Evaluation

Finally members were invited to compete a simple evaluation form.
    A selection of their comments reads:

> It was fun, helped me be with others, yet not with them all the time.

> Well, I stayed and it was OK.

> I enjoyed being silly without being laughed at.

> It helped me to write letters.

> I could do it.

> It was good.

Towards a therapeutic theatre

The members of this group formed the core of the therapeutic theatre group which forms the main body of this chapter.

    The joint work with Proper Job Theatre continued for a further four projects, since when they have retained a close relationship with the current group in various ways, often being welcome visitors during the rehearsal period. During this time more and more people became involved. Hospital staff, including secretaries, joined for a Christmas show and we received help from occupational therapy groups who made costumes designed by group members. Properties were made in woodwork sessions. Within the ethos of this activity, the confidence of group members grew and the performances became very important to them.

    Visits to the theatre combined with their own work increased their awareness of such things as acting styles, pace and theatrical conventions.

    According to group members, their performances were declared to be important for several reasons, for them the importance of giving something to others, in this case, a piece of theatre that they had created from their own ideas. In contrast they described their feelings of impotence about their previous experiences which always involved being passive recipients so that they had learned to feel out of control of their own needs. The experience of being listened to and provoking emotions in others combined with an ownership of their own creation and a sense of responsibility for their own performance in the play as they learned how to be fellow members of the same cast was stimulating and produced a sense of well being.

Endings and beginnings

The group stayed together for three years, with new members joining only at the start of a new project.

When the time came to disband there was little sense of a group ending because those involved continued to be associated, to a greater or lesser extent, in their own way with drama projects outside the hospital or would continue with a re-formed group.

People seemed to be saying 'I know I can do drama, therefore I can join other groups on an equal basis, as an actor with experience rather than as a raw beginner.' For example some of the group participated in a lengthy community project run by Opera North.

On reflection it seems to me that this level of involvement in community theatre, while not being orthodox dramatherapy, had a very strong therapeutic effect. In particular, the devising and taking part in plays that could be shown to an audience within the hospital, gave people confidence in drama as a means of self-presentation which could become part of their lives in the future. The feelings of uncertainty about life without the support of the group which so often accompanies the closure of well-established dramatherapy groups was absent. Instead, the continuing presence of drama itself provided an ongoing link between group members. There was a sense of people looking forward to new experiences of theatre as well as back to the ones they had enjoyed together.

People were aware of feeling better than they had done and wanting to develop new found skills in this craft. The project had opened a door which, they felt, would remain open in the future. Carers reported observations of improved fluency in speech, lessened psychomotor retardation, increased spatial awareness and a marked awareness of social skills including dress sense. The recipe we followed may be different from the one used in dramatherapy but the basic ingredients were the same.

This point marked the end of the first phase when I was still working in the exploratory mode. Now having satisfied myself that this approach was fundamentally viable I wanted to build upon the therapeutic value of the medium; to aim at a kind of dramatherapy which depends structurally on theatrical performance in which the relationship between actors and audience is crucial to the therapy that takes place.

In other words I have tried to use the experience gained from a community theatre project and my own theatre background and training as a way of doing dramatherapy which calls on the total theatrical event, rather than confining itself to the process of dramatic imagination which itself needs no audience. By doing this, I have tried to bring this dramatherapy, with this group, more strictly into line with those theories of a therapeutic theatre which go right back to classical times – theatre as the liberatory celebration of personal relationships.

Forming the Therapeutic Theatre Group

Membership

The group was formed from those members of the previous group who wanted to engage in therapy, having become aware of changes within themselves as a result of their experience in the group plus clients from open dramatherapy groups who desired and required a therapy intervention in the climate of a closed group.

Members were required to have had some experience of drama and to agree to take part in performance.

Assessment and evaluation

A formal assessment procedure was undertaken so that evaluation could be based on a comparison with initial assessment.

The form has undergone changes during the years but the essential components have remained unaltered. Information required for the first part of the form is standard. Details such as name, age, address, medical conditions, other agencies involved, mental health history and medication are taken from client, care workers and records.

The second half is concerned with information specific to the therapy. On one side of the form are headings; voice, body, movement, spatial awareness, imagination and concentration. These are then broken down into details. For example, in the voice category the following are listed: inflection, intonation, tone, audibility, appropriate volume and fluency. These are then graded between one and ten (one – speaks in monotone; to ten – varied undulations in voice).

General questions relating to voice are asked and responses of various kinds are recorded (for instance, 'When you raise your voice does it seem to get stuck anywhere in your body?' and 'Do you use your voice for anything other than saying words?' 'Can you think of other ways we use our voices?').

Next, imaginative processes are recorded in response to the meaning of proverbs; sentences are completed, such as, 'one day a little boy woke up and looked through his bedroom window; he was surprised to see...' and 'a woman sat at the side of a road, she was startled to see...', small objects are sculpted to create a story.

It was noticed that the people who had been involved in the community theatre project scored significantly higher than other potential group members.

This initial interview closes with a general discussion centred around the clients' understanding of theatre and drama.

I have found this to be an essential and very important process as great difficulties may be encountered if the clients' view of theatre were to be centred on actors performing in a box set behind a proscenium arch, in a naturalistic mode, while the dramatherapist is concerned with a different view of theatre, maybe, imagistic styles or physical theatre. In order to promote the feedback necessary for group drama, it is important that discussion on theatre should take place as an ongoing part of the whole process and not only during the initial interview.

During the time between the interviews, the first group members were encouraged to think about which potentially sensitive areas they would be interested in exploring (some of them would, of course, have been discussed in the initial interview).

The group

Our first two plays were story-making projects in which self-contained stories created by group members were linked by a central theme and structure presented in a non-naturalistic style. However, in order to convey a sense of our rehearsal processes I shall focus on other plays which, I hope, will illustrate how an understanding of theatrical genre provides the impetus and structure for the therapy. The two contrasting productions are a melodrama and our adaptation of *A Christmas Carol*.

The Melodrama

The group's aim

The first meeting for any project is always tense, cautious and slightly chaotic. People seem to be feeling that the last production was the best they could do and 'how can they follow it'.

New members are given a short history of previous productions. In fact, they have usually already seen them as an audience member.

From the chaos of apparently lost creativity an idea of the kinds of risks that people want to take both as individuals and as a group start to emerge.

On this occasion, individual risks were specified as: being a character of a different age than myself; being alone on the stage, making long speeches and showing a lot of emotion. Group aims were: to work with music; to express lots of emotion; to put together a complete play with a simple storyline; to develop characters; to 'move a lot' and to produce a play where the audience can understand what is happening without needing to hear it all. (This last comment refers to performances of plays where the actors have had to cope with various hazards – audiences who talked in the wrong places or were hard of hearing or background noises that were over-loud.)

As a dramatherapist I was also keen to work on some unexpressed areas of difficulty that were still present, for instance appropriate touch was still hard for some members and, as they had expressed, fluid movement and the bodily expression of emotion were definite areas of difficulty.

Thinking about these requests I decided that a strong yet simple structure and a contained yet fluid style of theatre were needed.

One genre emerged as a the solution – melodrama. Yet how to sell this particular approach to the group? As I suspected and feared, group members produced all of the stock responses to melodrama. The form was stated to be insincere, 'over the top', funny, unperformable and silly. Some group members also contributed their insight that they had often been accused of being melodramatic in their everyday lives and to attempt to produce this on stage would be unhelpful to say the least. As the term melodrama is indeed often used in a derogatory manner, it was difficult to persuade the group that this form would most closely fulfil their proposed purpose.

I did not want to cajole members into doing anything with which they felt uncomfortable, yet I felt sure that the genre would be helpful to them if their knowledge about this product of the Victorian theatre could be enriched and their interest stimulated.

As an undergraduate drama student, my own interest in melodrama was fired by the lectures given by Chris Meredith, whose knowledge and enthusiasm for this period of theatre has inspired generations of students. I asked the group if I could invite him to come to talk to them before a final decision was made. Slightly puzzled that an academic could be interested in melodrama, they readily assented.

Chris kindly agreed to talk to the group and thus awakened their interest so that they became quite enthusiastic. Practical work on acting styles produced excitement and a profound change of attitude. We were ready to begin work on our melodrama, supported at intervals by Chris.

Taylor (1989) describes the Victorian theatre as a 'theatre of feeling' and I started an 18-week rehearsal period with exercises centred on emotions. We used well-known theatre exercises and others that I invented on the theme of opposing emotions, gradually making these larger and larger expressions of the life of the body.

In melodrama, the emotions conveyed are not complex. Only one emotion was conveyed at a time, this had to be understood by an often noisy audience in a large theatre responding to actors who performed without the aid of sound systems. Emotion was shown by movement which was often almost balletic in form and style.

From working with the familiar dramatherapy method of sculpting, we moved to using our bodies to reproduce tableaux from contemporary illustrations of Victorian melodramas.

The emphasis was on first of all finding the emotion and then allowing it to flow into every part of the body, from the tips of the toes to the ends of the fingers and finally the face. Without words we developed the tableaux into short scenes; next we moved in slow motion to hug or embrace another person, to comfort a griever, to express joy to a bringer of good news and to react to an intruder.

During the weeks, members busily and voluntarily engaged themselves in research of the period. They brought back information about social conditions, costumes and photographs of family groups and music from the period.

As we worked to find and embody the acting styles as sincerely and as accurately as we could across the intervening culture gap, I slowly introduced music which enabled the movement to flow in more fluid and expressive ways. I had left the addition of music to this point as I wanted it to enhance the acting style rather than dominate stage movement in a way that would start people dancing.

Only now did we start to think about our characters or casting.

During the improvisations, people had tried a range of the stock melodrama characters – the young hero, the heroine, the mother, the villain, the exotic outsider and the old person, etc. They had embodied them and brought them to life; now they needed to choose one to further develop. A difficult decision. It was interesting to see how people chose a character rather different from themselves.

In dramatherapy terms we often speak of dramatic distance; regarding it as one of the most important therapeutic factors in dramatherapy. This gap or distance between ourselves and the character we elect to play can permit us to examine traits, emotions and their corresponding body positions that we would not, for a variety of reasons, choose to associate ourselves with in other circumstances.

The idea of playing a character removed from themselves was one of the risks that group members initially set for themselves. Members were now asking 'Will people believe in us if we play against appearance?' For me, as a therapist, this sentence contained several layers of meaning. Was it a straight unambiguous question about the performance, a metaphor for life or an expression of change?

Their question was not replied to directly but facilitated into a discussion about the nature of truth in performance and how this can be conveyed to an audience. The group's conclusion was that if they believed in themselves, the art form and the character, then the audience would believe. We could enable the audience to enter into a willing 'suspension of disbelief'. As is usual in dramatherapy practice no one was cast by the director/dramatherapist, each role being negotiated; smoothly in this instance as only one person wanted each part.

The male juvenile lead was taken by our oldest male group member, the corresponding female part by the oldest female, the outsider by one of the core group members who often took on a welcoming and helping role within the group. The heroine's mother by one of the youngest members and the old villain by a gentle young man who was a group member. In addition, a participant who was constantly aware of his working-class origins and his 'lack of style' chose to be a rich and benevolent aristocrat. We also had an orphan boy who wanted to be on the periphery of the play and finally a messenger.

Before moving on to create a plot we worked on character.

The characters in melodrama tend to be one dimensional rather than the kind of rounded characters detailed by E.M. Forster, for instance. They are not psychologically complex and there are no subtexts. What the characters want is clearly stated in each line. Similarly there is no point in searching for objectives or super objectives, yet Stanislavsky himself (Magarshack 1950) had a great respect for melodrama when it was truthfully portrayed.

Our aim here was to make our play as truthful as possible according to the rules it must follow in order to be a genuine melodrama.

Our starting point was to build upon the relationships between the characters and their environments. As we did not know what might happen, we started with tableaux that reflected the relationships, going on to experimenting with as many variants of the relationships as we could. For example, the outsider became a gypsy who had travelled to strange lands and learned many exotic customs. Back in England he struggled to earn a meagre living by telling fortunes. The villain was a landlord who wanted to marry the heroine, who, of course, loved the hero, the nephew of the benevolent Lord Bootlace. What would happen in the course of the play to this collection of characters?

To start off, we decided on an opening tableau, a device we had used before. This gives characters a chance to introduce themselves. In this case it was to be a silent tableau accompanied only by taped music.

The photograph of a Victorian family was our focus. What was the heart of the family? We decided that this was the mother and daughter (who became Mrs Worthing and Miss Constance Worthing). We also decided that mother and daughter should be seated, so two chairs were set for them. What was their relationship? They loved each other. Where is Mr Worthing in this picture? It emerged that he had been killed at sea! The start of a plot! How could this have happened? The villain caused his death. Why? Because he wants to marry Constance. Questions and answers came tumbling out as we blocked the opening sequence.

The movement between Mrs Worthing and Constance was dictated by their relationship and carefully selected music. Mrs Worthing entered slowly and sat on a chair, gracefully but rather tired and pre-occupied. From the opposite side of the playing area Constance appeared happy and lively. She curtsied to her mother who rose to greet her, cheered by her daughter she embraced her and they slowly sat down, touching hands, a still picture of a close mother and daughter relationship.

Now, coming from the audience area Lord Bootlace appeared. He removed his top hat (by this time actors already had one item each to aid their character's movement) and bowed, a complicated gesture for this actor who lacked coordination but who practised and practised between sessions until he could proudly display his perfected movement.

Lord Bootlace moved behind the two women and gestured for his nephew to join the group. The nephew, Oliver, entered, acknowledged his uncle and greeted Constance in different mode: this was the woman he hoped to marry! It was this happy group that the appearance of the gypsy interrupted. As he reached out to them for inclusion, they recoiled at the strange sight he presented, then suddenly everyone's attention was captured by the landlord villain! Their gestures of rejection turned to fear as he viciously threatened them before he turned to leave, followed by the rejected gypsy. The nephew, bidding Constance an extended fond farewell departed following Lord Bootlace. At this point we paused to devise a rough outline for the plot and the further interactions between characters.

The conventions of domestic melodrama demand a particular structure for the events in the play. These usually involve distress on behalf of the hero and heroine, particularly the latter, who is wooed by the villain for evil purposes.

The forms of good eventually triumph over evil. This is often coupled with a revelation which causes surprise to both the characters and the audience. Rather than hindering the process of dramatherapy these structures, which are similar to those in myths and fairy-tales, can act as containers for creative ideas to flow within, providing a catalyst for the construction of group and individual inspiration and for interpretation of how the story of the created characters may develop.

In this particular group, each participant was now familiar with his or her character and had some idea of their relationship with other characters. The next stage involved starting to build a scenario, hesitantly at first, and then as things started to gain momentum, ideas flowed and a storyline was formed.

In order to sustain dramatic tension we decided not to reveal Jasper's involvement in Mr Worthing's death until the finale, when it was also to be discovered that Jasper was the gypsy's long lost brother.

At this point our running order was as follows:

Scene 1: Tableau and introduction to the characters.

Scene 2: The delivery of the letter containing news of 'Seadog' Worthing's death.

Constance and Mrs Worthing are destitute.

Scene 3: Carlo, the gypsy, gives his history of travel in strange lands and laments his present state of destitution. In his crystal ball he sees danger for Constance from Jasper. Oliver enters and the gypsy warns him of impending danger. Oliver ridicules Carlo's warning and he leaves.

Scene 4: Oliver, alone on stage, starts to wonder if there could be some truth in the gypsy's warning. He declares his love for Constance.

Scene 5: Constance is distraught, Jasper demands the rent.

She cannot pay. He demands her hand in marriage or she and her mother will be sent to the workhouse or debtors' prison.

Scene 6: Lord Bootlace muses on the sights he has just witnessed in the workhouse he has visited for the first time. Oliver enters and begs help from his uncle.

Scene 7: Mrs Worthing begs Constance not to marry Jasper. They try to console each other, Constance will marry Jasper to save her mother.

Scene 8: Jasper comes for his answer. Constance refuses. Jasper decides to kill her so Oliver cannot marry her. He renders her unconscious and turns on the gas taps so that it appears to be suicide.

Scene 9: (To be played in front of the tableau of Jasper and Constance.) Lord Bootlace, Oliver and Mrs Worthing express their distress.

(This was performed in silent movement with a photograph of Constance as the focal point.) Carlo reads his tarot cards and sees grave danger for Constance. He rushes to her aid and rescues her just in time. He is shot by Jasper, but before he dies, reveals he is Jasper's long-lost brother. Jasper sees the error of his ways when he is reminded of his tragic childhood. He shoots himself.

Scene 10: Alerted by the shots, Oliver, Lord Bootlace and Mrs Worthing rush to the house. Oliver and Constance are reunited. They find a letter in Jasper's pocket which shows he planned Seadog Worthing's death. Lord Bootlace invites everyone to share his house. They honour the gypsy and see his final card which foretells future happiness for everyone.

How were we going to make this come alive? Several issues needed to be considered. Although some group members had elected to take small parts in the performance, it was important that they were as active in the rehearsal period as those with larger parts. Our contract required us to meet each week as a complete group, so the activity needed to be structured in order for everyone to have the chance to be involved all the time unless they actually chose not to be. This should be a personal choice, not one dictated by some kind of 'leading actor' hierarchy. In fact, my main aim in all this was to make it possible for the whole group to be involved all of the time.

In performance we never had an 'off stage' area. Everyone was on stage for the whole performance. In this project the playing area was framed by a row of chairs on each side. Actors not actually in the scene 'framed' the action by sitting in the chairs, sometimes reacting, sometimes comforting someone, sometimes making sound effects. This was the first way the aim was achieved; the second was by using the kind of exercise which would help us develop particular styles of acting; the third, by improvisation-based relationships between the characters and the plot.

Certain scenes were improvised which were never intended to be performed. The total area of the room was used for rehearsal workshops. These had three main aims: to explore acting itself; to examine a particular acting style (in this case that of melodrama) studied by means of pictures and traditions of Victorian acting, and that style expressed in a particular melodrama – that is, melodrama style as we had discussed it and practised it ourselves during the rehearsal period.

For example, the scene between the villain and heroine came to life once the two actors involved recognised the real dramatic meaning of the scene and could combine meaning and form.

The danger of expressing genuine emotion, and of revealing oneself as a vulnerable human being was balanced by the ready-made 'mask' provided by theatrical convention. Risk and safety combined to permit a measure of self-expression. In other words, a basic – if not the basic – principle of dramatherapy shared itself within a traditional theatrical setting. The degree of identification with the characters they were playing was by no means perfect. Having discovered the dramatic reality of the characters they were playing, the actors sometimes found that they could not react to the plot as flexibly as they would like to have done without getting out of character. For example, the actor playing Lord Bootlace had, through this dignified and controlled man, found what he described as 'a centre of stillness!' This was very precious to him and quite a startling discovery, as he had previously viewed himself as a very agitated and restless person.

At one point, the plot formulated by the whole group seemed to demand that he confront the villain. We rehearsed this several times but he always resisted the interaction. Somehow, working with stillness as the essence of Lord Bootlace and added concern, loneliness and sadness without problems, somehow working with stillness and confrontation confused him. It was a combination he could not yet understand physically or emotionally. I suspect, however, that all actors are forced to come to terms with similar problems at some point in their characterisation. After all, drama and theatre are about our ability to play a range of roles, some, if not many, of which we will find difficulty in associating ourselves with. In this case, it was a problem of role flexibility. He had achieved a significant change in the way he was able to be himself; he hesitated to put his new understanding to the test. He understood that it was through the character that he had found something for himself, his fear was that another, more familiar aspect of himself, his aggression, would surface and destroy the very stillness he now cherished in increasing areas of his life.

As a dramatherapist I felt that I could afford to wait until he was sufficiently confident to continue his journey, in his own time. Appropriate clinical consideration here took priority over artistic aims and this scene was not included in the performance. The actor did, in fact, find gentleness in confrontation through another character, Jacob Marley, in another production. This was all part of the rehearsal process, leading towards the actual performance.

In the following section, Anna Seymour, an actor and director, describes the play as performed.

Response to the melodrama (by Anna Seymour)

The performance took place in an airy basement on a sunny day, for a 'Friendship Club' at a technical college. A performance space had been cleared with two plain screens providing a backdrop. The audience chattered noisily. There were no reverential silences, no blackouts or explosions. The overture insinuated itself from a modest tape recorder. The actors, dressed in period costume, simply made a tableau for us to look at and through their quiet conviction engaged our attention.

They began their melodrama – a form maligned and exploited in pastiche by the makers of TV comedy shows. Yet what the group managed to do was inject life into the form by making it their own rather than presenting us with a trite piece of entertainment.

What I experienced was performance of such refreshing honesty that many a professional actor could envy.

The fact that the juvenile lead in his striped blazer was a lined man in his 60s or that the daughter Constance was considerably older than her mother was of no consequence. We could believe these stage relationships because they believed them and presented them with total commitment. This was important. It is easy to mock melodrama and the term 'melodramatic' is generally used in a derisory way. The impulse at first may be to laugh at the convention. Moral structures are clear, the heroes and villains unmistakable and the plot is always predictable.

Here young Constance and her mother face the workhouse if she doesn't agree to marry the wicked landlord. But her heart 'belongs' to another. Through the twists and turns of evil threats, declarations of love, predictions by the travelling gypsy Carlo and the discovery of a crucial letter by the romantic hero, the plot finally reaches its dramatic conclusion. The villain dies but not before the revelation that he and the gypsy are long lost brothers. They share a poignant deathbed reunion followed by the joyful realisation that now the lovers will be free to marry. At this point the benevolent Lord Bootlace intervenes putting his home at the disposal of the family and thus secures their future. This final resolution is gratifying and we leave the performance with a sense of well being. The circumstances of the story have been chosen by the actors and resolved through the theatrical convention. This was significant. The form enabled the relationships to be examined rather than restricting the exploration. This is made clear in the importance of physical posture and stage groupings in melodrama. Far from being dismissable as an excessive show of emotion, attention to the detail of large and clear gesture can actually focus on the truth of that emotion. The sincerity of the actors' approach removed any ambiguity of meaning. This was immensely satisfying, to see simple feeling expressed on stage, unadulterated by clever tricks or irony. At times things went wrong and there were moments of nervousness but this didn't matter, the actors were sufficiently supportive of each other to allow the action to continue. The Victorian costume was carefully designed and the actors were as at ease in their clothes as they were with their characters. Similarly the incidental music was appropriately atmospheric but was also used to advantage in highlighting moments of dramatic tension.

I was aware of the performers' vulnerability but at the same time realised how this was exposed in a situation made safe by the conventions of a particular theatrical genre. Not only was the devising of the play a therapeutic means for the actors but it invited the audience to share in the idea that showing vulnerability is legitimate, often necessary and can be respected. The artistry of the theatre supplied a way of dignifying the personal relationships and individual journeys which became collectivised through the play. Thus the audience were able to engage fully with the performance. This was creative work in progress which could be shared. What better recommendation could there be for a piece of theatre?

A Christmas Carol

Introduction

This was another project based on material from the Victorian era. However, our approach was completely different. The decision to work on this text was influenced by the group's desire to present a seasonal performance for Christmas and an interest in adapting a well-known text.

During our work on the melodrama and the following project on myth and story telling people had started to discuss, albeit in a limited way, the relationships between the personal and the political, and the individual and society. The choice of *A Christmas Carol* provided a focus for these concepts to be examined and developed.

Aims and objectives

When I came to draw conclusions from our experience in previous groups I could distinguish some areas in which there had been definite and recognisable change. Using the actual formal evaluation techniques confirmed this. These were: increased spatial awareness, a recognition of the boundaries of self and others; appropriate affect; and a more expressive use of the voice.

Assessment prior to this group defined some shared areas of difficulty.

The story-making elements highlighted problems with abstract thought processes, confusion about the differences between engagement and distance, and the differences between social and personal role interactions. (We had already worked in the areas of family and friendship roles and understanding of these had substantially improved but we had not focused on social/public roles.)

At our first group meeting the formal setting of our aims and objectives was, as usual, based on the interface between theatre and therapy and divided into individual and group aims.

Aims included those identified in the assessment/evaluation process and also: to play more than one character and to establish changing character without the aid of costume; to work as an ensemble; to determine how interactions between people are determined by status and class; exploring and experimenting with different forms of anger; responding non-verbally to other people; and using our voices in different ways. Our proposed adaptation of *A Christmas Carol* was to provide the framework for these in both a direct and an indirect way.

The preparation

At the next meeting we used a very large sheet of paper, ruled into columns. On this we set down characters, scenes and important objects (such as Scrooge's front door and bed). The scenes were then broken down into units and the characters and objects added to each unit.

As a method of starting to create our own dramatic images we divided into small groups. Each group took an equal number of these and devised a still, sculpted, non-verbal image for each of them. Thus, the whole plot was presented by showing each image in sequence. We further developed this by adding sentences from the characters and each group wrote a short statement about the attitudes and motives of the characters, not as the character, but as a commentary about what was happening.

This exercise helped us to prepare for the imagistic style we were aiming to achieve and formed the beginning of our experimenting with distance, starting to view our own actions from without!

The commentary statements were then transferred to large sheets of card and placed on the floor.

Our next move was to make a link card to go between each placed card. For example, the description of one unit read 'Marley had been punished for the way he lived his life, cheating people. He wants to warn Scrooge about how awful hell is!' The link card read 'So – Marley decided to visit Scrooge one Christmas. A time when he could be very good to other people!'

The cards were eventually placed in a circle, starting and ending with the unit in which Scrooge was handing out Christmas presents. From here we looked at different ways to tell the story. In pairs, the participants chose different styles of story telling and decided upon contrasting presentations. One pair decided to tell the story as a ghost story, imagining that we were all in an old house on a dark and windy night, another pair relayed the plot as journalists, another as two excited children on Christmas Eve suggesting the setting of a warm room heated by a huge log fire with falling snow visible through large bow windows. Each method gave a different emphasis to the tale and allowed us to view the text from varying perspectives.

Before we began the process of casting, I set one more exercise in order to gain further perspectives. We broke the text down into sections in which objects were important. We decided upon a Christmas tree for the beginning and ending sequence, Scrooge's school and office desks, his front door, a candle, the Cratchitt's oven and table and a pawnbroker's shop.

The whole group sculpted each object and, while 'in role' as the object, discussed the scenes they imagined being played around them. The effect of this was quite powerful. The actors experienced a sense of frustration and a loss of power as the inanimate objects, as they were unable to intervene in order to change the sequences of action, but we also achieved a sense of the kinds of choices that characters were making as the plot unfolded in their imaginations.

We had previously decided to perform the play without props or period costumes and with everyone active within the playing area for the duration of the performance. The experience of 'being' the objects brought them into prominence during the process of choosing parts. I view this as very important as it provided people with the option of actively choosing to play an object rather than passively opting for this as a negative choice. We also listed other characters who would be essential for our particular adaptation. These included beggars, carol singers, party guests and scavengers.

Casting took place quite swiftly as people had already formed ideas of the kind of risks they would like to take during the rehearsal period. Some negotiations were needed but we completed the task to everyone's satisfaction.

As group members wanted to spend some time on the story, we decided to spend the next few sessions blocking the play through improvisation in an imagistic mode.

The units of action became:

(1) Scrooge distributes Christmas presents to a group of people who have been decorating the Christmas tree.

(2) Back to Scrooge's past. Scrooge and Cratchitt in Scrooge's office, surrounded by beggars.

(3) Scrooge returns home through streets full of beggars.

(4) As Scrooge reaches his house the door knocker turns into Marley's face.

(5) Marley meets Scrooge inside his house.

(6) Scrooge eats his supper and retires to bed.

(7) The Ghost of Christmas Past takes Scrooge back to his apprenticeship and school days.

(8) The Ghost of Christmas Present shows Scrooge the way that his nephew and the Cratchitts celebrate Christmas and shows him the children, ignorance and want.

(9) The Ghost of Christmas Yet to Come takes Scrooge to look at his gravestone and to witness his possessions being sold.

(10) Scrooge awakes and decides to change his ways.

(11) Scrooge distributes Christmas presents to the people who had decorated the Christmas tree.

The link between units five to ten was the bed created by seven actors with others playing a large bedside candle and a bedside table.

Now that we had a clear idea of how we could present the story we needed to work on each unit in fine detail.

Each sequence was built up in a different way but all were informed by our declared intentions to look at the relationships between the person and society.

To describe some of our rehearsal processes in some detail, I will concentrate on how two units were developed for performance.

The opening sequence was devised through improvisations based on the standard drama format: Who? – Scrooge and friends (people whose debts he had discharged). When? – Christmas Day morning. Where? – Scrooge's sitting room. Why? – Scrooge had opened his house to all the people he has made destitute from loans and loan interest, to provide them with a celebration he had purchased a huge Christmas tree and decorations. What is the scene about? A celebration of Scrooge's change of attitude and people's willingness to accept it.

One actor played the Christmas tree and stood arms-outstretched on a chair singing the carol *O, Christmas Tree*, while the other actors, in mime, excitedly passed the baubles to one another and decorated the tree.

We decided upon the carol for several reasons. First, singing was to be one of our new uses of voice; second, because we needed a device to call the audiences' attention to the start of the performance; and third, because the melody to the song is also the tune of *The Red Flag*. Some members suggested this would be in keeping with the interpretation that we were working on. As the carol ended, Scrooge gave out the presents to the delighted recipients, who proposed a toast to Mr Ebenezer Scrooge – a generous and kind-hearted man! As the merrymakers sang the praises of Scrooge, the actor who was to be Bob Cratchitt stepped forward and the action froze. The actor informed the audience that things had not always been this way. He introduced Scrooge, standing in his cold and bleak office, counting his money and bemoaning the fact that some of his cargo ships had sunk and he had lost expensive goods. As if this wasn't enough he would also have to pay for stamps to send letters to the drowned sailors' widows. This convention of actors stepping out of the action and narrating or commenting on the play was repeated, in differing forms, throughout the performance. Sometimes people commented on their own character, sometimes on the sequence of events and sometimes on wider issues of a social nature. For example, poverty, ill health and charity. As Scrooge lamented his losses, the other actors joined the scene. A cold and weary Bob Cratchitt bent over his work, his freezing fingers hardly able to hold his pen and two groups of beggars, hunched and frozen in the howling wind framed the action.

Our first attempt at this scene was superficial and stereotyped. The beggars slapped their hands against their bodies with enormous vigour and their begging actions were quick and active. Scrooge and Cratchitt improvised their lines with gusto, resembling a quick-fire interaction between two friends and with a sense that, as the audience would already know the content of the scene, it could be rushed.

In order to bring a dimension of truth to the performances, I adapted exercises from Augusto Boal's *Theatre of the Oppressed*. Each actor defined the nature of their oppression. These were – Scrooge/money; Cratchitt/Scrooge; beggar/class systems; beggar/the rich; beggar/hunger; beggar/the cold, etc.

Pairs were then formed and divided into person A and person B. Person A then sculpted person B into their character's oppression and showed them the kinds of movements and sounds they would make. Person A then placed themselves in relation to the oppression. Person B responded to this stance, person A reacted to person B which caused a counter-reaction. We continued to play with the format of reaction and counter-reaction, initially in silence, then sounds (not words) were introduced. As the exercise progressed, we moved from a cerebral response into spontaneous and expressive movement. The sequence was then repeated with the roles reversed.

This very simple game allowed the actors to respond with total expression of self and to find a pace and movement for the character.

We then replayed the scene, imagining that the oppressors were also present. Not surprisingly this gave the acting an animation and power that it had been lacking. The interactions between Cratchitt and Scrooge gained a sense of urgency and immediacy and became an illustration of a real relationship between a mean and unscrupulous employer and his meek and mild employee. It was both a representation of the relationship between this particular employer and employee and a universal image of the oppressor and the oppressed, portraying both the general and the specific. The beggars became still and really seemed to be frozen through to their bones!

The actors had come some way to feeling and understanding the frustrations and constraints of the characters. The form of theatre style we were working with was also allowing us to experiment with distance, engagement, commentary and involvement.

Our next step was to probe further into the essence of the characters. We were starting to set up the contrasts between emotional and social engagement with the characters, and objective views of them. The actors returned to their sculpts of oppression and embodied them more fully. Making them larger and larger so that their bodies covered the maximum possible floor space, we then progressed to sculpts of the characters performing everyday actions. From these sculpts each person found one movement which represented the character in an abstract way. These movements were then taken into different dimensions of space and style; flowing, angular, straight, curved and squat. This progressed to conveying emotion via the movement, and discovering how the emotion affected the movement and how the movement could affect the emotion.

Following this we re-ran the scene with the movements informing the words rather than the words informing the movement. We found that another layer had been added. Scrooge discovered that his movement kept his body, mind and eyes closed from pity and compassion while Cratchitt's movement kept him in his place.

When we later returned to work on this scene I employed some Brechtian rehearsal methods to allow us to explore the conflicts between involvement and detachment. The purpose of these techniques is to allow the actors to become clear about what the characters are choosing *not* to say. During the interactions between Scrooge and Cratchitt this emphasised the status and class difference between the two men:

CRATCHITT (actual text): Mr Scrooge, sir – would it be possible... er, I was wondering – I wonder, could I – may I, have Christmas Day off?

[*Not*: I want Christmas Day off.]

SCROOGE (actual text): Christmas Day off! What are things coming to? I give you money for the little bit of work you do and you stop work to ask for time off!

[*Not*: Yes, you have worked hard all year and you deserve a rest.]

and

CRACHITT (actual text): Mr Scrooge, Sir, it is a little chilly in here. Would it be possible to have just a little more coal on the fire?

[*Not*: I am very cold and need more heat.]

SCROOGE (actual text): More coal on the fire. Good heavens, you'll have me in the workhouse with your extravagant ways.

[*Not*: I am concerned for your welfare and safety and you need more heat.]

BEGGAR (actual text): Please, Sir, a small crust of bread, a sip of hot drink.

[*Not*: I am cold, thirsty and hungry. You are rich. Give me food, drink and warmth.]

Both the lines of actual text, the *Not* and the following words are said by the actor. The sequence served to heighten awareness of how the perceived status of the characters informed their speech and movement. It also encouraged the separation between the personal and the political as we explored the conflicts of interests that each character, as a representative of their class, brought to the scene.

We continued with different rehearsal methods from political theatre until the week before performance. Each unit was rehearsed in a slightly different way but with our aims and objectives underpinning all of the preparation, and they all added different perspectives.

Unit eight, the ghost of Christmas Yet to Come, was concerned with the way Scrooge would be remembered after his death, if he persisted in his uncharitable ways. The sequence of the scene in performance was as follows: the ghost of Christmas past emerged from her representation as part of the bedhead and created a deep chill in the room, rendering Scrooge as cold as the beggars he had refused to help. The bedroom was transformed into a bleak, deserted graveyard. Scrooge checked his gravestone (which was not represented but imagined). The other actors stood at the back of the playing area with their arms folded, hard and rejecting. Horrified, Scrooge read the brief inscription on the stone – 'Here is Ebenezer Scrooge'. The ghost in an accusing tone asked 'Where are the mourners?' 'Where are the people to tend your grave?' 'Where are the people to weep for you?' 'Who cares, Scrooge?' In response to each question, an actor turned their back on Scrooge, mirroring the way he had literally and metaphorically turned his back on the needy during his life. Scrooge stood alone and frightened. Suddenly the actors behind him burst into hurried and brisk movement. Each one had an item that had belonged to Scrooge; a watch, a hat, a stick, a snuff box, books, cash boxes, sheets. They rushed to the front of the stage attempting to sell their wares. Scrooge recognised all of the precious goods he had amassed being sold on the open streets. He rushed into the group weeping and trying to reclaim his possessions.

This ended in a scream of 'Who are you?' Slowly and in one unified movement, the crowd turned towards him and pointed accusing fingers. One by one they detached themselves from the group and faced him speaking their lines. 'Remember me – you forced me into debt and debtors' prison', 'Remember me – I starved when you refused me a crust of bread', 'Remember me – you passed me when I was cold and thirsty'.

Repeating lines like these, people moved down stage to regroup into an accusing image. From this image emerged Mr and Mrs Cratchitt mourning their son, Tiny Tim. They were joined by other mourners who lamented his death and spoke kindly of the poor sick boy who cared so much for everyone else. The image portrayed was in stark contrast to the attitudes to Scrooge.

Scrooge was distraught and saw how he could have prevented Tiny Tim's death. He recognised how he had oppressed himself and others and determined to change. He reached out to the Cratchitts, and the scene dissolved as the actors reformed the bed. Shocked and genuinely repentant Scrooge wandered around the empty space seeking solace but finding none.

This was the scene as performed for an audience, the result of an exploratory rehearsal process.

Although we had the set framework of Dickens's story, we spent some time in experimenting with how the power balances could be redressed and changed by the other characters, through changes brought about the oppressed rather than by the central oppressor – although we had already identified that Scrooge, himself, was also oppressed to some extent.

However, the two areas that I intend to focus on are our successful explorations of anger and methods that enabled the actors to gain insight into responding intuitively to others.

To begin with the latter; this was worked on throughout the group but specifically in this unit via the improvisations around the attempts to sell Scrooge's goods.

Many of the group members still experienced difficulty with 'reading' the body language of others. The drama exercises that we used were intended to heighten this awareness. People were willing to enter into this, for them, quite threatening area because they were preparing for a performance that was very important to them. In order to understand more about the non-verbal signals generated by others, we needed to start to gain more knowledge about the energy generated from our own bodies. To achieve this we reverted to some exercises that were already partly familiar to the group. This familiarity added another dimension of safety. We started by finding a safe space in the room to stand in to find a stance that created a centre of balance in the body. This centre of balance was imagined as a colour which then expanded to flow through the whole body, creating a line of colour and harmony.

Once everyone had discovered their 'line of balance' we started to generate energy from this line by rubbing our hands together. Once people could feel the warmth created by the friction of their hands, we parted them and experimented with holding the hands in different positions to feel the changes in the energy flow. Then we passed our hands, palms inwards, around the whole body, varying the proximity of the palms to the trunk, legs, arms and head.

We discovered the varying degrees of heat generated by different areas. The sequence was then repeated with the body in an unbalanced state. The differences between the two experiences were then discussed. Our previous experience of these exercises was then to create two characters each, one from the balance and one from the imbalance and to take these characters into improvised scenes.

We formed pairs and the sequence was repeated; this time hands were passed around the partner's body without actually touching the person. In pairs participants discussed the energies they had exchanged with each other.

Returning to work as individuals again, we found colours for different emotions and portrayed the effect they had over the body. Pairs were reformed, standing back to back, and defined as person A and B. We worked to the following format: person A stood still with eyes closed while person B concentrated on a colour and emotion which they passed through their own back to their partner's back. Roles were reversed and the pattern repeated. In discussion following this sequence, it was quite remarkable that the majority of colours and emotions had been correctly identified. I would suggest that there was nothing mystical about this; the results were achieved by pure concentration on the energy (or what we colloquially call 'vibes') being transmitted to them.

We progressed to short, silent improvisations in which people reacted to the emotions being shown to them. Within this context we produced vignettes of Mr and Mrs Cratchitt comforting each other, Tiny Tim's mourners reacting to them and eventually to the line of people who were rejecting Scrooge. The preparatory exercises enhanced the performance and gave the actors more confidence in their abilities. For example, when they were standing in the downstage line they were now able to stare straight ahead instead of indulging in their previous practice of casting furtive glances at the person next to them in order to check when to move. People could now sense the movement of another person and respond appropriately.

This newly developed technique was also in evidence within the grouping that turned to accuse Scrooge. People talked about the difference they felt during the two structures.

In the former they described a chill radiating from the others, and in the latter a charged and heated energy. Both of these sequences contained a form of anger. In fact, the whole unit dealt with different types of anger; the cold, rigid anger of the rejecting group, the revengeful anger of the vendors, Scrooge's dismay mixed with anger, his anger with himself for the way he had lived his life, the distraught anger of the Cratchitts and the sorrow and anger of Tiny Tim's mourners.

Responses of anger had formed a substantial proportion of the previously described work. This was extended by in depth dramatisation of the characters expressions of anger. We worked with a variety of empty chair techniques (the characters literally expressed their anger to empty chairs), extensive voice work and soundscapes.

The soundscapes were instigated as a progression from the voice work. While taking part in the soundscapes, participants lay prone on the floor to give maximum body space for inhalation and exhalation. The lights were dimmed to protect eyes. We started with breathing exercises to enable people to work with maximum lung capacity and to prevent damage to the throat. Then, verbally with people contributing sentences when they wanted to, we built up a picture of a cold, dreary and dark Victorian street. When our description was completed we started to make all the sounds that might be present in the visual images we had created together. There was the sound of howling wind, feet crunching on crisp snow, horses hooves on cobbled streets, the cries of street vendors, beggars calling for alms and people greeting each other with 'Merry Christmas'. The intermingled sounds and calls created an atmosphere of poverty juxtaposed with wealth and well being. I then asked the group to imagine that they were all poor people and that they could see Scrooge's coffin being carried through the street. What would be their reactions? At first one or two people made a muted response, then others joined in and they started to jeer, shout and express their anger. After this had climaxed I took the group back to the street sounds and then to just the noise of the snow fluttering softly to the ground. Every soundscape followed this pattern, ending with peaceful sounds so that group members were able to discharge emotion and then relax. Each one was directly linked to the play we were rehearsing. The clients' real struggles to express anger were projected into the fiction of the drama. They were totally involved with the sounds they were creating, and the distance of time, place and person enabled them to obtain an emotional release that would have been far too terrifying for them to attempt in a direct way.

Working with the soundscapes also helped to prepare for the penultimate unit, which was celebratory. In rehearsal I usually worked on these two units together so that the celebration became part of the de-roling process. It was a structure in which the energy generated by the anger could be re-worked into joy.

This then was part of our rehearsal for the play. A rehearsal process that followed the standard dramatherapy format: warm up, enactment and de-roling.

The period of rehearsal allowed us to explore, re-explore, invent, re-invent and discover new meanings within familiar territories, to change our perceptions of self, others and the world, allowing the imaginative process to become actualised in a helpful, powerful and cooperative way.

Reflections

There were two main aims. First, to explore dramatherapy processes and a dramatherapy awareness within the format of rehearsal for a piece of orthodox theatre – that is, a dramatic sequence of scenes presented to an audience; second, to explore the therapeutic experience of theatre in the light of dramatherapeutic processes. In many ways the two are interchangeable.

I would argue that dramatherapy does not just make use of theatre and drama within a clinical context but the therapy itself is a particular application and ordering of these very structures.

Within the rehearsal period of *A Christmas Carol* exercises from the work of relevant theatre practitioners, Bretch and Boal, were selected to give a specific style to the performance and to meet the aims and objectives set by the group. These were evaluated by both the benefits that they afforded to individuals with the group and the group itself, and the audience's response to the play. For example, one set aim was to use the voice in a variety of ways. The device of commentary from the actors from within the play entailed experimenting with voice tones to produce a difference in delivery between the actor as character and the actor as an actor, speaking directly to the audience. Playing a variety of characters, of different ages and social classes demanded attention to accent, intonations and pitch in conjunction with experimenting with how different characters may express emotion; the difference between how the beggars and the vendors express their anger.

Singing was a new addition to the actors' repertoire. Christmas carols were sung to establish scene and mood, often undercutting a speech to add atmosphere and emotion. During the scene between Scrooge and the Ghost of Christmas Yet to Come, actors representing the people who refused to mourn Scrooge sang *In the Bleak Midwinter* to create the chill of the winter in the desolate graveyard, in contrast *Deck the Hall with Boughs of Holly* was sung by party guests to provide music for their dance. The penultimate scene was performed to *Ding Dong Verily on High* with altered words becoming 'Ding dong, verily on high, I'm alive, I'm alive, I'm alive' as Scrooge invited everyone to dance in celebration of life. The play dealt with life and death, and death in life, and these became themes we worked with as they emerged. They were not pre set but issues that were grappled with as they emerged. These are huge issues but the play allowed us to enter into these with the safety of structure and containment. The play, itself, also became a boundary for the group to work within. We worked with boundaries of the group therapy and the play and within these we could become clear about other boundaries.

The performance element required us to define further boundaries, the relationship with the audience, defining playing areas and, importantly, deciding upon how to respond within discussions with our audiences. People often invited us to talk about our rehearsal processes and how the performance was created. We needed to decide on how to do this without breaking the confidentiality of group members. Another aspect is the definition and practice of the relationship boundaries between the dramatherapist and group members. I go with the group to performances and on visits to the theatre. As in all group therapy, struggles between dependency and independence are often played out during the group time. The performance is a time of independence, and the pre-performance warm up that I lead becomes symbolic of a preparation for becoming self-supporting and self-sufficient.

The group have created a strong and unique identity which can contain conflict, dissent, anxiety and distress. Humour plays an important and often uplifting role and members have developed a huge sense of fun.

Our current project is our first attempt at comedy and has already enabled a different form of play and energy to be created.

Conclusion

Typically, theatre's aim is to produce a play. The play is the raw material and the finished product. The director has an image of the play in her/his mind and directs the actors to develop performances that will illustrate his or her idea – more precisely; the director's vision is the raw material, the actors' performances are the way in which the vision is given living form, and the finished product is performance. This is a crude description of plays that are director controlled and while it does not correspond to every director's approach, it is authentically theatrical in the sense of being the realisation of a theatrical idea. Some directors work in the opposite direction, towards a vision rather than from one. In other words, they explore feelings and ideas, attitudes and experiences suggested by a scenario and move into presentation of material originating in the life of a group which finds expression and embodiment in terms of a particular scenario. This approach, although genuinely dramatic (and consequently potentially theatrical), gains strength and definition by building on, or having at its disposal, a body of theory and practice evolved from the exploration of human awareness as it is dramatically expressed in human relationships. In dramatherapy the basic imaginative experience which underlies theatre is explored and developed, and time spent in moving towards clarity and definition of feeling along dramatherapeutic lines can only intensify the truthfulness of drama which is staged and presented theatrically.

From another point of view presenting their work in theatrical form can contribute to the healing experience of clients who are involved in dramatherapy by bringing a real sense of shape, definition, clarity of statement to the dramatherapeutic process. Members of this group felt it easier to express themselves in circumstances where the actions and ideas contributed to a tangible goal, a real life event – in other words a definite performance.

Acknowledgements

These performances could not have taken place without the cooperation of all the people who invited us to perform and organised the venue. I would like to thank them for their efforts. Thanks too, to Roger Grainger, Hazel Krzywicki, John Edmondson and, of course, to the players themselves who readily consented to this publication about their experiences.

Note

I make no claims that this assessment is objective, scientific or complete; it is not intended to be so. My approach to audit, evaluation and assessment continues to grow as I read books and studies on new paradigm research and I acknowledge a great debt to Roger Grainger for his publications on dramatherapy and research methods.

References

Magarshack, D. (Trans) (1950) *Stanislavsky on the Art of the Stage*. London: Faber and Faber.

Taylor, G. (1989) *Players and Performances in the Victorian Theatre*. Manchester: Manchester University Press.

CHAPTER EIGHT

Dramatherapy in Acute Intervention

Pete Holloway

The Setting

The work included in this chapter takes place within a day unit offering an alternative to hospital admission for patients with acute psychiatric problems. The day treatment unit was developed in its present form some four-and-a-half years ago, and while its relocation from an old Victorian asylum to brand new premises within the last year has presented many practical problems, the client group and philosophy of treatment have remained relatively consistent. The unit's primary function is to offer a service to ten day-patients who are either experiencing major difficulties within the community or are making a fragile recovery following an in-patient stay. Many of the people we see have survived a recent suicide attempt; some are experiencing their first or second psychotic breakdown and most are attempting to cope with acute crises in their lives that have either precipitated or exacerbated their psychiatric difficulties. Day-patients are referred by members of the local community mental health teams, by ward-based staff, or by their consultant psychiatrist. They attend the unit on a five-days-per-week basis for approximately six to eight weeks. All day-patients have a keyworker whose responsibility it is to devise a programme for the individual patient that meets their needs and addresses their current difficulties. Such programmes are a varying balance of diversional activities (arts and crafts, swimming, badminton), remedial or skill-centred activities (home rehabilitation), symptom-focused groups (agoraphobic and anxiety management programmes, confidence building) and psychotherapeutic exploratory work and 'process' groups. The majority of groups run to a weekly cycle – the exceptions being the agoraphobic treatment and an intensive dramatherapy group that is held when the demand and opportunity arise. Dramatherapy input has developed over the years to fulfil four major functions:

(1) The establishment of peer interaction as people come into the unit.

(2) A forum for exploring process issues as they arise within the patient group; e.g. feelings of 'stuckness', or fear of returning to everyday life.

(3) A psychotherapeutic modality focusing on common experiences; e.g. relationship difficulties.

(4) Individual work for people with a turbulent personal history and/or personality difficulties.

The focus of particular group interventions varies according to the needs of the patients present at any time, but one major group structure has emerged as the most practical and useful, given the intensive nature of the unit. This is a ten-session group of two-hour sessions held twice weekly; the first three sessions of which are open to new referrals and the final seven closed.

At the heart of the unit's ethos is a multimodel, multidisciplinary approach and I positively welcome staff from other disciplines joining me in running the dramatherapy groups. As well as offering an immediate feedback and support process, such involvement greatly helps to dispel some of the myths and fears about dramatherapy which may arise in any institution (cf. Jennings 1990, pp.18–20). Further, it ensures a clarity of focus in explaining theatrical and dramatherapeutic concepts, thus helping to 'ground' the practice. Despite the multidisciplinary ethos, however, we maintain our distinctions between one discipline and another. In the following section I will discuss the contribution that my training as a dramatherapist brings to the eclectic, organic ethos of the unit.

The Theoretical Orientation

The role of a creative arts therapist is a complex one. Even within our own professional and training associations there is much debate as to whether we are, primarily, creative arts workers who choose to work in therapeutic milieu, or whether we are psychotherapists who use creative arts experience as our therapeutic modality (cf. Meldrum 1994). Clearly, working in an acute psychiatric establishment there is an in-built tendency and expectation to view the work that we do as essentially psychotherapeutic – aiming for the amelioration, if not alleviation, of suffering through effecting cognitive, emotional and behavioural change. If we are to venture down the psychotherapy road, however, we must be relatively clear what we are doing there and how we can meet the expectations and demands of that particular journey.

My starting point is that drama, in its simplest form, is the essentially human act. It is the capacity that differentiates us from the rest of the animal world: 'Humans are capable of seeing themselves in the act of seeing, of thinking their emotions, of being moved by their thoughts. They can see themselves here and imagine themselves there; they can see themselves today and imagine themselves tomorrow' (Boal 1992, p.xxvi).

As such our dramatic capacity is a primary resource at our disposal when we attempt to make sense of the world around us. We could go further than this and say that it is precisely this reflexive capacity which allows psychological and emotional development and change to occur in the first place. Successfully managing the complex interface between self, other and world at large requires a high degree of dramaturgical skill – to simultaneously perform, and evaluate the reactions of others; to be actor and critic within the same corporeal and chronological space. None of this is new of course: Goffman (1959), in his seminal work *The Presentation of Self in Everyday Life*, presents a sociological perspective of our dramatic capacity; Kelly (1955), in *The Psychology of Personal Constructs*, creates a complete psychological framework upon the actor – self-critic paradigm; Boal (1992), in *Games for Actors and Non-Actors*, considers the political and transformative potential of this essentially human capacity. The cannon of dramaturgical analysis of human action is, indeed, broad and ever growing. All such analyses suggest to me that the dramatic capacity for simultaneous action and reflection is precisely the very stuff of which psychotherapy is made, and which it relies upon to effect change. The ability to bring past experience into the consulting room and make sense of it in the here-and-now; the ability to feel one thing and understand it as something else (i.e. issues of transference); the ability to evaluate, monitor and modify behaviour in order to achieve future goals, are all testaments to just how much 'talking therapies' rely on the primitive dramatic capacity of the client.

If traditional psychotherapies already utilise the human capacity for drama, then what more can the dramatherapist offer? The answer is both simple and complex – theatre. Two thousand years of theatrical history with its richness, complexity and diversity do not tend towards an easy definition of this apparently simple word. Yet all theatre forms, to a greater or lesser degree, share some common features. We will therefore take a broad and uncontroversial definition as our starting point: 'Theatre is a direct experience that is shared when people imagine and behave as if they were other than themselves in some other place at another time' (Neelands 1990, p.4). The theatrical tradition which the dramatherapist brings into the clinical milieu, then, is essentially experiential, collective (shared by people) and has that quality of make-believe, or 'as if' reality. In short, this tradition provides a repertoire of forms and structures which offer the potential of 'dramatic distance' – a dramatic reality which is both born of our experience and yet distinct from the everyday world; it is both intrinsic to 'me' and yet is shared and recognised by 'others'. The capacity of theatre to enable us to put our experience at one remove from real life has crucial therapeutic impact. For many of my patients their real life 'dramas' have already proved to be too close for comfort, precipitating major suicide attempts, psychotic break-downs or the threat of confinement in hospital. Therefore, a form of therapy which allows for objectivity, reflection and collective identification in an area that has proved to be overwhelmingly subjective can provide a degree of personal and emotional safety that more cathartic and revelatory therapies are unable to offer. Another common feature of this client group is their feeling that they cannot cope – that somehow the rigours of life have proved too much for them; in essence, that they are not strong enough *in here* to deal with what is hitting them from *out there*. Hence the guilt, the blame, the self-reproach and the fatalism of the depressive view of the world. The pervasive sense is that they have, indeed, become passive victims in the face of powerful life events. A major criticism of medical-model psychiatric interventions is that they mirror just such passivity in the patient. The agents of change are psychotropic medication or benevolent and quasi-omniscient analysts, anything but the clients themselves.

As Boal (1979) points out in *Theatre of the Oppressed*, such a criticism may also be levelled against traditional theatre. The agents of theatrical action are those specially selected, trained and talented individuals – the actors. The audience, by far the majority of those present at the theatrical event, are confined to the role of passive spectators. As such they have only a negligible capacity to influence the view of the world they are being presented with.

At the heart of my notion of dramatherapy is the invitation to become the active agents within our own dramas. For me there is no room for a passive audience of spectators within the clinical space. Such a role mirrors far too closely the inevitable fatalism that many of my patients only too easily fall into.

An invaluable antidote to such passivity is the theory and practice of Augusto Boal. His work with a variety of oppressed and dispossessed groups throughout South America and, latterly, much of Europe provides a wealth of exercises and games through which participants can easily enter into theatrical action. Likewise his theatrical forms, such as *image theatre* and *forum theatre*, provide accessible means of tearing down the paralysing, mesmerising 'fourth wall' between actor and spectator.

Within the field of formal psychology we find an echo of Boal's (1992) 'spectactor' (pp.xix–xxii) in the theories of Kelly and his personal construct psychology. Kelly's central thesis is that we, as individuals, are engaged in a constant process of actively attempting to make sense of our experience. He equates this to a scientist experimenting in order to prove or disprove his hypotheses. For Kelly, our experience of the world around us produces certain hypotheses; we then test these out in our active engagement with the world. Of course, unlike scientists, we do not have at our disposal a range of specialised equipment or a controlled environment, and Kelly suggests that our behaviour is our only experimental tool. Thus we behave in certain ways to enable our hypotheses about the world and our place within it to be tested, and hopefully validated.

Kelly starts from the philosophical position 'that we have created ourselves and can therefore re-create ourselves if we so wish' (Fransella 1984, p.139). His theory 'remind[s] us that all our present perceptions are open to question and reconsideration, and… broadly suggest[s] that even the most obvious occurrences of every day life might appear utterly transformed if we were inventive enough to construe them differently' (Kelly 1986, p.1). For patients who are struggling with a chaotic, defeating and fatalistic sense of their experience, Kelly's concentration on the fluid potential of our interpretations is of great value as well as being ultimately re-assuring. This idea of Kelly's, coupled with some of the philosophical underpinnings of classical *crisis intervention* (cf. Ewing 1978) forms the kernel of my practice within the day treatment unit.

The vast majority of our patients come to us as a result of a perceivable crisis in their life. Handled sensitively, the experience of acute crisis – with its need to gather helping resources, and receptiveness to intervention, its self-limiting nature and openness of outcome (Ewing 1978, p.14) – can lead to what crisis intervention practitioners refer to as a 'teachable moment' (Parad and Parad 1991, p.10). In Kellyian terms, acute crisis can be a time when deeply entrenched personal constructs are adapted and modified, so that behaviour becomes a rich experiment – opening up new possibilities and explorations – not just a dogmatic circle of attempting to validate redundant hypotheses of worthlessness, powerlessness, fatalism and the like.

This is the aim of my dramatherapy sessions: to provide a process where people can move from a sense of being overwhelmed by external events to opening up new ways of seeing themselves as actors in their own lives. This aim is largely achieved through the active process of democratic theatre making along the lines of Boal's *image theatre* and *forum theatre* techniques. It is a complex and difficult undertaking, dealing with the crises of being human, for as Kelly (1955) notes, our experience of the world is constantly shifting and changing:

> The substance that a person construes is itself a process – just as the living person is a process. It presents itself from the beginning as an unending and undifferentiated process. Only when man attunes his ear to recurrent themes in this monotonous flow does his universe begin to make sense to him. (p.53)

Maybe the democratic theatre forms and our active participation within them, provide us with a laboratory of human action and interaction. A forum in which we can take stock of our capacity to effect our world and to be effective within it.

The Practice

In a room that doubles two mornings a week as the ECT treatment area we set up our laboratory. For the duration of the sessions the space is exclusively ours, stripped of all clinical trappings: the trolleys consigned to an ante-room along with the oxygen cylinders. All that denotes our space are the four walls, enough stacking chairs for the group members, and the minimal equipment I may use in a session. This is our empty space – the injunction is to fill it with our imagination and our serious playing. What we create is a 'rough theatre' (Brook 1968), full of mistakes, suggestions, heckles, a distinct disunity of styles and an urgent sense of energy, sadness and much good humour.

The process of forming a group from those attending the unit starts at the multidisciplinary team meeting. Here, I (and my assistant, when possible) put forward a loose proposal, vaguely sketched around current issues among the patient group. (One of the accepted ground rules of our team-working is that information about individual patients is confidential to the team as a whole, therefore all the workers are regularly updated on concerns, progress or otherwise of all the patients.) The assessment of those patients identified as suitable candidates is a relatively informal affair. Given the degree of sharing within the staff team little further personal history is necessary. The assessment, therefore, tends to focus on their conception of what dramatherapy might involve, any concerns they might have about such conceptions, and their willingness to attend for an initial group session. I purposely do not attempt to give a full rationale of the group, or too rigid an indication of what we might do at this stage, rather I stress the basic form and structure of the group. My reason for not giving a great many details of the content of the group and not being at great pains to allay much of their anxiety, is that their staying with whatever moderate apprehension they have, and allowing themselves to test it out in practice, is the first action of the group experience. Obviously, if their anxiety is overwhelming, or comes from totally erroneous beliefs then some attempt at reassurance is made.

By the end of this process we arrive at a group of between four and eight people who have tentatively agreed to 'give it a go'. The first meeting is crucial in terms of establishing a culture of action, and overcoming that initial sense of 'what have I let myself in for?'; it is my first chance to emphasise, in practice, the fact that this is an active group. So, we start with the standard name game, throwing a ball to someone and saying their name. I then develop this into more complex interactive variations, requiring increasing concentration, differing rhythms, until we are engaged in the task of 'juggling' three balls as a group. In the process of playing, any initial embarrassment and awkwardness quickly dissipates, as people become en- gaged in the developing task. It never fails to amaze me how quickly relatively disorganised and pre-occupied people settle into this exercise, appreciating the structure and rhythm of it, and finding a sense of achieve- ment in working towards a collective goal within minutes of joining the group. From very simple beginnings we are building a sense of collective action and interacting with people in startling new ways. This exercise also serves a diagnostic purpose in that it allows me, relatively quickly, to gain a sense of levels of concentration, commitment, anxiety, explosive emotions and variations of energy within the group.

I then introduce a simplified version of a tai chi exercise which requires coordination of breathing and movement in a very basic, rhythmic routine. This exercise becomes a 'framing device' for all the creative drama work we do throughout all ten sessions. Thus it serves to signify that the time for sitting and talking is over and the time for action has come; likewise, towards the end of each session, we use it to close the dramatic action and to signify the move to reflection and feedback. The use of a standard exercise from session to session serves to create a containing ritual; group members often feedback as to how comforting it was to have such an exercise that they could take for granted. For much the same reason, the group ball game serves as another constant reference point, although rather than this being a repeated ritual, there is always some variation around the theme from session to session, thus actively conveying the idea that in our playing we will be risking new experiences. Another such reference point is a group 'pulse' exercise. (The group stands in a circle holding hands – I squeeze the hand of the person next to me, sending a 'pulse' up their arm, across their shoulders, down their other arm, they then squeeze the hand of the person next to them and so on.) As with the ball game, there are a myriad of variations, and I tend to use these for specific purposes: to focus the group after a high-energy exercise, I may send round a steady, continuous, repeating pulse; to gain some momentum after a very quiet or detailed exercise, I might make a competition of how quickly or accurately we can send the pulse around. The final reference point of each session is a closing ritual where I go around each member of the group and offer them a sheet of paper and a pen. This is for them to use as they wish and whatever they write, squiggle, doodle or simply fold away remains entirely confidential – enabling each member to individuate from the highly collective nature of the group experience. These four structures punctuate each session. They have the security of familiar territory (particularly the tai chi exercise and the closing ritual), but also underline that the group is about developing new ways of using familiar structures.

As well as these ongoing structures, the first three sessions of the group have a more global governing structure which focuses on building a vocabulary for the more intense work of the closed sessions. In the first meeting, as well as introducing the 'reference points' outlined above and establishing basic ground rules, I introduce the notion that as we meet the challenge of our everyday lives we become 'mechanised' to think, feel and respond in certain ways (Boal 1992, p.40). In order that we can use our dramatic capacity to the full we need to be able to be both aware of our 'mechanisations' and to free ourselves from them. To this end, in the first session I employ a lot of physical actor training exercises, particularly those that involve basic body awareness and what I call 'dislocation' exercises. I mean by this, exercises which serve to break up natural everyday movements – examples might be 'grandmother's footsteps', 'musical statues', caricaturing of other people's walks and so on. These then develop into more complex movements, such as moving around *as if* being pulled or pushed from certain points of the body. For the first session the majority of the time is spent with each member working individually, but we close the session by some pair work around the notion of pushing, pulling and finding points of balance. All this is done with a lot of side-coaching from me and much chance to feedback on what it felt like, and what was comfortable and uncomfortable. The reason that I conclude with balancing exercises is that I am eager, as early as session one, to introduce some form of physical contact that involves a level of trust, but without it being seen immediately as a 'trust game'. Many of the people I work with have lost their capacity to trust, or to risk trusting, and therefore introducing exercises as 'a trust game' immediately generates much anxiety and resistance.

In the second session, the focus is on introducing the idea of *image theatre* (cf. Boal 1992, pp.2–6). The concept is a very simple one: that we use our fellow actors to create an image of a particular theme, experience or issue; we do this without giving direct commands, but by physically manipulating the actor(s) into our desired image – hence the introduction of physical contact and negotiating balance in the first session. Initially, I introduce this as a game with people working in pairs; one is sculptor, the other is 'a lump of clay'. After each image they swap roles. We work very quickly – no more than a minute for each image – around stereotypes, basic emotions and on to more complex themes. The speed at which we work aims to guarantee an emotional distance so that the participants can become comfortable with the form prior to using it in a more closely emotionally identified way. From the work in pairs, we come together into a whole group (or two groups if we have the full eight members) and begin work on a group image. Often at this stage I select a particular scene from a fairy-tale, or other well-known story – again aiming for emotional neutrality as we learn the form. One of the group members will make an image of that scene (say the Ugly Sisters discovering that the slipper fits Cinderella), she will then take on the pose of one of the actors that she has just positioned, and he will make his own additions and alterations to the image, and so on until all the group members have actively put in their suggestions. Making an image in this way creates the notion that we are debating a view of the world, in action; it also ensures that the image remains a collective expression and that no one individual has sole ownership or is overly emotionally identified with the end product. This is crucial when we come on to working with more complex and potentially disturbing themes – we are not in the business of catharsis, and the sharing of ownership of these collective images helps to generate the necessary reflective distance that I have referred to earlier (see above).

In the third session we make a change of gear and begin to introduce words into the play. This may be gently structured in one of two ways: either through beginning to develop characterisations, or through generating narrative stories. As in the image work, however, the process of building a character or making a story is a collective one, and is not left entirely to each individual. In a character 'hot seat' exercise, for example, there is always a balance between suggestions from the 'audience' and improvisation from the 'actor'. Thus if someone asks, 'what's your relationship with your husband like?', and the actor cannot come up with an answer *in character*, it is up to all of us to offer suggestions. Likewise, story-making becomes a game in which we all take part, are put on the spot, and help others out when need be. These are the first stages of what Boal refers to as 'simultaneous dramaturgy' (Boal 1979, p.132), an active collaboration between audience and actor, where the actors perform the audiences' 'script' as it organically develops. Here, again, I am attempting to introduce a structure in emotionally neutral terms before we employ it within the more problem-focused work of later sessions.

In attempting to build a basic vocabulary throughout these first three sessions we broadly follow Sue Jennings 'embodiment–projection–role paradigm' (Jennings 1990, p.10), but with the extra dimension of the whole process taking place within a collective framework – thus corresponding to the theatrical notion of building an *ensemble*. By the end of these three sessions there is a developing sense of collaboration and commitment within the groups, as can be witnessed by the fact that out of 58 people taking part in the groups over the last year, only five have not continued beyond the third session. For the next seven sessions we follow one of two broad strands; which of these we pursue is partly dependent on the size of the group and partly on the homogeneity or diversity of their problem areas. If the group is small or has a variety of difficult precipitating experiences we tend to stay with the *image theatre* structure. If, on the other hand, the group is larger and has some crucial experiences in common, the work develops into *forum theatre*.

An Image Theatre Group

Andrew, Barbara, John and Roy were always a pretty diverse bunch.[1] In the general group work within the unit, Andrew remained painfully quiet; Roy and Barbara would often be in tears; and John for the most part gave the impression of being far, far away. In their individual work, little was different, although Andrew talked of having had some plays that he had written performed at a notable London fringe venue; Roy spoke of the pleasure in playing with his five-year-old nephew who was currently staying with him; Barbara talked of the creative woman that she had once been prior to becoming seriously depressed; and John was always full of (fairly unrealsitic) plans for his future. All had recently considered suicide as the only option left to them, although only Andrew had seriously acted on this thought.

In the sessions they all responded very well to the four recurring structures I referred to earlier (see above), where the direction came very much from me, but when we moved into the more improvisational mode of working, the momentum became very flat (which may have been partly due to my concerns about taking too many risks with this fragile group). After a couple

1 All names have been changed to protect confidentiality.

of weeks of going through the motions in the image work Barbara suggested that we look at the idea of being trapped by other people's expectations and demands. The group produced what was really their first dynamic image which they entitled 'the tender trap'. As each person made their alterations the image became more and more tortured and claustrophobic. When we could hold the image no longer, all of the members relaxed out of it and started talking at once about the discomfort, the feelings of being pulled in so many directions, and as Roy said 'not feeling like your own person at all'.

When working with images such as this I follow Boal's model of generating an image of 'reality', then moving to an 'ideal' image and then creating an image of 'transition'. As we moved to the ideal image it became quite clear that there was to be little agreement as Barbara and John wanted the bodies in the image to support each other, whereas Roy and Andrew wanted all the bodies to lend their support to just one of their number. We tried out a variety of physical combinations, but still could not gain consensus. Talking about the pros and cons of the two positions and trying out compromises in action, dominated the whole of the next week, but finally they came up with a very strong image which relied as much on personal space as it did on physical support. The image of 'transition' showed a slow unfolding, a letting go of the desperate grips and holds that each had on the other. Up to this point all the characters remain amorphous 'bodies' and it is only after mapping out the progression of images physically do we begin to ascribe roles and definitions to the various positions taken within the sculpt. The roles were, almost inevitably, those of family members and the story that the group told to bring the whole experience to a close was one of finding enough space from the 'ties that bind'. In feedback they all talked quite animatedly of their problems. Andrew of his mother who still treated him as a sickly child; John of his father who never liked him as a youth and liked him even less as a man; Roy of his large family who always turned to him in times of trouble, but didn't want to know when he was having a hard time; and Barbara of her attempts to juggle the demands of her elderly mother and two daughters, while only really being interested in her son. From the hesitancy of the early stages, this group managed to find some kind of a shared understanding and a clear articulation of what they wanted from and were able to give to their various families.

The Forum Theatre Groups

Where the group size is sufficiently large (as is often the case, most groups being between six and eight people, plus myself and an assistant), we attempt to develop our image work and *simultaneous dramaturgy* into a narrative theatrical scene. In devising these theatrical pieces we split up into two sub-groups. Over the course of trying out various image themes such as 'suffering', 'frustration', 'isolation', 'oppression' there comes a point where each group will find an image with sufficient dynamic tension to allow us to develop it further. The rules for making these images are essentially the same as above, but with the important extra rule that the burden of the theme should be focused on one 'body'. Thus just one of the characters in the image will be the victim of the suffering, frustration, etc. All other characters will be contributing to their burden. Again, it is not until the group has decided on a collective image do we begin to ascribe status, role and characterisation to the 'bodies'. Once we have some idea of the characters involved in the frozen moment of the image, we give it a title. We find just one line of monologue for each of the characters in the image. As the actors hold the image; I go round, one by one, touch them on their shoulder and they voice what the character might be thinking, feeling or imagining at that moment in time. The actors then swap roles again and again, so each actor has the chance to see the image from the perspective of every character. From there we make the story of what has brought the characters to this situation. We start with the facts: who the characters are, what relationship they have to each other, where the scene takes place, what they are all doing there and so on.

Over the years I have found that while this client group can cope relatively well with clearly structured physical work, and are prepared to be verbally quite spontaneous, when I have asked them to attempt to improvise through movement or to layer verbal spontaneity on top of physical activity, they become very self-conscious and guarded. I now attempt to enable them to make a cognitive map of where they are going in any improvisation, hence the focus on the basic facts of a narrative scene prior to improvising it in practice. I also point out that any decisions taken at this stage are always open to revision and even key details as to character, location and situation can be altered.

The scene is then improvised, refined and rehearsed until we have what Boal refers to as 'the model' (Boal 1992, p.19). In the process of creating the scene I take responsibility for ensuring that the 'victim' is not totally and inevitably annihilated from the outset, that there are still options open to him at the start of the narrative, and that the end point flows from poor choices made by the 'victim'. Examples of such scenes have been a single mother attempting to cope with the conflicting demands of her children; a man trying to create a life for himself on release from prison; an old woman trying to convince her son and daughter-in-law that she didn't want to go into a nursing home; and many, many more. All detailed scenes of a broad and hard experience of life. The 'models' are always primarily fictional, they are about make-believe characters in make-believe places, but the emotional identification involved in making that make-believe together means that there is a level of connection in the situation for each one of the participants. This is true even if their suggestions have been revised beyond all recognition, or have had to be compromised along the way: the fact that those suggestions were made, evaluated and acted upon in one way or another gives them an essential validity.

As the two sub-groups arrive at a finished model, they come together again. One group to present their piece and the other, initially, to watch. Now the game of *forum theatre* (Boal 1992, pp.17–26) begins. The audience, here, has a responsibility – to change the mistakes and the situation of the 'victim'. First they watch the model from beginning to end. Then it is presented again, and any time an audience member thinks the 'victim' is making a mistake or could be doing something more effective she can stop the action, take the place of the 'victim', start the action from wherever she wants and try out her proposal in practice. The actors also have a responsibility: to ensure that the proposed solution is met with realistic reaction in order to keep the 'victim' where she is. The forum may go on and on, as there are often many more not quite good enough proposals than there are clear-cut solutions. The point is not to achieve a cathartic release from the suffering, but to test out, in our laboratory, the ideas, the strength and the stamina we need to take back with us into our encounter with the real world.

Despite our not aiming for a cathartic release, however, it is not to say that it does not come. In the forum about the man returning to life from a prison sentence, Ray (who had been very suicidal and withdrawn for many weeks prior to attending the unit following the sudden collapse of his marriage) found a way of disarming the victim's wife and her new lover through a direct account of how he (the victim) was beginning to see the shades of grey that had existed in their relationship, rather than desperately clinging on to an idealised past. This was clearly a case of Ray rehearsing a new personal construct which he could take away with him through which to re-construe his own experiences.

Clinical Conclusions

While much of the theatrical work of these experiences draws heavily on Boal's models, I am not convinced that the structures themselves are inherently therapeutic (despite Boal's (1990) claims of them being a 'method of theatre and therapy'). The therapeutic power of these experiences lies in the interface between the injunction to be an active participant, rather than passive victim; the ongoing containing reference points of the group experience; the collective nature of the creative process; the use of 'dramatic distance' and, lastly, the image and forum structures themselves. For such an acute population, the need for containing rituals and 'dramatic distance' is paramount for any partial alleviation of their suffering to occur. Once these therapeutic structures are in place, and the security that they offer is recognised by the patients, then the task of tackling problem areas and re-appraising our sense of the world can begin.

For many of our patients their time at the unit is merely a first step in beginning to tackle these areas in an active and dynamic way. Therefore our goal is only very rarely to effect fundamental intraspychic change. We aim, rather, to provide just enough encouragement and challenge to allow people to begin to feel back in control. Such is the nature of acute psychiatry, and as such it requires more direct intervention than exploration, more containment than catharsis, and more distance than emotional proximity. We must first provide the safety, before we invite our patients to take the risk of experimenting with their conceptions of self, others and world at large. This safety, ultimately, comes from our ability to create a laboratory through which to explore the complexities of being human, and to utilise our dramatic capacity in that task.

References

Boal, A. (1979) *Theatre of the Oppressed* (translated by C.A. and M. Leal McBride). London: Pluto Press.

Boal, A. (1990) *Méthode Boal de Théatre et de Thérapie – L'arc-en-ciel du Désir.* Paris: Editions Ramsay.

Boal, A. (1992) *Games for Actors and Non-Actors* (translated by A.Jackson). London and New York: Routledge.

Brook, P. (1968) *The Empty Space.* London: Penguin.

Ewing, C.P. (1978) *Crisis Intervention as Psychotherapy.* Oxford: Oxford University Press.

Fransella, F. (1984) 'Personal construct theory.' In W. Dryden (ed) *Individual Therapy in Britain.* London: Harper and Row.

Goffman, E. (1959) *The Presentation of Self in Everyday Life.* New York: Doubleday.

Jennings, S. (1990) *Dramatherapy with Families, Groups and Individuals.* London: Jessica Kingsley Publishers.

Jennings, S., Cattanach, A., Mitchell, S., Chesner, A. and Meldrum, B. (1994) *The Handbook of Dramatherapy.* London: Routledge.

Kelly, G.A. (1955) *The Psychology of Personal Constructs.* New York: Norton.

Kelly, G.A. (1986) *A Brief Introduction to Personal Construct Theory.* London: Centre for Personal Construct Psychology.

Meldrum, B. (1994) 'Historical background and overview of dramatherapy.' In S. Jennings, A. Cattanach, S. Mitchell, A. Chesner and B. Meldrum. *The Handbook of Dramatherapy.* London and New York: Routledge.

Neelands, J. (1990) *Structuring Drama Work: A Handbook of Available Forms in Theatre and Drama.* Cambridge: Cambridge University Press.

Parad, H.J. and Parad, L.G. (1991) 'Crisis intervention: Yesterday, today and tomorrow.' In N. Rao Punukollu (ed) *Recent Advances in Crisis Intervention, Volume One.* London: International Institute of Crisis Intervention and Community Psychiatry Publications.

CHAPTER NINE

The Seeds of the Pomegranate
Images of Depression

Brenda Rawlinson

An exploration of the pathological images of depression, panic, and anxiety, which have emerged through the working of dreams, sandtray therapy and dramatherapy

I'm in a painting workshop, the painting I'm involved with is of a morbid nature. The colours are black, dark blue and green, browns and grey; the painting has the quality and feeling of a crucifixion, with much angst and suffering, there is little hope. Leaving my painting for a moment, I notice a woman, she walks over to my painting and begins to modify the image. When I return to the painting, I observe that she has painted a tree, on the dark background; the tree is covered with golden pomegranates, I know that these are the fruits of the underworld.

(The dream of a middle-aged woman, during a depression.)

When my mother was pregnant, she had an intense craving for pomegranates, and I, deep within the darkness of her wounded womb, ingested the sacred fruit of Persephone.

(A woman's reflection of her mother's memories of pregnancy.)

In this chapter, I will be exploring the pathologised images of depression, panic and anxiety which have emerged from work utilising dramatherapy, sandtray therapy and dreams. Styron (1991) in his book *Darkness Visible* describes his own journey through depression, with a clarity drenched with passion and images of terrible beauty. He skilfully mixes stark and powerful memories, connecting the reader with what he describes as:

> I stood there helpless... aware
> for the first time that I had been
> stricken by... a serious illness
> whose name and actuality I was
> able finally to acknowledge

(p.46)

Later he writes:

> My brain... had become less an
> organ of thought than an
> instrument registering minute
> by minute, varying degrees of its
> own suffering

(p.58)

The focus of this chapter will be on pathologised images from both the personal and collective areas of life and psyche. I will seek to explore the work through an archetypal perspective, attending to messages which emerge from imagination and soul. After taking a brief look at the working of dreams, I will be giving a place in the drama to the Greek God Dionysus. I will then look at the images which I have shared with three women who have entered the underworld of depression. Their therapeutic image-making will be linked to passages from William Shakespeare's play, *The Tempest*. The play expresses a powerful relationship between alchemical process, sleeping, shadow and dream:

> We are such stuff as dreams are made on;
> And our little life is rounded with a sleep

(*The Tempest* IV:i)

Dreams... as Interior Drama

I have always been interested in dreams. As a child, dreams always had a special significance for me. I imagined the experience of dreaming as a sacred and religious event. The feelings I had on awakening, were focused on a sense of being granted entry to a very special location. This place had a very different perspective than that of my waking state. Within this space, I entered and became part of a huge drama, which was enacted through a theatre of the imagination. The intuitive wisdom of the Child-archetype guided my understanding into an awareness of depth, meaning and truth, which dwelt naturally within this mysterious place. A world which not only consisted of my personal story, but also a vision which touched the heart and the soul of the world itself. The dreamscape contains and moves the images of life and death in a fantastic kind of spiral movement. My childhood fantasy encompassed the notion that the dream world was a place people entered after their death (*the underworld*). These creative nightly journeys moved my soul – through sleep – into a ritual of 'little deaths' in life. The aboriginal people talk of *dreamtime*, describing it as all our personal individual dreams, merely resonating with the bigger dreams of the whole universe.

As an adult I returned to a more conscious exploration of dreams, through therapy. For me, the mystery of the dream still remains; particularly in two areas: first, who makes the dream? And second, where does the dream come from? I find it difficult to answer this with any certainty! Staying with the not knowing would appear to be a powerful requirement when working with the dream, since it would appear that the ego does not initiate or control the dream. The quality of the dream moves us away from the sole perspective of ego-consciousness, encouraging a creative and playful approach. In order to do this we need to look at the dream with an imaginal eye. In this manner we can suspend an over-dependence on only one type of logic, that which has a tendency to over-control. Freud's very valuable work led us into an interpretive approach; while this has a place, there can be a real danger of fixing the image. This does not allow the imagination to shift, deepen or move the image on towards new possibilities.

The psyche would appear to regulate dream work, but does demand trust in the process, allied to an attitude of non-interference, when working with images which emerge from the unconscious. This inherent regulation of dream material helps to provide protection from the desire to over-analyse. When giving attention to dreams, it is important to recognise that the dream is telling us something we do not know. The images from the unconscious are presented to us as a guide towards an understanding of information that may not yet be apparent on a conscious level. Therefore it is meaningless and unhelpful to rush into an interpretive mode, when the messages and wisdom contained within the dream could, through imagination, allow us to move on and through without destroying the potential for future development. Sometimes images will return in the same or in a different form. If they have been dismissed, on the basis of being 'understood', the deconstruction of old ideas and the discovery of new ones can be lost.

The dream could be viewed within the framework of an alchemical process, which 'cooks' the prima-materia of soul, while providing a vessel or container through which we can learn our lifework, through soul-making.

Bosnak (1988), in his illuminating book *A Little Course in Dreams*, looks at the three major alchemical stages of Nigredo, Albedo and Rubedo. He then explores the various images associated with these stages through their spontaneous emergence within dreams. He also reminds us that this is not a linear process; he guides us back through space and time, illustrating the importance of these images in the present, past and future. In our present age and culture we tend to regard alchemy with a rather simplistic attitude; reducing it to an ancient and outmoded form of chemistry, which attempted to turn base metal into gold. Here we can observe a too-literal position of a subject, which is, in fact, complex and beautiful in its associated imagery. Alchemy can provide a powerful and deep model for viewing the dream-world.

Rubedo Stage

Within our Western culture, we put greater emphasis on the Rubedo stage. Rubedo carries images of light, it expresses a kind of sun consciousness, based largely on the principle of logos, and indeed on all aspects of life which value the heroic. The focus is placed on enthusiasm, clarity, energy, strength and endurance. The colours of the Rubedo stage are red, orange and gold, holding the image of the ultimate marriage between masculine and feminine. The quality of thought is of action rather than of reflection or musing, there is a driven energy; allied to a will and a requirement towards power. If the Rubedo passion becomes too hot and frantic, the gentle golden light, which guides our conscious lives, can become a manic whirling sun, which breaks through with ever-intense heat, burning us out. We run ever faster, over-achieving, ever pushing towards absolute perfection, not sleeping, over-working and worshipping material images which imprison us in debt and envy. We over-value youth and have no place for the natural ageing process, there is constant craving for instant gratification and we find it almost impossible to wait. When the fire of the Rubedo becomes too hot, the vessel breaks, shattering the narcissistic mirror, returning us to the leaden darkness of Nigredo.

Nigredo Stage

Within the world of Nigredo, we feel heavy, pathologise through our body and symptoms have feelings of sadness, or sometimes no feeling at all. There is a lack of clarity, imagination, concentration, thoughts of death and despair, shadow and suicide prevail. The journey has taken us down, we stumble in a nightmare world, which comprises hopelessness and terror. In this world dwell the pathologised images of melancholy, fear and panic. It is in this place that we learn about the deep shadows of our age and culture. Nigredo is an important part of the process, if we choose to ignore it, both within our personal lives and on the collective, the fear of the shadow and darkness is projected on to others who carry it for us. There is value and wisdom in the images contained within Nigredo. I believe that therapists have a powerful requirement to meet this shadow, with humility, imagination and integrity.

Carl Jung gave us a theatre and dramatic model for dreams, as follows.

(1) *Location* – The place where I am.

(2) *Dramatis Personae* – People, animals, etc. in the dream.

(3) *Exposition* – Action, who is the dreamer with?

(4) *Development of Plot* – What is the dreamer doing? Moving on.

(5) *Culmination* – Something begins to change.

(6) *Lysis* – Solution.

Jung did, however, point out that the two final stages are not always apparent, also that dreams do not offer a purely linear explanation or culmination of events and that it is necessary to look at a whole series of dreams in order to observe important patterns emerging. Dreams can have a powerful healing dynamic, but it is often difficult to understand dreams with only an upper-world perspective. Jung also made the suggestion that the dream is 'nature itself speaking'. There is often something of the Trickster archetype present, within the language of the dream. For this reason, it is important to adopt a flexible, playful and creative approach towards the dream. The Trickster teaches us that things are not always as they might appear to be. To find the qualities of the Trickster nature, playfulness and an ability to deconstruct, we need look no further than towards the patron saint of drama, the underworld God of the Greeks, the great loosener – Dionysus.

CHORUS: Oh, blessed he in all wise,
    Who hath drunk the Living Fountain,
    Whose life no folly staineth
    And his soul is near to God;
    Whose sins are lifted pall-wise,
    As he worships on the mountain,
    And where Cybele ordaineth,
    Our mother, he has trod:

(Euripides 1902, p.83)

The Bacchae by Euripides is a play about a society ruled by a great and powerful king. King Pentheus holds the rational and logical as a complete basis for civilised life. Here is a man who is rigid, clinging to pragmatism, logic and order, ruling through organised systems of control. Although it could be acknowledged that all these qualities are required in order to facilitate the development of a stable society, there is also a requirement for an instinctive life which enjoys the use of the senses. Within this realm of life (in its purest sense), there is no desire to analyse.

The God Dionysus arrives in disguise (in mask), he enters his kingdom offering the missing link – the spirit of nature. He is in the animalistic, displaying the essential essence of instinctive life, for its own sake. The logic of Dionysus moves us into liberation from boredom, repression, rigidity and stuckness. King Pentheus rejects the gifts offered by this God, which in turn provokes an angry response from Dionysus and his band of followers. Havoc breaks loose within this ordered society, King Pentheus attempts to imprison and bind Dionysus, it proves impossible; you cannot bind a God whose motivation is directed towards loosening. The divinity of Dionysus is shunned, not given a sacred place within a society ruled by over-control.

Depression and anxiety are often difficult to work with because control is a major factor in the culture and history of the person involved. It would be fair to state that most of us have an innate fear of losing control of ourselves. I believe that Dionysus can offer us an archetypal solution to this fixity. We often regard Dionysus as an archetype whose main motivation is to move us into states of uncontrolled frenzy and emotion. In the early days of dramatherapy, the Dionysian element of loss of control was often cited as a strong case for not using the therapy within a clinical setting. Dionysus has much more depth than can be understood from this over-simplification of his function. He is not purely a force which moves us from the opposite positions of control and the lack of it. There is a third choice: a process of loosening.

In her book *Pagan Grace*, Paris (1990) firmly connects Dionysus with drama, theatre and mask. She states that 'Dionysus is not the God behind the mask. He is the mask.' Further that:

> In our psychological culture, the quest for the true self conceals an anti-Dionysian fantasy and typically monotheistic one. We do not easily recognise Dionysus, patron of actors, who invites us to play every role, tragic as well as comic, grotesque as well as solemn, with intensity, with brio. To know Dionysus, we must accept identification with the mask, instead of searching for something behind it. The identification, intense as it may be temporary... As God of carnival of

masquerade, he is concerned with the constant metamorphosis of identity and opposed to any fixed identity with role. (p.49)

Dionysus brings us the gifts of dancing, acting, masking, dressing-up or down, the heady wine, the exultation of group experience, intense emotion and important ritualistic practices. Dramatherapists are interested in groups, also the processes contained within them. We are taught to observe and respect Apollo's great rules of listening, understanding, concentration, clarity and synthesising. There can be a tendency to ignore the Dionysian influence, due to a fear of identification with his wild side. I believe that this is more likely to occur when, what Ginette Paris calls – 'his true divinity' – is not recognised.

After many years of therapy, people can still carry the hunger for expressing intense emotion and ecstasy. This longing often manifests in a kind of acting-out and is strongly related to an emptiness – in soul, in nature. All therapists recognise the problem of people becoming almost addicted to therapy and group work. We could view this as a kind of Dionysian intoxication allied to incomplete attempts truly to deepen and let go; also a difficulty to express (through the senses) an intensity, that touches life and the world beyond therapy and the personal. The sacred wine of Dionysus is consumed unconsciously (without spirit). It is important to recognise that Dionysus is not the God *of* the wine, he is *in* the wine. The increasing thirst for intense experience is related to sensitivity and pain, a longing connected to an ever-deepening emptiness, requiring nature and the instinctive life of the senses. Dionysus is there, working through the group, but not recognised or given his rightful place; he then becomes an archetypal force which is rejected and repressed. Wearing the mask of wild intensity, he works through the shadows of collective projections of terror and madness.

> Dionysus is usually presented as an extravagant, intemperate figure, which is certainly an important part of the archetype. But this keeps him within the boundaries of carnival-like occasions, or tragic and intense situations, and so includes him from everyday life. And we lose the day-to-day Dionysus, the God of mask. To know him is not to unmask him, but to take a deeper look at the mask.

> (Paris 1990, p.50–51)

When Dionysus enters the kingdom ruled by King Pentheus, he arrives bearing gifts. The very gifts that are required to balance the format of the society created within the land. Dreams bring us gifts, with similar intentions; but they speak in a different language, from our more conscious understanding of wisdom. We need to listen to our dreams with a different ear, to understand them with a kind of paradoxical logic. Maybe Dionysus can help us! The attitude of deepening to the language of masking can be applied to therapy and dreamwork and the following passage from *The Bacchae* illustrates this particular paradoxical nature beautifully.

PENTHEUS: And whence these revelations, that thy band spreadeth in Hellas?

DIONYSUS: Their intent and use Dionysus oped to me, the child of Zeus

PENTHEUS: Is there a Zeus there, that can still beget Young Gods?

DIONYSUS: Nay, only He whose seal was set Here in thy Thebes on Semele

PENTHEUS: What way Descended he upon thee In full day or vision of night?

DIONYSUS: Most clear he stood, and scanned My soul, and gave his emblems to mine hand

PENTHEUS: What like be they, these emblems?

DIONYSUS: That may none reveal, nor know, save his Elect alone

PENTHEUS: And what good bring they to the worshipper?

DIONYSUS: Good beyond price, but not for thee to hear.

PENTHEUS: Thou trickster! Thou wouldst prick on the more To seek them out!

DIONYSUS: His mysteries abhor The touch of sin-lovers

PENTHEUS: And so thine eyes Saw this God plain; what guise had he?

DIONYSUS: What guise it liked him. Twas not I ordained his shape.

PENTHEUS: Aye, deftly turned again. An idle jape, and nothing answered!

DIONYSUS: Wise words being brough to blinded eyes will seem as things of nought.

PENTHEUS: And contest thou first to Thebes, to have thy God established?

DIONYSUS: Nay; all Barbary hath trod his dance ere this.

PENTHEUS: A low blind folk, I ween beside our Hellenes!

DIONYSUS: Higher and more keen in this thing, although their ways are not thy way

PENTHEUS: How is thy worship held, by night or day?

DIONYSUS: Most oft by night; tis a majestic thing, The darkness

PENTHEUS: Ha! with women worshipping? Tis craft and rottenness!

DIONYSUS: By day no less, Whoso will seek may find unholiness

PENTHEUS: Enough! Thy doom is fixed, for false pretence corrupting Thebes.

DIONYSUS: Not mine; but thine, for dense blindness of heart, and for blaspheming God!

(Euripides 1902, 100–102)

The Tempest

It is believed that *The Tempest* was first performed in 1611 and was probably written earlier in that same year. At that time there was a fashion for masque drama. Although Shakespeare himself did not write in this particular style, *The Tempest* displays some aspects of this particular form of dramatic writing. This is particularly interesting when considering the political and religious climate of the time. Alchemy was still practised, but had lost favour. There was in fact quite large-scale persecution of all so-called occult practices within this period of history. Cobb (1984), in his book, *Prospero's Island*, explores the many alchemical themes, which manifest throughout the play. He also places Shakespeare's most magical play firmly within the context of these difficult times. We can only admire Shakespeare's courage, wit and great psychological insight, as he both explores and presents this heretical material to the King himself. Since parts of the play are presented in a kind of modified masque format, he was able to inform his audience in a manner which was both acceptable and entertaining, although containing very powerful and topical content. Many Jungian psychologists view this play as an illustration of Jung's theory of individuation; sighting Prospero as a character who portrays aspects of Shakespeare's own particular life journey. Whatever the real truth may be, we can only imagine. What is clear is that the construct of the play is both clever and complex, displaying a wonderful depth of understanding about the structure of psyche, soul and their relationship to the world.

The Island: Location and Dramatic Personae

I am going to explore the play through images which emerge from the rich and symbolic narrative. Initially, I would like to return to Jung's first section, his dramatic dream structure – *the location*. The island is the most perfect landscape, in which to explore the great wealth of psychological material in the play, which connects us to therapeutic process and the archetypes of the collective unconscious. We could hold the fantasy that the island is always *in-dream*. It is a dream island. *Even if the island was not inhabited, the location itself would carry on dreaming.* The characters in *The Tempest* are *in* the island, the island is not *in* them. This is an important distinction to make, and useful to consider if we connect back to the Aboriginal definition of dreamtime, which was mentioned earlier. The idea of moving into a dream landscape is a most helpful aid in avoiding the real danger of over-identifying with powerful archetypal material, in a too personal way. It also offers a more imaginative way of not allowing the work to fall or rise into a state of inflation, giving us an opportunity to discriminate what actually belongs to us and the personal, and what needs to be returned to culture, history, race, ancestry and the world.

> CALIBAN: Be not afeared, The Isle is full of noises,
> Sounds and sweet airs, that give delight and hurt not.
> Sometimes a thousand twangling instruments
> Will hum upon mine ears; and sometimes voices,
> That, if I had then wak'd after a long sleep
> Will make me sleep again; and then in dreaming
> The clouds methought would open and show riches
> Ready to drop upon me, that when I wak'd
> I cried to dream again.

(The Tempest III:iii)

Within the play there are constant references to time and sleep. These represent some of the most important factors in both the play and therapeutic work. The quality of sleep that is mediated by Prospero, is essentially concerned with loosening ego consciousness, in order to allow the richness of important and relevant unconscious material to manifest, and move the work (or action) on without interference. The particular quality of this special sleep, also represents a beautiful mode of *stopping*, in order to prepare body, spirit and soul, for the next stage of the journey. This sleep is very powerful and has to be administered with great care and integrity by Prospero's deep understanding of alchemical process. The island itself (location) allows the images to rest; this is a deepening event! Therapists encounter sleep in its many guises, when engaged in their work; indeed it is quite common for therapists to experience the sensation of the person they are working with, putting them to sleep. There are, of course, many differing levels of sleep and it need not always be defined as literal sleep. The sleep, for instance, can be deadening, narcotic, escapist, defensive. When placed in the alchemical stage of Albedo, it can represent a kind of moon-consciousness, dreamy and reflective where things are not quite as they may appear to be. There is the sleep that is refreshing, cleansing, relaxing or full of dread, fear — an encounter with 'The Dark Night Of the Soul'. One of the most distressing symptoms of depression is the inability to sleep and often to dream; there is no imagination, and sleep, the blessed gift of soul, is kept from us. This is the darkest of depressive positions, and the most difficult to deal with and go through. All the different aspects of sleep are important medicine in the healing process. Nature itself bears this gift, Prospero learns to respect this natural power, understands its function as he harnesses sleep to help him in his greatest and most important work.

> PROSPERO: By accident most strange, bountiful Fortune
> Now my dear lady, hath mine enemies
> Brought to this shore; and by my own presence
> I find my Zenith doth depend upon
> A most auspicious star, whose influence
> If now I court not, but omit my fortunes
> Will ever droop.

(*The Tempest* I:ii)

When working with depression, time would appear to be one of the most important factors. In truth, we do not know how long a depression will last, or how often in a person's life it might re-occur. The very nature of depression is a kind of slowness allied to a leaden and heavy sensation of nothing moving. But within this heavy Nigredo blackness are images, which indicate when the time is right, for some movement; as the blackness, begins to transform into dark blue. This stage requires very sensitive handling. It is imperative that the illuminating light of understanding is not focused too brightly into this changing blue hue, but is encouraged to stay with the mood of the blue, as it expresses aspects of the black, after endless nothingness. This is the 'darkness visible' which Styron (1991) describes so poetically in his thought-provoking book. As therapy continues, there are often frustrating phases when the process appears to stop (or takes a meaningful rest); these periods of stopping, if honoured, can offer great riches (rather in the way that Caliban describes the dream), towards the creative fulfilment of the work. Like Prospero, we need to know, intuitively, when it is appropriate to take action, and when it is time to wait, trust and reflect. As Prospero discovers, to control the elements is only one side of the business. The thing that is impossible to manipulate, either through magical art or therapeutic technique, is the role of the heart, and the journey of the soul, within this mystery of life and fate.

Dramatic Personae, Exposition, Development of Plot, Culmination

Sandtray therapy is a playful and imaginative way of working with images, both on a personal and collective level. The process is simple in operation and practice, but complex in its way of weaving the various images, which permeate our life and culture. Sand is contained within shallow square containers, small figures and objects are placed into the sand, which can itself be moulded and given shape in order to enhance the final structure. The small figures and objects are placed in a manner which presents and displays an outer and inner dramatic vision of material which is difficult to express in a purely literal way, that is, verbal communication. The movement is spontaneous, demanding a playful attitude, also an intuitive trust of imagination, in order to hermetically draw attention and concentration towards information which is relevant to the present, while having vast implications connecting past and future. It is a containing and magical way into the unconscious, and providing the therapist and client have due respect for the power of unconscious images, is safe gentle and reflective in application. Bridges can be constructed, linking inner and outer worlds, encouraging discovery and movement between the two. The figures and objects become players and props, given script and movement by the constant flow of energy mediated by the unconscious. These are little talismen which can illuminate our lives through play, as in the way of the child-like potential and acceptance of a fruitful life, which exists within the limitations of our human experience of the journey between life and death.

I work with images which emerge from the unconscious through dreams, sandtray therapy, creative movement, improvisation and play. The image is not presented or given to us, in order to serve the ego or offer a quick breakthrough within the therapeutic process. Although there are times, when the gentle light of conscious understanding, can illuminate the work suddenly, after weeks of struggling with the heaviness and stickiness of the congealed prima-materia. The importance of returning to the original image cannot be over-emphasised. The process of interpretation can lead us away from the image by making associations and, by isolating aspects of the image, can imagine its contents for the sake of clarification and meaning. This may be necessary, and fruitful, but always, after the associations, we need to return to the original form, in order to honour the integrity of the gift from the unconscious.

A 20-year-old girl with an eating disorder constructs a sandtray, entitled 'My New Year'. She fills the tray with her hopes and wishes, in the bottom left hand corner, she includes a beautiful black snake. She explains that this is not a negative image, but one which she feels is important. That night she dreams:

> I look at my reflection, in the mirror, I notice a large spot on my chin. I squeeze the spot and the pus begins to emerge, followed by blood. The spot becomes my mouth, a large snake appears, it felt as if it came from the pit of my stomach. More of the snake appeared, it becomes thicker and bits of its skin keep catching on my teeth, finally it is fully emerged, I wake up.

The disgorging was a release, she had found the snake impossible to ingest and had vomited it up. She described the process as one of becoming lighter, of feeling that the snake was now in the right place. She no longer felt at the mercy of an internal demon, having changed to a sense of reverence towards the powerful collective archetypal image of the snake. The snake was in the world and not in her, returned to its rightful place, in its own image.

Janet is a young woman who has suffered symptoms of depression and anxiety, for most of her adult life. Janet has very little emotional language and keeps feelings tightly under control. The main reason she was referred to dramatherapy was because of an inability to use words to express her thoughts. Because of this I asked Janet if she would like to find a new way of expressing, other than by using words. I introduced her to the sandtray room. She and I spent our first session exploring the hundreds of objects and figures displayed on shelf.

She then picked some and placed them in the sand, under the title of 'Important aspects of my life'. Having enjoyed the experience of discovering a new way of communicating, Janet was eager to continue working with sandtray therapy. As the depression deepened to the darker stages of the Nigredo, she communicated a growing dependence on alcohol. It was felt by her Care Manager that Janet might benefit from work where the emphasis was focused on image and metaphor. The work began on a one-to-one basis, as Janet found communicating with people very difficult and also required time to establish a trusting relationship with me. She told me that she did not dream and was at present not sleeping very well. We agreed to work with sandtray therapy, as this offered the most simple, playful and loosening way to get into the work, without it becoming too threatening.

The first image or dream expressed in therapy is of prime importance, it will often set the scene, so that the stage is in the right perspective and light, for the ensuing drama to unfold. Janet's first sandtray depicted a mandala shape, with rings of sand fences, surrounding deep ridges, placed in the centre was a dragon completely covered and imprisoned by a large spider's web. Janet described this powerful image as the way she felt, also how this young dragon, was not able to express itself, in the manner which was most natural to its true nature. She also recognised her own powerlessness in being able to begin to make contact with the frightening aspects of the creature, while feeling overwhelmed by the enormity of its needs. Her compassion for this animal moved me, it is unusual for people to express such feelings for a mythical creature, which carries huge archetypal projections of disgust, repression and fear. Baring and Cashford (1991) in their book *The Myth of the Goddess* state:

> What was feminine was the dragon-mother, the earth and moon, darkness, chaos confusion, nature as emptied of spirit; and what was masculine was the sky-father, the heaven and sun, light, order, clarity, spirit as freed from nature. That these simplistic assignations of value, originating 4,000 years ago, are only recently being challenged on a wide scale indicates how deeply they have entered into our culture without our noticing. (p.285)

Janet's heroic battle was beginning, but was tempered with an awareness of her responsibility to respect and honour, the darker and repressed elements of the image.

Janet continued working with the sandtray, which in turn stimulated the imagination, producing fragments of dream material, enabling her to begin to build bridges between the unconscious and conscious areas of her psyche. Later, she joined a dramatherapy group, where she discovered others who also experienced similar feelings of loneliness and isolation. Working within the group, Janet discovered another way of expressing her anger and frustrations through the exploration of creative movement. As she slowly began to discover the power of her own body, the variety of ways in which she could both celebrate and mourn the essential aspects of the feminine which were lost for her, she moved her life into the world, strengthening her ego, while holding compassion for the lost and fragmented elements of her childhood. Her original description of this feeling of not being held was based largely in her experience of 'being put to sea as a small child, without a vessel strong enough to ride the stormy waves.'

PROSPERO: In few, they hurried us aboard a bark;
                    Bore us some leagues to sea, where they prepared
                    A rotten carcass of a butt, not rigg'd,
                    Nor tackle sail, nor mast; the very rats
                    Instinctively have quit it. There they hoist us,

To cry to th' sea, that roar'd to us; to sigh
To th' winds, whose pity, sighing back again
Did us but loving wrong.

(*The Tempest* I:iii)

Being cast adrift on a stormy unpredictable sea is a fitting and almost archetypal image for the overwhelming feelings presented by people in the initial stages of depression and anxiety.

The Homeric Hymn to Pan

(HESIOD): And in the house she bore Hermes a dear son
who from his birth was marvellous to look upon,
with goat's feet and two horns – a noisy merry
laughing child.

(Lopez-Pedraza 1989, p.123)

When I first read *The Homeric Hymn to Pan*, I was astonished. Is this really the description of an archetypal force, which – within psychotherapy – presents a pathology, which can appear intransigent in its ferocity and unpredictable in its nature. Lopez-Pedraza (1989), in his book *Hermes and His Children*, offers an explanation:

Pan creates most panic when his image is presented under the historical disguise of the devil. With this sort of appearance in psychotherapy, there is only a very slight possibility of reverting to the image of the 'God of Hellas' as seen by the English poetess... (who revives) the image of Pan as a true God, and not merely as one side of the split between God and the devil. (We have to remember that throughout Manichean Christianity Pan alone has carried the 'Shadow of God'.)

(p.132)

Here we can observe once again, as in Dionysus, a despised and rejected archetypal force, carrying projections of darkness and madness. No longer does Pan run and play freely in the open spaces and mountains, but surprises us in supermarkets, on crowded transport and in busy town centres; it is no great mystery that we, and he, panic in this manic whirlpool of what we call a civilised society. Pan is another nature God, Pedraza describing him as 'The psychotherapy of the body'.

Panic is a highly distressing symptom, being important for people who experience this presence to understand cognitively what is happening to their body. Breath work, relaxation techniques and an understanding of the sympathetic nervous system are important factors when learning to deal with panic. Alongside this work, we can work the body through imagination. Bodywork often reveals a sensation of being paralysed, unable to run, unable to fight, usually because the person involved has no image on which to focus the panic. The legs and feet are heavy and leaden (Nigredo), while the head is in a kind of manic, dizzy spin (Rubedo). There is a physical split between these two sensations; and rather like Pan, within our Western culture, they are in the wrong place. Working with creative movement can be helpful in this context, exploring ways in which the body is given the opportunity to express its own distress; especially if the person can construct appropriate rituals, which express the elements of containment, holding and reflecting; moving Pan into the feet and legs, wherein he can use his goat-like qualities to traverse the difficult and rocky terrain of depression, with the sure footing of the animal, which is his familiar. Meanwhile, the slow Saturnine qualities can be experienced, as moving towards the head and torso, slowing the heart, allowing the thinking to connect with the frightening and overwhelming feelings. This can offer an opportunity for discrimination to function again, strong enough to contain the heat of the alchemical fire. People who suffer panic often describe the sensation of burning – as if they are 'on fire'. This image once again connects us with Christian ideas of hell and the devil. Other images have presented themselves through movement work, descriptions of being 'cast adrift on a very stormy sea', being overwhelmed by huge waves, the fear of being swept away with nothing to hold on to. It is as if there is no comfort, nothing to contain what is experienced as a threat of complete annihilation. The ego is in a state of not being able to contain the contents of the unconscious, which floods the conscious life; transforming the world into a place of confusion and terror.

Helen's experience of depression, which had been with her since her childhood, presented in the way of alternating periods of depression and panic. Many of the images mentioned above, were described to me by her, when using movement and sculpting. We constructed locations, using furniture flats, props and soft play equipment before moving the improvisations into the body and feelings. In this manner, Helen was able to create boundaries, in which she could explore her intense and deep feelings. Helen's sense of isolation and worthlessness echoed clearly through her own Tempest; Helen discovered her wounded child, and attempted to find a source of holding, someone or something to carry a small light, to enable her to make her journey into the depths of the underworld.

Sandtray 1: Holding the Opposites

This Sandtray illustrates that Helen's tension is continually falling between a state of panic and depression. She stands in a circle constructed of wooden beads, glass pointed strips, which connect her to the images, which represent the two sides of the split. Behind her is a dragon, guarding a large white egg. At her feet is a mask, which she uses when necessary. The place of depression, she called 'Saturn's kingdom', it carries all the leaden heaviness, and is dark and black; there is just one small candle, which Helen decided to light. There is a critical old man, books are scattered around him, he represents discipline, patience, endurance, endings and a sense of death; a snail begins its slow journey towards the other side of the circle. The opposite side is full of fire and bleeding. There is a tall masculine figure praying, a small horse, raised on its back legs; the horse is trying to make contact with the praying man. Both figures are encircled by an open wound, which will never heal completely. Behind these two figures is a snake encircling a staff, in front of the snake two red flowers push through the earth, while the God Eros points his arrow towards the opposite side. The sandtray is very complex, Helen and I worked with these images in some depth, but for the purpose of this chapter, there are two major areas which I would like to highlight.

The journey of Eros and the snail

These two images were connected to the movement work (with the panic) which I mentioned earlier. The experience of moving the slowness into the hearth and head – easing the burning heat, the bleeding wound, the frantic feeling – this steady influence was represented by the snail, while Eros carried his message of relatedness and love to the cold, icy, hopelessness of what Helen perceived as Saturn's world. These two images helped us loosen the stuck nature of the situation portrayed in the sandtray. Through imagination, Helen could move the images towards new and unexplored areas of her world, without destroying their intrinsic basic nature, or transforming them into something else. The biggest danger when working the image is to move it too far away from its original source and meaning in a desire to find a major breakthrough.

The dragon and the egg

The dragon was guarding something very special. Helen described this 'special thing' as the essential life-force. Helen questioned whose egg it was; this suggested that maybe we could talk to the dragon figure and try to find out a bit more about it. After a series of role-play situations, Helen identified aspects of the mother in this image – but of a dark and devouring nature. She knew that the egg had something to do with her, and that the dragon was holding it in a manner which gave her no access to its potential. The image of the dragon became stronger in its association with mother, as we kept returning to the original representation in the sandtray, that of the nesting, brooding, warming and protection of the egg. As we continued, the darker aspects of Helen's relationship with mother became stronger; after a session in which she attempted to set up communication with her own personal image of mother, she wrote the following passage:

> There are knives in my heart, the blood can not flow. The white fat, of my mother's mother's mother. Generations of these blown-up, congested women. My heart is beating. I know I'm alive! My heart is heavy, I carry generations of guilt and shame, Rage and fear. My mother's, mother's mother, weeps in the grave, Screaming from the place of the living dead. She drinks my birth blood I stand in my whiteness, limp, lifeless. I fall in the barren womb of blackness and terror.

Helen's experience of depression and anxiety had been with her since her childhood. Her relationship with her mother had been particularly difficult. People who suffer panic often describe a feeling of 'not being held' by their mothers, also that mother was not strong enough to help them contain fear. A clinical definition of panic is often described (in psychotherapeutic terms) as an inability of the ego to hold and 'sift' the contents of the unconscious, particularly the collective unconscious; if the ego is not strong enough to perform this task the conscious life is flooded with archetypal material which feels totally overwhelming. When the personal mother appears weak and unable to contain, the child will often look to the archetypal mother. The archetype of the great Mother is very complex, having many parts, one of which is the witch or 'dark mother'. In the archetype of the dark Mother we can observe another, repressed and dark archetypal image, which manifests within human life, as terrible and death-like. Helen experienced her in this way; her sense of isolation and worthlessness echoed clearly through the symptoms. Helen also required a source of holding, someone or something to carry a small light in the dark world of her whirlpool of emotions.

PROSPERO: I must, Once in a month recount
           What thou hast been,
           Which thou forget'st
           This damned witch Sycorax
           For mischiefs manifold, and

sorceries terrible
To enter human hearing.

(*The Tempest* I:ii)

Prospero's attitude to Sycorax is very heroic. He projects total evil on to her and indeed, from his intellectual viewpoint, she fulfils that role beautifully. In many ways, Sycorax is one of the most important elements of the play; she is the most elemental of all the elementals on the island. She is the deep primal essence, her realm the deepest level of the collective unconscious, encompassing the deepest recesses of the fathomless depths of our location. But she has a son who loves her, and he feels a deep sense of loss at her passing.

CALIBAN: This island's mine, by Sycorax my mother,
which thou tak'st from me.

(*The Tempest* I:ii)

In her novel *Star Dancer*, Sampson (1993) explores the myth of the descent into the underworld of Inanna, where she meets her dark sister Ereshkigal, queen of the underworld. The image Fay Sampson creates of the dark Mother, evokes both terror and pity within the reader:

> She lay sprawled across her throne in an abandonment of suffering. Her hair was wild flowing, like neglected leeks. Her nails, like copper rakes, drew fresh blood to add to the hardened crust that streaked her face. No skirt hid the knotted-veined thighs, where purple snakes seemed to struggle round the darker hole. The blood that crept from this was black, unwholesome. Ereshkigal was bewailing the babies she could never bear live. Her miscarriage, who had robbed the world of so many babies, who snatched some many mothers into Kur, was, in her own body, agony. She rocked herself nursing the searing fire of emptying, biting her lip to fight the pain of tearing away. 'Oh, my insides! Oh, my outside!'. (p.459)

The dark Mother is part of the whole, but split off. It is interesting to note that many of the darkest elements of the feminine that occur in myth and story are often in that position because of their anguished response to rejection, pain and suffering. While I'm very mindful of the purity of the darkness and evil that is intrinsic within these images, also that they cannot be transformed or pulled up into the light, it is important to give them a place in nature and life. In this way we can begin to explore the image with discrimination, to move from the more primitive images to goddesses, such as Hecate, who carry great wisdom in their darkness, who can see above as below, who sit at the crossroads of death, and like the midwifes of birth, initiate us into death.

The rejecting and negative Mother is a constant theme in therapy. We blame Mother for many of the ills that blight the individual and the world, and often have to hold the necessary transference of Mother in the initial stages of therapy. Berry (1982), in her book *Echo's Subtle Body*, explores this theme in her chapter 'What's the Matter with Mother':

> When heroically opposed, the mother turns monster. The religious sense of her is lost. Her nature as non-being, absence, lack, is no longer part of her mystery – that which makes her greater than our own narrow sense of life and achievement. Rather she becomes a contrary force, to rule over and conquer. Her earth becomes replaced by our ego-centricity, our illusions of competence, self-sufficiency, ego capability. We deny the earth's divinity and exchange her ground with its complexities, its twisted chthonic, creatures, and shame for our goal-directed, clean, ever-bettering fantasies of goodness, health and achievement. (p.13)

Further that:

> The hero's mother complex is characterised by his struggles to be up and out and above her. And because of his heroic labors to free himself from her, it is he who is most surely bound to her. Better service to the earth mother might be to assist her movements down to the deepest regions of her depths. For the mother's depths are the underworld. (p.14)

Sandtray 2: Homage to Hecate

A pathway of stones leads to the sacred home of the Goddess Hecate. Hecate sits at the opening, a large pot in front of her, around her feet and moving out into the world is a large and beautiful snake. Around Hecate are the images of her being – winter trees, black feathers, a healing wand entwined with a snake, snakes, frogs and spiders, dark stones, eggs, death masks and a black cat. Before the cave, Helen, kneeling, offers her gift of recognition.

Helen was able to reproduce the sandtray by using props and sculptured shapes; she then sculpted, moved and role-played the images with other members of the dramatherapy group. Although regarded as a largely malignant force, we should not forget that Hecate has associations with Persephone, and is the third part of the triple moon Goddess of daughter (Persephone), mother, (Demeter), Crone (Hecate). Hecate is the only one who witnessed the rape and abduction of Persephone, into the underworld; she has an innate knowledge of above and below. She is the mistress of souls.

In her book *Conscious Femininity*, Woodman (1993) says of the crone:

> The third is the Crone, the woman who has gone through her crossroads. Hecate, the goddess of the crossroads, is the Crone. The crossroads in Europe still have little cairns where people drop their stones in honour of the Goddess. Those cairns have always been the place of Hecate. The crossroads represent a place where consciousness is crossed by the unconscious – in other words, a place where you have to surrender your ego will to a higher will. The Crone has gone through one crossroads after another. She has reached a place of surrender where her ego demands are no longer relevant. This is the positive side of the Crone. She is a surrendered instrument and therefore detached. (p.87)

MIRANDA: Alack what trouble was I then to you.

PROSPERO: O, a cherubin
Thou wast that did preserve me! Thou didst smile,
Infused with fortitude from heaven
When I have decked the sea with drops full salt,
Under my burden groan, which rais'd in me
An undergoing stomac, to bear up
Against what should ensue.

(*The Tempest* I:iii)

We could see Miranda (the inspiration for Prospero's courage) as *Anima*, the illuminating soul quality, which can endure the gravest of situations. Miranda is the inspirational child in this context. Helen could only hear the cries of the wounded child, this has a very different resonance from that of the joyful, playful child. This part of the child archetype represents the pathologised aspect of the child, which we encounter so often in therapy. It requires a delicate touch to care for the damaged part of the child archetype, without fixing it in a dependent mode. Helen was able, through the language of play, to release aspects of the positive child, while not falling into a transformative attitude with the wounded child, who still required full gestation in the darkness and depth of the Great Mother's womb. In one sense, we can observe Miranda and Helen as positive parent, offering the wonderful spark of potential, which can be found in even the most difficult circumstances.

Jane was referred to the Creative Therapy Unit, after being involved in talking therapy for just over a year. Jane was in a deep state of depression, her world was bleak and cheerless, she was isolated, afraid and lonely, she mistrusted people and attempted to drown her very powerful feelings, by consuming large amounts of alcohol. The situation was made worse by the fact that Jane was a woman of few words, finding it almost impossible to describe her situation through speech or conversation. Her dreams consisted of fragmented images of being 'pulled down', 'walking down dark tunnels, and meeting with frightening male figures', who had no personal identity for her. There was some speculation that Jane had been sexually abused by her father, but she was sceptical about this, as she could remember very little of her childhood. After discussing this possibility, she and I decided to not take the position of concretising this, but to allow the dreams and work in the sandtray to render information about this wounded child, of whom she could remember nothing. Jane enjoyed working with the sandtray, and was able to communicate much more about her feelings through making images, than she had ever done through purely talking. The sandtray images were also encouraging dreams; the evidence of a highly predatory masculine figure was becoming far more evident. Her memory of childhood was still vague, but she could now begin to communicate images of a very critical father, who was never satisfied with any of her academic achievements. One of the most powerful images presented at this time was of Jane kneeling in front of her father begging him not to punish her. It was still difficult to give words to the image, but she was able to write a short script, which she then read to me. It was beginning to look as if the father had been abusive; the tone of the narrative was very sadistic.

After working with me on a one-to-one basis, Jane very bravely agreed to join a dramatherapy group. This was a big step for her to take, and was the start of a process geared towards rehearsing social contact and sharing with other people. The group explored the images connected with the fairy-tale *Cinderella*. Jane identified in a very powerful way with an image, which she sculpted, of lying down, curled-up in the cinders or ashes. Through role play, using a double, she revealed feelings of intense fear, of being abandoned and despised; she stated that she was unclean. There are obvious implications of sexual abuse here, but what was also interesting was a statement about the family and its collective shadow. The father's family were Jewish, living in Germany at the time of World War II. He and his sister escaped the holocaust, but many of the family had been murdered in the concentration camps. The subject was never mentioned within the family, and was buried under the pretence of it never having happened. Somehow, Jane felt that she had had to carry this knowledge of pure evil, alone, no one would talk of it; she could remember times when she had been intensely pre-occupied with her father's history. It was beginning to look as if the abused father had become the abuser. The ashes were a chilling reminder of her family history. We continued to work on the dream images, of abusive male figures; these were occurring in dreams more often, becoming more sexual in nature. Jane did not want to take these figures too literally, she needed to make more contact with her personal memory. Her childhood was still lost in a foggy murky landscape.

MIRANDA: Tis far off,
And rather like a dream than an assurance
That my remembrance warrants. Had I not
Four, or five women once that tended me?

PROSPERO: Thou hadst, and more Miranda. But how is it
That this lives in your mind? What seest thou else
In the dark backward and abysm of time?

(*The Tempest* I:ii)

Jane had a requirement to retrieve her memories of her lost childhood; unlike her father, she wished to acknowledge her past, even if much of it was filled with pain.

Who planted the yellow flowers around my childhood home? Why was my mother happy there? I'd like so much for her to tell me what I was like as a child. If no one can answer my questions, I'll invent a plausible response, blending memory and imagination as in the Renaissance. I need those memories because they carry my identity!

(Paris 1990, p.119)

Miranda knows on an intuitive level, that fragments of her past are beginning to reconnect consciously, although the memories hold the atmosphere of being dream-like. As before in the play we can observe that 'The time is right'! Prospero helps her to unravel the mystery of her forgotten childhood. Miranda has asked before, but it would have been too soon to make the best sense of it. In this great work of Prospero, the timing is of the greatest importance. This is also true of therapy, it is necessary to stand the tension of waiting, so as not to panic the fragile nature of the wounded child by imposing ideas that do not emerge from the archetype, inner truth and the individual's personal fiction. There is at present much debate centred around 'false memory syndrome'. May it not be wiser to wait for the details of the traumatic event to emerge from the unconscious, rather than planting a suggestion of what might have happened, based on collective diagnostic criteria? For Jane, the imaginative work with image was beginning to stir and animate the congealed nature of the prima-materia of her childhood enabling memories to present themselves at their own pace. It is the image that keeps the memory alive – as in the way of the dream – and imagination is bound in the image of what the memory is, not always in a literal sense, sometimes as a hunch. it is always important to remember that inner truth may differ considerably from collective and cultural truth.

Sandtray 3: I Will Go into the Hare

There is a large mountain of sand, which Jane describes as a mountain. Standing on the top is a large two-headed monster, with large sharp teeth, ready to attack. Behind the monster, stands a woman, wearing a long robe with a cowl covering her head and face. She carries a pot and has a submissive nature. A white bird is on the ground, beside them, unable to fly. At the base of the mountain and along a small path, is a shallow indentation in the sand; in it sits a hare.

Although Jane was not sure what the sandtray meant to her, she could describe who the various images represented, also that the image filled her with foreboding. The monster was her father, the woman her mother, the bird freedom, and the hare was Jane herself. She took a photograph of the image home, in order to reflect on it further. I received a phone call the next day: she wanted to see me, as she had had a short nightmare, after which memories had begun to flood in. During the following session, she disclosed sexual and physical abuse. Her naturally pragmatic nature trusted these memories as true. For many weeks, more memories returned, and she was able to express her anger and confusion about these horrific childhood events. Jane began to reclaim her identity, which she felt her father had stolen from her. There was huge sorrow regarding her mother's inability to protect her from this violence. It was some time before we could look in depth at the image of the hare; when we did, it revealed a mix of the personal, collective, archetypal and the Shaman.

The hare carries deep collective symbolic material and is a powerful religious image in both east and west. The hare was the symbol for Aeastre, the Celtic Goddess of rebirth. This animal was connected with witchcraft. The Christian Church fed its flocks with stories of witches, who turned themselves into hares, in order to outrun the men of the inquisition. The hare then became a hunted animal. On a collective and cultural level, this symbolic material is important and gives insight into myth and history, but it is important to stay true to the original image. Maddy Prior (singer and songwriter) in her beautiful *The Fabled Hare* (1993), states:

I sall goe until the hare,
Wi sorrow and sick mickle care.
Here's the tractor here's the plough,
And where shall we go now
We'll lie in forms as still as the dead.
In the open fields the hares said
No cover but the camouflage
From the winter's wild and bitter rage
All our defence is in our legs
We run like the wind the hare
said

(Side 2, track 2)

It is tempting to view the hare as a symbol or representation of Jane's situation, but maybe this is a too literal position. Jane 'went into the hare', she took on the behaviour and display of the animal, in order to cope with her situation; this is a Shamanistic act. As a child she was the hunted one, every evening she would stay as 'still as death' in her room, in order to fool her father that she was not there. If this did not work, she would run 'like the wind' to a secret place, where, at the age of 12, she discovered the deadening power of alcohol. As Jane and I explored her pathology, through the image of the hare, we were able to focus on the instinctive and animalistic side of nature, thereby giving it a place in life. Memories continued to present themselves, through dreams and the images which Jane produced; slowly she is beginning to reclaim her identity and rescue the wounded child, with love and respect for the dark nature of its being.

Lysis (solution)

CALIBAN: When thou camest first,
Thou strok'st me and made much of me, wouldst give me
Water with berries in't, and teach me how
to name the bigger light, and the less,
That burn by day and night; and then I loved thee,
And showed thee all the qualities of th'isle,
The fresh springs, brine-pits, barren place and fertile
Curs'd that I did so! All the charms of Sycorax,
toads, beetles, bats light on you!
For I am all the subjects that you have,
Which first was mine own king; and here you sty me

In this hard rock, whiles you do keep from me
The rest o'th'island.

(*The Tempest* I:iii)

Caliban is shadow; for Prospero he is the inferior despised, rejected, unwanted aspects of Prospero's vision of himself. But as we can observe, it is unlikely that Prospero would have survived his first years on the island, without Caliban's help. Prospero has to some extent tamed and enslaved the elementals – in the guise of Ariel and Caliban – but not completely. The basic nature of Caliban is retained, it cannot be transformed, or resurrected into something which it is not. Caliban stays true to his nature, true to his source, Prospero's art could be seen as a work against nature. Within depression, the shadow aspects of the psyche manifest with great force, we cannot ignore them or push them away; they will not be transformed or taught another language which replaces their own.

CALIBAN: You taught me language, and my profit on't
Is, I know how to curse. The red plague rid you
For learning me your language

(*The Tempest* I:iii)

Prospero, at the end of the play finally acknowledges this part of himself, he also understands the absolute necessity to respect this dark and natural power 'this thing of darkness I acknowledge mine'. The shadow aspects of ourselves are purposive in their inferiority, as part of the healing process. For Prospero the island magic is powerful, he respects this, and harnesses its energy with care. It is Ariel, as hermetic and imaginative messenger, and Caliban as shadow and essential, dark moist soul (who knows that he has lost something very essential), who are the catalysts for some of the most important movement in the drama.

If it appears that my writing contains a somewhat morbid pre-occupation with the dark and repressed, it is because I believe that the dark images of Nigredo are not there in order to be pulled upwards towards the light, or transformed into a more acceptable aspect of the archetype. The darker phase of the process, rather like the darker phase of the moon cycle in nature, has importance in the work, it is part of the whole. There is a tendency, particularly in the more 'new age' therapies, to see the final alchemical opus as the complete transformation of these darker aspects of human life and psyche. There is a strong desire to drag the perceived inferior material upwards towards the superior. This can manifest in an inflated perception of the heroic, causing too much hot air to fill the alchemical container, activating an explosion which fragments the material, splitting, dividing and burning, until the ashes and waste products settle once more into the shadowy depths of Nigredo. It is necessary, when working with shadow, to draw the superior downwards, encouraging the inferior to engage at a level which feels safe, where the light is not so bright as to send the seeds of life scuttling back, before there has been an opportunity for a true meeting, with mutual respect. The light in this phase of the work is not black or white but grey. We take the middle way! We could ask the question, why do we always insist that roses should grow out of the muck, why can't the muck be valued in itself? Of course, the fact that roses grow more beautiful if fed on muck, is a hopeful and positive image for our fear of the inferior, but maybe the muck has more to show us, than its ability to turn ugliness into our cultural idea of beauty.

Bleakley (1989), in his book *Earth's Embrace*, takes a critical look at humanistic psychology.

> We might fruitfully contrast a text of Maslow's, packed with jargon such as 'deficiency-needs', and 'being-needs', with Medieval and Renaissance language, that is closer to the soil, to the earth herself, both less personalised and less abstract. The latter is animated language, mythical yet earthy and sensual, shot through with soul-talk and talk of the soul, which, in seeing through to the world as it is, allows the world to individuate in its own images. It is deadly, rather than deadening, stunning us into a deepening or putting us into a state of suspension, as our best poet Shakespeare does at every turn. This, rather than puffing us up with false hope of salvation in self actualisation, where the person becomes a world explained and contained. (p.189)

PROSPERO: Have I made shake, and by the spurs pluck'd up
           The pine and cedar. Graves at my command
           Have wak'd their sleepers, op'd and let them forth,
           By my so potent art. But this rough magic
           I here abjure; and when I have requir'd
           Some heavenly music – which even now I do –
           To work mine end upon their senses that
           This airy charm is for, I'll break my staff,
           Bury it certain fathoms in the earth,
           And deeper than did ever plummet sound
           I'll drown my book

(The Tempest V:i)

Prospero calls his work 'art', he utilises the energy and forces of the landscape and the creatures around him to create his final work of alchemy. Having achieved this, he can throw away his magic and connect with his humanness again. He gives the symbol of his borrowed power (the staff), back to the earth, from whence it came. When we as therapists work with this 'stuff', which we call the unconscious, our task is similar, that of working with art, through art, mediating the imaginative messengers which flow, through us, from a source which is still the greatest mystery. Like Prospero, we are required to respect the images, which are related to us, through dreams, fantasy and pathology. Prospero does not own this power, he is fully aware of its ownership; that of life itself.

> PROSPERO: Let us not burden our remembrances with
> A heaviness that's gone

(*The Tempest* V:i)

References

Baring, A. and Cashford, A. (1991) *The Myth of the Goddess*. London: Viking Arena.

Berry, P. (1982) *Echo's Subtle Body*. Dallas: Spring Publications Inc.

Bleakley, A. (1989) *Earth's Embrace*. Bath: Galeway Books.

Bosnak, R. (1988) *A Little Course in Dreams*. Boston and London: Shambala.

Cobb, N. (1984) *Prospero's Island*. London: Coventure.

Euripides (1902) *The Bacchae*. Translated by G. Murray. London: George Allen and Unwin.

Hillman, J. and Roscher, W.H. (1972) *Pan and The Nightmare*. Dallas: Spring Publications Inc.

Jung, C. (1945) *Collected Works*. London: Routledge, Kegan & Paul.

Lopez-Pedraza, R. (1989) *Hermes and His Children*. Einfiedeln: Daimen Verlay.

Paris, G. (1990) *Pagan Grace*. Dallas: Spring Publications.

Prior, M. (1993) *Album-Year*. Oxford: Park Records.

Sampson, F. (1993) *Star Dancer*. Glasgow: Headline Feature.

Shakespeare, W. (1951) *Collected Works* (Players Edition). London and Glasgow: Collins.

Styron, W. (1991) *Darkness Visible*. London: Jonathan Cape.

Woodman, M. (1993) *Conscious Femininity*. Toronto: Inner City Book.

Suggested Viewing
Kidel, M. (1994) *A Kind Of Blue*. Channel Four Productions.

CHAPTER TEN

Dramatherapy and Clients with Eating Disorders
Fragile Board

Ditty Dokter

Letting Go

I love you but don't ask me to eat
I love you but don't ask me to fight
my hunger is of a making just beyond my reach
but I cannot quench my thirst with mothering milk
nor return to a life rejected in youth.
I love you but don't ask me to live
I love you but don't ask me to breathe
this hurting of life is not for you to heal,
this body, your creation, is not yours now to feed
you set me free at birth, set me free now.
You love me so allow me to leave
I love you so please let yourself free
I wear your guilt around my neck and slowly I drown
as I leave my embodied life behind
my soul begins to fly.

(Warriner 1994, p.228)

Many women in current western society, American research quotes up to 80 per cent, have problems concerning food intake and body image. This chapter is about one pole of the continuum of obsessions with food; people suffering from eating disorders to such a level of self-destruction that it dominates, ruins and ultimately destroys their life.

The fragile board in the title of this chapter is based on a piece of sculpture by Elise Warriner. This sculpture depicts a life-size dining table and four chairs constructed of barbed wire; the chairs lack seats and the table surface is made from insubstantial clingfilm. This 'dinner setting', the name of the piece, stands on a carpet of foodstuffs such as pasta, rice and cereal. This image embodies for me the battlefield and fragility of family relationships as represented by the family dinner table. Elise's images and poetry are a strikingly eloquent expression of the struggle with life of someone suffering from anorexia nervosa (Dokter 1994).

In this chapter I will outline the attempted definition, diagnostic criteria and aetiology of eating disorders. The treatments provided are contextualised in the setting where the dramatherapy practice took place. The six-month dramatherapy group in the case-study illustration forms the main body of the chapter. I conclude with some reflections on the methodology and complexities of this work.

Throughout history women have used the control of appetite, food and their bodies as a focus of their symbolic language. Brumberg (1988) shows how the understanding of food-refusing behaviour evolved between the sixteenth and nineteenth century, in response to new developments in religion and medicine. By the nineteenth century the refusal of food had become transformed from a religious act into a pathological state; from sainthood to patienthood. However, even when an illness is organic, being sick is a social act. Expressions of physical anguish and mental stress are selected quite unconsciously from a repertoire of symptoms which we learn by being part of a culture. When attempting to understand the aetiology of eating disorders, different explanations can and do exist simultaneously. Presently there is still no definitive answer to what anorexia nervosa really is, although attempts at definition have been made since the nineteenth century. Bulimia nervosa, as a much more recent concept, was incorporated in the DSM-III (Diagnostic and Statistical Manual of Mental Disorders) in 1985, and is even more undefined. That any definition will need to incorporate the biological, psychological and environmental factors, is now generally accepted. Eating disorders are not merely a social construction. They have physical consequences and involve a level of self-destructive behaviour, which makes them qualitatively different from chronic dieting. They show the reciprocity of biology and culture.

Eating Disorders; Diagnostic and Clinical Features

The following diagnostic criteria of anorexia and bulimia nervosa exist (DSM-III 1980, 1985). These medical criteria focus more on illness than health. They emphasise the biological and, to a lesser extent, psychological factors.

Anorexia nervosa

(1) Refusal to maintain body weight over a minimal normal weight for age and height, e.g. weight loss leading to maintenance of body weight 15 per cent below that expected; or failure to make expected weight gain during a period of growth, leading to body weight 15 per cent below that expected. For men 25 per cent below (Margo 1987)

(2) Intense fear of gaining weight or becoming fat, even although underweight.

(3) Disturbance in body image, e.g. the way in which one's body weight, size or shape is experienced. Feeling fat when emaciated, or experiencing one bodypart as too fat, even when underweight.

(4) In women, absence of at least three menstrual cycles, when otherwise expected to occur (primary or secondary amenorrhea).

(5) In men, a high incidence of over-activity (Margo 1987). NB women increasingly show zealous commitment to exercise too.

Bulimia nervosa

(1) Recurrent episodes of binge eating; rapid consumption of a large amount of food in a discrete period of time. Fifty per cent of anorexia sufferers also experience intermittent loss of control over eating.

(2) A feeling of lack of control over eating during the eating binges.

(3) The person regularly engages in either self-induced vomiting, use of laxatives or diuretics, strict dieting or fasting, or vigorous exercise in order to prevent weight gain.

(4) A minimum of two binge-eating episodes a week for at least three months.

(5) Persistent over-concern with bodyshape and weight. NB bulimia sufferers are often of average weight, 25 per cent have a past history of anorexia.

I have given a fuller description of the clinical features of anorexia and bulimia nervosa as well as the surmised aetiological factors elsewhere (Dokter

1994) there is also a wealth of other literature on the subject. The subject of eating disorders is of growing concern. It is widely accepted that a combination of biological, psychological and social factors are of importance in the aetiology of eating disorders (Garner and Garfinkel 1985). Predisposing factors for anorexia tend to be a family history of eating disorders and affective disorders, a personal history of affective disorder and a fear of maturity. In bulimia, predisposing factors considered are a family or personal history of affective disorder, and a predisposition to obesity. The connection between eating and affective disorders was shown in the acute psychiatric unit where I worked as a dramatherapist. The unit offered specialised care for clients with affective disorders and/or eating disorders.

For both types of clients the social pressure to be slim is an important factor. The socio-cultural context provides reasons for recruitment to fasting behaviour. The subsequent anorexic 'career' includes the physiological and psychological changes which condition the individual to exist in a starvation state. Bruch (1973, 1985) subscribes to this when saying that the cultural emphasis on increasing slenderness can never be the sole determining factor. 'Normal' weight control is distinctly different from the frantic obsession with thinness of the anorexic sufferer. Bruch suggests that the changing status of, and expectations for women play a role. The contradictory expectations of achievement and dependence create severe personal self-doubt and uncertainty in women, particularly in adolescence. The psychological genesis of eating disorders are considered as largely familial and individual. However, the present cultural aesthetic contributes to an acceleration in dieting, which increases the number of people at risk. This is reinforced by the fact that the incidence of anorexia and bulimia is different for women from different ethnic groups in Britain. Those with culturally less emphasis on a slender bodyshape tend to have a lower incidence. When western values are adopted more, the incidence rises (Holden and Robinson 1988). In practice it is important to consider different cultural values concerning food, eating and the body (Badrinath 1990, Jennings 1994).

Susie Orbach (1978, 1985) shows the double bind in expectations regarding successful femininity for women. She argues that the psychological consequence of the suppression of women's desires for both dependency and autonomy is that women do not feel worthwhile in themselves. This psychology is brought to mothering, particularly the mother and daughter relationship. Because the daughter does not receive adequate gratification of early dependency needs, she has difficulty in the separation process, for she still needs an experience of consistent nurturing (Chodorow 1978). Through the idealisation and alienation from the female body in modern society, the adolescent girl is learning to develop a split between her body and herself. In her attempts to conform or reject contemporary ideals of femininity she uses the weapon so often used against her; she speaks with her body.

Orbach's view reflects a wider one in which eating disorders are seen as obsessional behaviours, connected with dependence versus independence issues (Lawrence 1984) and the family as a predominant factor in the development of eating disorders. The central relationship focused on in literature is the one with the mother. Winnicott (1965) discusses how a child needs to learn that it has a voice. If the mothering is 'too good' the child does not learn this. It can only express itself in its actions and often only learns to do what the parents approve of. For these individuals it is difficult to achieve and maintain a sense of self as a free and autonomous person. The relationship with the mother is often the central idealised relationship. The mother may be the preferred ideal object, but if she is not available a friend, partner or sibling can fulfil the same function. This was certainly the case for dramatherapy group members. The dynamics of these relationships were regularly brought to and explored in the group. The idealisation is a particular difficulty; ambivalence, the coexisting of positive and negative feelings, is very difficult to acknowledge openly. Instead, it is expressed physically.

The above argument is female centred; 5 to 10 per cent of eating disorders sufferers are male. They mainly suffer from anorexia and the fact that this is seen as a predominantly female disorder increases their problems. They tend to be diagnosed later, their weight loss tends to be more severe and their self-image regarding their masculinity problematic. Some arts therapists have described their work with individual male clients; this illustrates their predicament well (Sloboda 1993, Luzzatto 1994).

The Treatment of Clients with Eating Disorders

The aetiology stresses a combination of social/cultural, physiological, psychological and family dynamic causes. Most modern treatment programmes address the complexity of these aetiological factors. The treatment has two aims. First, it focuses on the physical well being and survival of the client. Second, it focuses on understanding the issues underlying the difficulties with food. One of the problems with this is that too much focus on physical well being can reinforce the concept of the disorder as an illness in itself, where underlying factors are not relevant.

Treatment involves a combination of re-feeding and re-establishing regular eating patterns, a cognitive–behavioural input on body perception and distorted thought-patterns and psychodynamic treatment on an individual, group and/or family basis. The psychiatric unit where I worked as a dramatherapist offered all these and added physiotherapy regarding relaxation and body image work. The re-feeding in this particular unit was negotiated with the client and involved intensive nursing care and the involvement of a dietician. The advantage of this multidisciplinary approach is that the psychodynamic input can focus on underlying conflicts and emotions. In this approach the difficulties around food are seen as a symptom. In an in-patient setting the arts therapies usually form one of the psychodynamic forms of treatment following or accompanying weight restoration. Certainly my own orientation is psychodynamic. Given the brief nature of a six-month therapy group and the context of the rest of the treatment I decided to focus on the difficulties in interpersonal relationships. A more creativity-oriented approach could focus on exploration through the art medium. This would aim to address and adjust fixed obsessional thought and behaviour patterns. A client with anorexia, for example, in an open dramatherapy group I facilitated always chose a solid piece of rock to represent herself. She described this rock as unwanted, ugly and unmovable. Working with other clients and their objects meant that the identity of her rock changed with other people's perception; they saw its solidity, its hidden attractive veins, its smooth shape. Staying purely within the story metaphor, alternatives to her perception were offered. She would not easily accept these other perceptions but recognised their possible validity. This type of more cognitive work is only possible once some nutritional improvement has been made. When clients are in a state of extreme starvation their mood is often too labile, their concentration too poor to participate in any group work. Schaverien (1994) shows that some form of engagement can begin even at that stage; she leaves art materials at the bedside for clients' use if and when they feel able.

Garner and Garfinkel (1985) actually reinforce that nutritional improvement and a resolution of psychological problems should occur in close interaction, because a lasting recovery requires a change of the inner-self image (very poor with extremely high ego-ideal standards). They formulate the therapeutic aim as encouraging the client in the search for autonomy and self-directed identity in the setting of new personal relationships, where what they have to say is listened to and made the object of exploration. This importance of returning control to the client is not easy when both complying and wanting to please are strong features of the client's psychological make-up. The focus within the therapy is that the clients have a consistent experience of being listened to as important. The therapeutic task is not to give clients insight into the symbolic significance of their behaviour, but to help clients face the realities of their past and present lives. Interpretation as a therapeutic tool is not acceptable. It is a painful re-enactment of being told what to feel and think. It interferes with the development of autonomy and trust in one's own psychological abilities.

In relation to group therapy, a small group is considered more containable (four to six clients). When recruiting, one needs to keep in mind the likelihood of a high drop-out rate. Mixing clients with anorexia and bulimia can be useful when selecting for a group. Although the bulimic and anorexic can represent each other's fears, the one out of control the other over-controlling, they can also be a good education for each other. It is important to have at least one member at the desired weight as a model and assurance that it is possible. When working with a group, offering individual sessions is helpful, both to prevent drop out and as preparation for revealing personal material later in the group. Keeping in touch through letters and phonecalls can be helpful for similar reasons (Dokter 1992).

The literature concerning dramatherapy work with this client group is limited. Young (1986) wrote about in- and out-patient group work. The American editors Hornyak and Baker in their book *Experiential Therapies for Eating Disorders* (1989) do not mention dramatherapy, but describe the use of poetry, family sculpting and psychodrama with this client group. The art therapists Schaverien (1989), Levens (1987) and Rust (1984, 1992) emphasise the importance of projective work for these clients. The dance movement therapists writing in Hornyak and Baker are the only modality which incorporated embodiment in their work, often focusing on body-image issues. The need to hunt out appropriate references in an area where arts therapists work encouraged me to attempt to bring together a body of literature on the subject.

Tolerating Chaos – A Six-month Dramatherapy Group

The clients I worked with in my group were not the adolescents often described in literature. The people I saw were in their 20s and 30s. They had usually been struggling with their eating disorder for more than ten years, with a history of several hospital admissions. The eating disorder might be the main presenting symptom, but substance abuse and self-harm were equally important, as was an overwhelming feeling of depression, emptiness and worthlessness. These clients were well aware that they had a problem (as opposed to common denial). They felt ambivalent and powerless to effect any change, and had frequently proved this to themselves and others.

With the multidisciplinary team at the unit where I worked, it was decided to offer a six-month dramatherapy group. One of the nursing staff would participate in the group as assistant to me, model for the clients and liaison with the rest of the team. As a dramatherapist I only worked one day per week at the unit; the eating disorders team met on a different day. Regular liaison between team members is very important to prevent splitting. In the context of treatment already offered, I suggested to focus on interpersonal relationships. The six months limit was due to restraints within the acute unit; the consultant did not wish to tie down an arts therapist to one particular group of clients for any longer than that. Usually a minimum length of one year is recommended (Garner and Garfinkel 1985) for clients with this degree of severity in their problems.

I saw clients once or twice individually for assessment before they joined the group. I discussed with them their expectations about dramatherapy and the group. I asked about other treatment received and what they might hope to get out of a group like this. I described what a dramatherapy group might entail (I needed to dispel fears about enactment) and the time-limited nature of the group. I then suggested trying out a technique we might use in the group as a 'taster'. Clients select objects from a basket with shells, stones, wood and other natural objects. The objects represent significant people in their life and themselves. They then sculpt these objects in relation to each other; close, far, on top, etc. It is an assessment structure I use frequently to look at client's interpersonal relationships. The sculpt is threefold; present, a significant past moment and some time in the hoped-for future (the client decides how far ahead this future is). I then often asked the first small change clients might wish for in the near future. This provided a good stepping stone to discuss client's aims for themselves and potential pitfalls. I also discussed a contract for ending. What might make people want to leave the group and what would be the best and worst way of leaving for them. Past experiences in groups provided another useful guide-line on this. I then gave clients a week to think it over and met them to discuss whether they wanted to join the group or not. I assessed ten people who were referred by their key worker, consultant or psychologist; eight decided to join. This was a high proportion, because clients agreed to be referred prior to referral.

During the group I saw people occasionally for an individual session; usually when problems became too overwhelming and clients needed to work through issues individually before bringing them to the group. This prevented drop-out on several occasions. Not all, however; over a period of six months, of eight clients attending the group, three dropped out. The first was the only out-patient in a group of past and present in-patients and found this too threatening. Another client discharged herself from the ward and with that from the group. The last decided to do a creative drama course instead. (She felt very ambivalent about the treatment as a whole.) On average, three to five people attended each session and for a period of between four and six months. Half were anorexic and half bulimic. The one male group member had already acquired and was trying to maintain the desired weight. The clients who attended had been troubled by their eating disorders for longer than ten years. The group was mixed anorexic and bulimic but often combined with alcohol, drug abuse and self-harming. Several of these features were and had often been present in one client. Given these chronic and complex problems, a six-month group duration was very short (the minimum recommended is a year), but the only possibility within the context. Many clients found commitment to a long-term group difficult. They hoped to be discharged soon, despite their history they did not want to acknowledge a need for long-term support. Ambivalence about wanting to change, gaining weight, looking at issues underlying the food problems, showed in ambivalence about commitment to treatment. The brief nature of the group work was supported by the other multidisciplinary treatment I outlined earlier. Some clients were also in individual arts therapy (art or music), while in the group.

Methodological Considerations

The dramatherapy techniques used in the group were mainly projective ones like sculpting, poetry and story-telling. Direct bodywork like movement was felt as too threatening. Johnson (1982) discusses developmental approaches in dramatherapy. The stages to move through are embodiment, projection and role. Jennings (1993) links these from birth to five years old as a child develops its play. First, bodyplay (movement), followed by projective play (sculpting, drawing and painting) and finally dramatic play (drama-games, enactment and improvisation). Johnson proposes that movement, drama and verbalisation correspond with the sensori-motor, symbolic and reflective stages. This developmental perspective is useful for those clients who have been blocked in their development. For clients with eating disorders this blocking of their autonomy and difficulty with verbalisation certainly applies. It might be useful to assess clients as to the most appropriate developmental stage to work in and base the choice of arts therapy modality on this: a blockage in the sensori-motor development, being in touch with your body – indication for dance movement therapy; in the symbolic stage – art therapy indication. However, for a dramatherapist this developmental perspective can also provide a guide for selecting the most appropriate structures and techniques. Young (1994) does so in her group work with bulimic clients.

The clients for my group tended to be very fluent in verbalisation. Mainly intellectualisation and defensive talking. Interpretation is not helpful (Garner and Garfinkel 1985), so to start at that end of the developmental scale and work backwards was not recommended. Embodiment, either in movement or enactment, was felt as too threatening. To stand up and be seen was a very prominent fear in the beginning of the group. I started with sculpting objects in the assessment and early stages of the group. In the later stages of group life-story and poetry work were an additional projective structure, which proved helpful. These projective techniques were felt to be helpful, because they provided people with an opportunity to express how they felt. The emphasis was on externalising internal issues, conflicts and ideas. In retrospect (at a follow-up interview three months after the group had finished), all clients said they found this helpful. At the time although, many expressed feeling threatened by the projected material:

> The only unhelpful part of art therapy, if you can call it that, is that it is like coming face to face with buried demons… putting down emotions on paper also helped to make them real… To draw and deal with the visually disturbing imagery unlocked emotions and feelings, which were hard to tidy away and leave behind after an hour.

> (Warriner 1994, pp.24–25)

My clients also viewed their sculpts, images and poems as taking on a reality of their own. Once emotions are perceived outside, denial is much more difficult. The process of engagement with the underlying issues had to start. These issues often concerned difficult, sometimes abusive relationships, which group members found hard to acknowledge. Flight into the symptom as a disease in itself, 'if only the weight was alright everything would be alright', was more difficult.

Elise Warriner's quote shows the importance and the difficulty of containment of the projected material. Processing needed to happen within the sessions. Tension mounted during sessions and, if not addressed, would result in bingeing or cutting to find release afterwards. Clients were taught some relaxation and self-soothing techniques, but what was most helpful was active reflection within sessions. Clients made their own connections and so gained some measure of control back. Each client also had an individual folder to keep their work in. They could leave material there for symbolic containment if it became too much, and return to it when they felt ready.

What was very important was the reflection during and at the end of each session. This was a structured reflection on the sculpts, poetry, images and stories, which included both positive and negative ways of perceiving what was there. As the group members had a very low self-esteem and a highly polarised way of viewing their material, working with a continuum or a cycle often facilitated a more nuanced approach to the reflection. This was so important, because the client's own interpretation tended to veer towards the negative, stressing self-worthlessness and hopelessness. Offering structures that did not deny the feelings, but offered the potential of re-framing was imperative, if people were to feel some sense of control over their material.

The use of the continuum (the two poles set along a line, exploring feelings and perceptions at different points of the line), cyclical stories (for example, that of Persephone, the different stages) and role reversal, were useful techniques to facilitate this process. An example of the use of the continuum was early in the life of the group. At the beginning of the sessions clients used little figures to sculpt some of the important interpersonal events of their past week. The theme arising from these sculpts was this week, and often, clients' total preoccupation with caring for others, losing themselves within the process. I suggested a continuum line, one pole the totally caring for others, the other pole total caring for oneself. I asked clients to select their preferred and feared places along this continuum and write some scenes connected with these points (past and present life events). These stories were then shared, or the title/some significant phrases if the whole story felt too much. A continuum, drawn this time, was then used to reflect on the gap between wish and action. If the clients felt able to, these drawings were then shared. Alternatively clients might write a poem about the feelings evoked by this work. They could read this out themselves, ask someone to read it for them, leave it to be read or share the title only. I always provided clients with alternatives to choose from (their control), and they also had the option not to participate. The latter option became an interesting arena for exploring autonomy. The continuum structures allow the clients themselves to explore their work, rather than relying on the therapist's interpretation. It also provides a structure to look at possible alternative perceptions or interpretations by the clients themselves.

Re-framing of perception if everything feels negative can be done through the use of stories and cycles, for example, a tree image in winter, spring, summer and autumn. Looking at self and life this way was very difficult for the group. As one client said: 'What is the use of enjoying summer, when you know that winter and autumn are coming again?' Working with the story of Persephone was a more symbolic way of engaging with, exploring and attempting to re-frame these themes of darkness and waiting, change and loss (Gersie and King 1990). Mostly, however, people created their own stories and poetry, rather than me providing them. The therapist is there for containment, too much direction feeds into the feeling of being controlled and manipulated. In the later stages of group life it became possible to do some reading and enacting of life scenes. Role reversal was then a useful technique to start engaging with and experiencing different perceptions. The need to externalise, engage with emotion and not feel totally overwhelmed, gaining some ability to look at and take in, then allowed clients to start looking at the painful underlying interpersonal experiences; Elise Warriner's buried demons.

This brings me to a few points about the role of the therapist in a group like this. Not that it is substantially different from that in other groups, but I found myself working in a slightly different way, and thought it might be useful to note these points. Some of those sprang automatically from the discussion before. For example the fact that the therapist is there to provide structure, but leaves choice within that. The role is not to interpret, but sometimes to model possible ways of expression and re-framing. The assistant was a very helpful model here too, because she was able to share that both negative and positive could co-exist, were not mutually exclusive. The only group member who had attained sufficient weight gain to aim for maintenance, was another model. This was so important, because the negative images and feelings could be overwhelming. The therapist is usually more active in a small group, and as eating disorders groups are often small, this also applies here.

Complexities and Conclusion

To express externally what has been expressed non-verbally through the body is very threatening for clients suffering from eating disorders. The threat is to experience emotions often deadened by the obsessive preoccupation with food and body shape and/or the physical effects of starvation and over-activity. Once the pain is externalised the engagement with underlying issues can begin. Learning to face and tolerate chaos requires a very effective therapeutic container. In an out-patient setting this may mean incorporating looking at food issues (Young 1994). In an in-patient setting close liaison with the multidisciplinary team is crucial. Dissociation and splitting are two defence mechanisms frequently employed. The arts therapy group could either be the 'good object', while the team members responsible for re-feeding carry the 'bad object' projection. Vice versa, the arts therapy group can be made into the place where 'I am made to feel bad'. Close communication is necessary to prevent collusion.

Related to this complexity is what happens when the unit team decides to discharge a patient who refuses to comply with the treatment contract, i.e.

does not acquire sufficient weight. Does the arts therapist agree to carry on working with the client as an out-patient after voluntary (client decides to discharge themselves to avoid – further – weight-increase) or compulsory discharge? These clients are likely to return sooner or later and the group could provide a holding environment. I would advocate a special out-patient group for these clients, rather than colluding with the client's avoidance and giving this message to the other group members.

Engagement in treatment is problematic. In a mixed client group the people suffering from eating disorders often distance themselves from other clients; 'I am different, not ill, do not need anything from you'. This can provoke much anger and/or rejection from other clients. Their neediness may also flood the group. A specific group for clients with eating disorders may be more useful, but is notoriously difficult to facilitate; eating disordered clients are experienced as extremely demanding and manipulative (as they also perceive others). Extreme anger and helplessness is a common feeling as facilitator. Co-working with good supervision, which looks at transference and counter-transference issues can provide the necessary support. Experiential staff training (Winn 1994) can also help team members to recognise the feelings evoked in themselves.

Concluding, notwithstanding what I have just said, I found this group very rewarding to work with. Despite the high levels of anxiety and relatively high drop-out rate (the usual trend), several members expressed that they felt they benefited from the group at the three months follow-up interview. They felt it complemented the treatment programme as a whole, because it focused on underlying problems and relationships. The creative work brought up more material than they thought, but this was felt to be beneficial, because it was combined with the re-framing structure. The feeling out of control and dipping into chaos would otherwise have been too great. All group members advocated a longer duration of the group, because of their initial fears of commitment. Most of them arranged to be in a different group or individual therapy after the group to continue the work which had begun. This makes me want to advocate a slow open ongoing group, wherever possible, especially for clients who are at the severe end of the spectrum and whose problems have become chronic. To be able to start tolerating chaos requires time, especially in the case of these clients, whose eating disorders had blocked out the rest of the world for many years. Time-limited groups can play a very effective role within an overall treatment programme, if they provide a clear focus and liaise closely with the rest of the team.

Recovery

Cutting through forever, the scarred tissues of remembrance,
unlayering the solitude that drowns me in its silence,
spitting out the wasted words and memories lost in time,
uncovering the wounded self that bleeds without a trace,
unmasking all the sorrows that crawl beneath my skin,
peeling off the childhood, outgrown and left behind,
unpacking all the burdened lies that tell me there's no hope,
sawing through the chains of guilt that bind me to life's hate,
and allowing myself to breathe in life and spit out the decay.

(Warriner 1994, pp.296)

References

Badrinath, B.R. (1990) 'Anorexia nervosa in adolescents of Asian extraction.' *British Journal of Psychiatry 156*, 565–568.

Bruch, H. (1973) *Eating Disorders. Obesity, Anorexia Nervosa and the Person within.* New York: Basic Books Inc.

Bruch, H. (1985) 'Four decades of eating disorders.' In D.M. Garner and P.E. Garfinkel (eds) *A handbook of Psychotherapy for Anorexia Nervosa and Bulimia.* New York: Guilford Press.

Brumberg, J.J. (1988) *Fasting Girls: The Emergence of Anorexia Nervosa as a Modern Disease.* Boston M.A.: Harvard University Press.

Chodorow, N. (1978) *The Reproduction of Mothering: Psychoanalysis and the Sociology of Gender.* Berkeley: University of California Press.

Diagnostic and Statistical Manual of Mental Disorders (DSM) III (1980) Washington D.C.: American Psychiatric Association.

Dokter, D. (1992) 'Tolerating chaos – dramatherapy and eating disorders.' In *Dramatherapy 14*, 1, 16–19.

Dokter, D. (ed) (1994) *Arts Therapies and Clients with Eating Disorders: Fragile Board.* London: Jessica Kingsley Publishers.

Garner, D.M. and Garfinkel, P.E. (eds) (1985) *A Handbook of Psychotherapy for Anorexia Nervosa and Bulimia.* New York: Guilford Press.

Gersie, A. and King, N. (1990) *Storymaking in Education and Therapy.* London: Jessica Kingsley Publishers.

Heal, M. and Wigram, T. (eds) *Music Therapy in Health and Education.* London: Jessica Kingsley Publishers.

Holden, N.L. and Robinson, P.H. (1988) 'Anorexia nervosa and Bulimia nervosa in British blacks.' *British Journal of Psychiatry 152*, 544–549.

Hornyak, L. and Baker, T. (ed) (1989) *Experiential Therapies for Eating Disorders.* New York: Guildford Press.

Jennings, S. (1993) 'The theatre of healing: metaphor and metaphysics in the healing process.' In S. Jennings, A. Cattanach, S. Mitchell, A. Chesner and B. Meldrum (ed) *The Handbook of Dramatherapy*. London: Routledge.

Jennings, S., Cattanach, A., Mitchell, S., Chesner, A. and Meldrum, B. (1994) *The Handbook of Dramatherapy*. London: Routledge.

Jennings S. (1994) 'A dramatherapy case history.' In D. Dokter. *Arts Therapies and Clients with Eating Disorders: Fragile Board*. London: Jessica Kingsley Publishers.

Johnson, D. (1982) 'Developmental approaches in dramatherapy.' *The Arts in Psychotherapy 9*, 83–90.

Lawrence, M. (1984) *The Anorexic Experience*. London: Women's Press.

Levens, M. (1987) 'Arts therapy with eating disordered patients.' *Inscape. Journal of Arts Therapy*, Summer. London: BAAT.

Luzzato, P. (1994) 'The mental double trap of the anorexic patient.' In D. Dokter (ed) *Arts Therapies and Clients with Eating Disorders: Fragile Board*. London: Jessica Kingsley Publishers.

Margo, J.L. (1987) 'Anorexia nervosa in males. A comparison with female patients.' *British Journal of Psychiatry 151*, 80–83.

Orbach, S. (1978) *Fat is a Feminist Issue*. London: Paddington Press.

Orbach, S. (1985) 'Accepting the symptom: a feminist psychoanalytic treatment of anorexia nervosa.' In D.M. Garner and P.E. Garfinkel (eds) *A handbook of Psychotherapy for Anorexia Nervosa and Bulimia*. London: Guilford Press.

Rust, M.J. (1984) 'Images and eating problems.' In M. Lawrence (ed) op cit.

Rust, M.J. (1992) 'Arts therapy in the treatment of women with eating disorders.' In D. Waller and A. Gilroy (eds) *Arts Therapy: A Handbook*. Oxford: Oxford University Press.

Schaverien, J. (1989) 'Transference and the picture: Arts therapy in the treatment of anorexia.' *Inscape*, Spring.

Schaverien, J. (1994) 'The picture as transactional object in the treatment of anorexia.' In D. Dokter (ed) *Arts Therapies and Clients with Eating Disorders: Fragile Board*. London: Jessica Kingsley Publishers.

Sloboda, A. (1993) 'Individual therapy with a man who has an eating disorder.' In M. Heal and E. Warriner (1994) *Anger is Red, Letting Go and Recovery*. In D. Dokter (ed) *Arts Therapies and Clients with Eating Disorders: Fragile Board*. London: Jessica Kingsley Publishers.

Winn, L. (1994) 'Experiential training for staff working with eating disorders.' In D. Dokter (ed) *Arts Therapies and Clients with Eating Disorders: Fragile Board*. London: Jessica Kingsley Publishers.

Winnicott, D.W. (1965) *The Maturational Processes and the Facilitating Environment*. London: Hogarth Press.

Young, M. (1986) 'The use of dramatherapy methods for working with clients with eating problems.' *Dramatherapy 9*, 2, 3–11.

Young, M. (1994) 'Dramatherapy in short term groupwork with women with bulimia.' In D. Dokter D. (ed) *Arts Therapies and Clients with Eating Disorders: Fragile Board*. London: Jessica Kingsley Publishers.

CHAPTER ELEVEN

Cues to the Dramatherapist from the Group

Katerina Couroucli-Robertson

Defining Dramatherapy

The British Association for Dramatherapists has now adopted the following definition for use in its literature and policies:

> Dramatherapy has as its main focus the intentional use of healing aspects of drama and theatre as the therapeutic process. It is a method of working and playing that uses action methods to facilitate creativity, imagination, learning, insight and growth.
>
> (British Association of Dramatherapists 1992)

As a dramatherapist I have often been asked what it is that one really does in a dramatherapeutic session. Very simply, the answer is, one works with the personal issues of the members and their relationships within the group, on a metaphorical and symbolic level.

In their book *Mutative Metaphors in Psychotherapy*, Cox and Theilgaard (1987) describe how a patient is facilitated to express his inner feelings through poetry and symbolism. The authors believe that, 'through the force of poesis and the aesthetic imperative, man defends, proclaims and becomes his history. It is possible to go blind (literally and metaphorically) if one sees too much; and the force of poetry can furnish both therapist and the patient with a "dark lamp".' In a dramatherapeutic session this poetry and symbolism takes on flesh and blood and becomes action. During the development of the session we have the opportunity to animate our symbols. Often the theme facing a group at a particular time is too painful to deal with directly and with words, consequently another method of working is necessary.

In every dramatherapy session there are four stages, the initial sharing, the warm-up, the main action followed by the de-roleing, and the final feedback. From the initial sharing (the first words members of a group exchange at the beginning of the session) and the development of the previous session, the dramatherapist takes her cues, which might be verbal, physical or circumstantial. For example, a group member may say that she is mourning, she may be wearing black, or she might just have a sad face. Another may be late or absent, another may have forgotten the time the group began or may have overslept, all these and many others are the plethora of cues one is given, all needing the right response from the therapist. The therapist receives both the group cue plus individual ones and she is called to decide which needs the most attention. In a dramatherapy session the therapist has the opportunity of changing the scenario, or guiding it in various directions. The therapist, like the theatre director, also decides who is to take the leading part at a given moment, always considering the pulse of the group.

The warm-up is used for the gentle initiation into the main theme which will be worked on during the session. It can be used more specifically in order to relax a group or it can be used in order to get the energy level lifted. It helps members to get in touch with their body and the signals they may be receiving from it. Or it can be used for the physical contact that it facilitates among the members and the trust this can provide.

During the main part of each session, I try to work with the group theme symbolically but also on a parallel level with the here and now. For example, in a new group where members were anxious to get to know each other but at the same time shy, I asked them to sit in a queue at a voting station waiting for their turn to vote. (At several poling stations in Athens this October, the legal representatives didn't turn up, which resulted in long delays and often the disappointment of having to go home and not voting at all that day.) This instruction not only matched the group issue, but was also a topical event, making the enactment easier to get into.

Through drama action, the unconscious is awakened and the members find themselves acting, drawing, making stories, and so forth, spontaneously. It is far more difficult to censure one's actions than one's words and as a result the actions are clearer and more straightforward. For example, in one of my therapy groups a member found herself in the very difficult predicament of an unwanted pregnancy. During the initial sharing everyone was very logical and told her all the good reasons why she shouldn't keep her baby. She was still living at home, she didn't earn enough money to support herself, she had just broken up with her boyfriend, and so forth. However, during the action, which involved some role playing of similar circumstances, the other members gave her completely contradictory messages to what they had told her in words. At the final feedback the group was able to see the two different angles to her predicament, which gave a better insight to what she wanted to do.

What is taking place may not become apparent to the individual at the time, but she or he will have the visual memory of it imprinted on their heart and at a later date the meaning of it may reveal itself to them. This visual memory of an event will stay with a person far more easily than a logical thought. Flashbacks to scenes acted out in a session may have an edifying effect on future behaviour. The visual memory of a part in a play or a painting that is kept can be seen as the transitional stage.

> The first object is the breast, but the development of a child's ability to form a 'mental picture' of his or her mother leads to the first relationship: when symbolism is employed the infant is already clearly distinguishing between fantasy and fact, between the inner and external events. (Winnicott 1971, p.6)

In one of my groups one member was coping with a dying father who had been in the intensive care unit for a month. Most patients going into that unit didn't come out alive, so my patient was in the process of mourning for someone who was not yet dead. She said that she felt she had to support her mother and be the strong family member in place of her father, but it was difficult and at the same time she also wanted to be the child. After sharing these feelings with the group, the other members all bowed down their heads and no one said a word; they were unable to support her. An exact mirroring of her relationship with her mother was taking place within the group. As a warm-up we did a few group hand exercises involving close physical contact without stress. These exercises were designed to help the members come closer to each other physically, thus providing comfort. For the main action I asked the group to paint a life-size door. After the painting had been completed I asked them to become this door, so they could experiment with its weight, its texture, its hinges, etc. During the final feedback of this particular session, the members were more open to sharing both what the door symbolised for them and the memories it aroused. The member who had been late arriving said she had just been to the funeral of a close relative who had died suddenly and this statement helped the others talk about death more openly.

This session had followed work done about the walls we build around us. Specifically we had worked with a poem by Cavafy which goes as follows:

Walls

Without consideration, without pity, without shame
they have built big and high walls around me.
And now I sit here despairing.
I think of nothing else: This fate gnaws at my mind;
for I had many things to do outside.
Ah, why didn't I observe them when they were
building the walls?
But I never heard the noise of the sound of the builders.
Imperceptibly they shut me out of the world.

(Cavafy 1948)

While working with the image of walls many of the group members had made very sturdy walls with no way out, so the image of a door came to me, not only as an opening to something new, but also as something which can be closed behind us; a door into safety or a door to a new road, a door to another world or a door separating two rooms.

What they drew in fact was an internal door of a house, with translucent glass, which allowed light to enter but one couldn't see through. It was a door which separated the sitting-room (a social room) from the more private rooms of a home.

It could also have be seen as a door from the intensive care unit to the outside world. I chose this way of working as it was a group activity where the members had a way of building something together, supporting the group as a whole, but at the same time personal memories were brought to the surface.

Dramatherapy Models

Because dramatherapy is based on theatre art, some have suggested that a better name might be theatre therapy, an opinion I don't disagree with, if it weren't for the fact that as a new modality dramatherapy needs stability. If a name change were to take place it would cause confusion and perhaps a feeling that there are different fractions, an impression we must avoid. Also, I am not sure whether the term theatre covers all the aspects of dramatherapy which I find so important, namely the use of metaphor and aesthetic distance. For me dramatherapy is a means whereby one can enter into an 'as if' situation on a metaphoric plane.

Another aspect which struck me only recently, while translating from English to Greek a dramatherapy workshop run by Steve Mitchell, was the use of the word 'drama'. While translating 'theatre and drama', I tended to translate only the word theatre as the word drama in Greek has different connotations (a theatrical play with a tragic theme, or a tragic happening). It then struck me that the correct translation would be that of the ancient Greek word drama, which means action. Perhaps the word action is our key word for explaining the meaning of drama in both English and Greek. In a dramatherapy session, the group members are expected to be mobile, words are put into action, images take on a life of their own, the whole person both mind and body is asked to be present and take part. I believe that through the spontaneous 'as if' action, the unconscious is freed and thus the dramatherapy session takes on the quality of a dream.

> 'The general function of dreams is to try to restore our psychological balance by producing dream material that re-establishes, in a subtle way, the total psychic equilibrium' (Jung 1964, p.4).

During feedback each member has the opportunity to decipher their actions with their own codes.

Although I believe that all dramatherapy groups have a similar core line, which differentiates them from other therapy groups, different models are referred to, which perhaps are better linked with the aim of each group rather than the way it is run.

Jennings (1990) talks of four dramatherapy models.

(1) Creative expressive, where emphasis is on the healthy side of the patient and enables a re-affirmation process through latent creativity.

(2) Task-centred emphasis is on the learning process involved in behaviour change.

(3) Psychotherapeutic intra-psychic processes and psychotherapeutic phenomena (transferences etc.) underpin group and individual practice.

(4) Dramatherapy model is strongly influenced by the in-depth study of drama and para-theatrical approaches and the human capacity to transform their experiences through the creative struggle between inner and outer worlds.

It is this fourth model I wish to expand on, and on which my professional experience is mostly based.

Dramatherapy being a new profession, its application varies from individual to individual, depending on their training and their other professional identity. Was their personal therapy dramatherapeutic? Was their supervisor a dramatherapist? What other influences have they undergone before starting up as professional dramatherapists. All these factors together with the personality of the dramatherapist will influence the way each one works and guides into action a particular dramatherapeutic session. Some might use role as the essential part of therapy, some might work with each individual's personal story as seen through their choice of story, film, play, etc. Others use stories which they choose for a particular group at the right time and others use free association and different creative methods each time. This may be a very simplistic way of describing the work of different dramatherapists. However, my intention is only to show how differently dramatherapy can be applied by different dramatherapists.

Directing a Dramatherapy Session

My own way of working is perhaps a combination of different techniques according to each group's needs at a particular time. With the cues the members give me I try to find a way of working with the particular theme in a symbolic fashion. To symbolise means to be able to experience the existence of links between objects which are also recognised to be separate and distinct. 'Thus a word or an image is symbolic when it implies something more than its obvious and immediate meaning. It has a wider 'unconscious' aspect that is never precisely defined or fully explained' (Jung 1964, p.34.) Ideas are taken from one point of view and seen in a parallel one, thus giving a new perspective. For instance, a group member during the initial sharing said that she had been very upset and confused after her meeting with a child she was working with as a play therapy trainee. While using finger paints, the child had finally overcome his initial disgust and inability to get his fingers dirty, and made a real mess. At the end of the session his mother was anxious about the mess and even noticed some paint on the child's socks. My client in her haste not to upset the parents grabbed the cleaning up cloth and cleared the table herself where they had been working. When leaving the child she found a conflict inside her of both wanting to please the parents and also helping the child in the way she felt best.

This stage was similar to the stage the group itself was going through. The group had reopened after the summer break with new members who were not quite sure how dirty they could allow themselves to get. What I worked with was the image of the washing-up cloth. The group as a whole became a washing-up cloth and cleared away what dirt it could find and then I asked each member to draw her own personal washing-up cloth. During the feedback members were allowed to reflect, if they wished to, on what this dirt was, which was their personal washing-up cloth, under what circumstances they used it, and so forth.

For each session I find I need a carefully thought-out plan, to use as a guide. Sticking, however, to this plan when the group has moved elsewhere may cause obstructions. While making this plan I consider how best I feel a particular group will work. I consider whether the group coherency needs to be developed or whether the members need to work individually. The media also needs close consideration according to how it might stimulate the group. If a story or a myth is going to be used, I always consider the issues these may bring forward. According to Lahad (1991), myths represent the id as they deal with gods, powers and characteristics which don't alter. Fairy stories represent the ego, where the heroes are more human but still they are fantastic and without emotion. Whereas modern novels have to do with the others, there are no gods or magic. Science fiction comes under this category and it offers good material for working with adolescents.

How the Calendar Influences my Work

The time of year and the customs this includes is also an aspect I find very important to work with, as this connects the group and its development with the outside word. Seasons and the meaning of each are very good subjects, as well as particular festivities. Through work with these themes the group can get a better understanding of community life. Autumn is the beginning of the new academic year, a time when many embark on new beginnings. It is the preparation for the winter to come, a sobering time after summer and the holidays. Also, a time when many people might decide to enter a dramatherapy group!

Christmas is a time of hope, birth, giving, families, and so forth. For a group which began in September or October, Christmas is the time when members have begun to feel safe with each other and the group may have started to represent a family.

Carnival time in Greece (which comes a month or two after Christmas in order to prepare people for the 40 days of Lent to come) is another widely celebrated time. It is a time when dramatherapy is practised by everyone, without them being aware of it! The costumes chosen to be worn and the personalities given to these, are always revealing of how a person is feeling at that particular time. The amount of whores and transvestites to be seen in the streets ought to be alarming!

Lent is another interesting time, which can be seen on a symbolic level. It is a time when people fast in order to purify their bodies in preparation for the sacrifice of Christ. One doesn't have to be religious to follow these customs, and of course many people don't, but it is surprising how many will refrain from eating meat during holy week. A group can also investigate what it needs to fast on in order to feel purified.

Next there is Easter and spring, perhaps the most important celebrations in Greece, which symbolise rebirth, new life, nature at her most profuse time. What are the fruits of the group?

And finally summer, heat and the slowing down of the winter rhythms. It is a time most people take a holiday and the long-awaited relaxation is in view. How can a dramatherapist not use all the above in order to enhance her or his work with clients!

My Experience

My experience mostly comes from ongoing dramatherapy groups which may contain members who have come either for their personal development (these could include trainees) or members with a specific aim such as coping with depression, eating disorders, bereaveavement, forming relationships.

I have also worked in groups of adolescents with learning difficulties. Some of my groups had a defined duration from their beginning, for example, two years. Others opened each September to new members and closed after three sessions, allowing each member to stay for as long as she or he chose. However, when a member wanted to leave, I strongly recommended that they do this during a natural break (summer, Christmas or Easter) and after the group had worked with the separation. And finally, other groups opened with a nucleus of clients and new members would enter when I felt this was right for the group, again each client would stay for as long as she or he wished, again with the recommendation to leave when there was a natural break in the group and after having prepared for the separation. The longest I have run the same dramatherapy group has been five years.

I believe that in an ongoing dramatherapy group the members have an experience on a different level to a short-term one. A long-term group has stability and gains maturity, not only in the behaviour of each member, but also in the group as a whole. Also, the members learn to understand the methodology used in dealing dramatherapeutically with each situation.

The numbers in each group I have worked with have varied from three (not an easy number to work with) to nine. More than nine members I find difficult to handle in a session of one-and-a-half hours. Also, one is no longer able to help each individual on a personal level if the numbers are high.

I have also worked with individuals using sand play and stories, and again I have found that they need time to get used to a new way of working and in order to feel confident with it.

After working in different ways in regards to the time contract, with groups opening and closing at different times, I have come to the conclusion that the best way, for me anyway, is the last example I mentioned. A group with a nucleus of members where new ones enter when I feel the group is ready to receive them.

In the two-year training dramatherapy group, I found that some members at the end were not ready to finish, and even although there was a two-year minimum stipulation from their training, they felt inadequate if they needed more time. Personal therapy is not something which can function with a time limit, on the other hand it should not become a crutch for endless years either.

How to Influence Group Dynamics

In a dramatherapy group the structure allows the therapist to influence the group dynamics by working in pairs, threes, small groups or focusing on one person.

For instance on the first day of an new group the members need to get to know each other, but at the same time they may feel self-conscious and unwilling to open up to the whole group. This difficulty may be overcome, to some degree, by asking them to work in pairs for the first warm-up exercise, and then slowly bring two pairs together, two foursomes, ending with the whole group taking part.

The therapist can instruct the members to choose a partner they don't know so well or they can be allowed to make their own choice. On the whole during the beginning of a group's life the therapist needs to build up group cohesion and trust so that the members feel safe to express themselves. This is the same whether the group has all new members or whether there are some new members coming in to an old group making the group's dynamics different.

The first sessions, as a result, will be planned with group exercises where the whole group is involved in the main action. When the members have got to know each other, smaller groups can be encouraged, as though the group has reached puberty, and towards the end when they are more mature they can work in couples.

When the life of a group has begun to get established and the patterns of this have become apparent, the therapist has the opportunity to guide the group depending on its needs at that exact time: out of the stagnant water when they are stuck, deeper into the mud if necessary, or back to the safety of the shallow waters when that is needed.

Alternatively, if the therapist feels confused, the structure that the members choose of their own accord might lead him or her to gaining the insight of what is taking place. Often during supervision it becomes apparent that the therapist's vision is not always as clear as that of the group's. It is also a point of learning for the members themselves to look back at the end of a session and register the schema they worked with and perhaps the reason for this.

I shall give an example of a closed dramatherapy group consisting of eight persons with seven members and the therapist. This group had been meeting for a year and had another nine months to run before it ended. So at this stage I felt that their feeling of security had been developed enough for the group to have a mask-making session (this is done with gauze and gypsum on each individuals face). This exercise I usually do over two sessions, in pairs, where one person makes the other's mask directly on her or his face. During the third session each member takes the mask of their own face and paints it or decorates it as they wish. This group, however, chose for each member to be done individually by the whole group, and so the whole process lasted for eight sessions. One member of the group, a person who had in the past taken a very prominent part, during this process retreated into the background saying he had done mask making in the past and didn't see the point of doing it again.

Just by their physical impute it was apparent at what stage the relationship of each member was in connection to the other members of the group, how they felt about the other members and how the others felt about them. Also, as this stage spread over several sessions, it was interesting to note the absentees on specific days when a certain member had been scheduled for.

The way each issue is focused upon in dramatherapy enables both the members and the therapist to enhance their understanding of the group process. It is impossible to give instructions on what should be applied in a given situation but it suffices to know that as a dramatherapist one has the opportunity to use a plethora of structures each with a specific aim.

Each group is unique and is facilitated differently. Members need to be trained gradually into working dramatherapeutically but even after some time certain groups react better to different stimuli. It is the therapist's job to find out what most motivates a particular group or individual.

Introduction to Practical Work

The following four headings give the essence of work done with different therapy groups: how each member evaluates herself or himself; helping group coherency; teasing out group aggression; and King Solomon's judgement.

These sessions are reconstructed from notes, hence the epigrammatic style. Different names have been substituted in order to protect confidentiality. I have chosen these four samples as they are fair examples of dramatherapy working symbolically with different issues.

I find it interesting how the length each group has been working, brings up different predicaments and the relationships between the members are at different levels.

They are all therapy groups meeting once a week for one-and-a-half hours. The holidays during the summer lasted between four to six or seven weeks. This may be considered long, but with the summer heat in Greece, the custom is for many people to be away for both July and August. The duration of each group described varied from six months to four years.

How each member evaluates himself or herself (session 45)

There were eight members in this group and one therapist. The group ran for 90 sessions so the work described below happened at exactly the middle of this group's life.

The members were Rose, Ann, Gina, Louisa, Helen, Vaso, George and Jenny.

The group began with three members late.

Gina asked to be allowed to sit on a chair instead of cushions on the floor which was our custom, as she was now heavily pregnant. The rest of group readily agreed and provided her with chair.

When Rose and Ann arrived four minutes late, they mentioned some man outside the entrance who had looked at them intensely.

Louisa said it must have been the cop who lived in the block of flats above, who was interested in dramatherapy. The possibility of a group for policemen was considered. Helen then said that she disregarded such people from the start, because they chose such a profession. She then went on to talk about the students' peaceful demonstration which had been disrupted by hooded men instigating violence. Those men were in fact policemen posing as hooligans so as to ruin the students' demonstration and make trouble.

Vaso said that it was the fault of the Albanian immigrants who had recently come to Greece. They were the cause of all the violence which had suddenly started to take place everywhere.

A conversation about the poor immigrants living in slums at the centre of Athens took place: how desperate these people were, and which way was the best for them to be helped.

Vaso said that her grandfather had told her about the Pondiac immigrants in his day, who used to parade with a card attached to them stating their worth for a day's work. It was like a real slave market.

At 20 minutes past, George entered.

George said that Athens was in an upheaval because of the student demonstrations, he couldn't find a taxi anywhere and waited for his bus for three-quarters of an hour at which time three came all together.

WARM-UP

For the warm-up the members were asked to walk in different ways impersonating a person they chose. After walking for a while they were asked to greet each other in different ways. First as acquaintances, then as good friends and finally as lovers. To start with their concentration wasn't very good, but they slowly got better at it.

I asked them to do this exercise so they could become more conscious of the different way we relate to different people.

ACTION

For this each member was asked to make a card stating how much money they were worth for a day's work and, if they wanted to, they could also state the kind of work they did.

At this time in Athens 10,000 Drs was considered a reasonable daily wage.

Jenny's card stated 10,000 Drs. Jenny was the eldest in the group, a social worker who had been working for some years in a state hospital for children. She had no problem recognising her value, but had some difficulty in getting this over to someone else.

Gina's card stated 5000 Drs. Gina was a kindergarten teacher, not working, with a young child of two, expecting a second in a month's time.

Rose's was 5678 Drs for a five-day week at six hours a day. Rose was a kindergarten teacher.

Helen's said 5000 Drs for building and roof painting. Helen was a working high-school teacher, divorced with two children, around 30 years old, who strongly identified with her students.

George's depicted a large bed with erotic connotations. George was an actor who worked periodically.

Louisa's had a list of all her qualities, the sum of which would describe the perfect wife, for example, good company, easy going, good mother, and so forth. Louisa was a primary school teacher, who was waiting to be appointed by the state and in the meantime had been working for the last ten years as a civil servant, she was married with a one-year-old child.

Vaso's card said she would undertake to do the most expensive job or the cheapest depending on what was asked of her. Vaso was a social worker with artistic talents.

Ann's card stated 10,000 Drs. Ann was a working kindergarten teacher considering marriage.

After each member paraded with their card the others were asked to choose someone they would be needing for a day's work.

FEEDBACK

During feedback, the choice of each person's profession, where there had been one, was discussed, together with the opinion each person had of themselves. Also, how they were perceived by the other members and who chose whom and for what reasons.

This theme of what value each person gave to himself or herself had been with the group for some time.

REFLECTION

The ages of the members varied from 24 to 42, although often their concerns resembled those of young students.

The theme of authority often came up, as although there was resentment and fear of it. Given the opportunity to choose a labourer put them each in that position and they were able to see up to a point how they themselves behaved in such a role. During the following session the group investigated more fully how each member was seen by the rest of the members.

Helping group coherency (session 10)

This group ran for 30 sessions as an introduction to dramatherapy training, what we called a 'creative journey' group. The session described below had been running for one-third of this time.

In this group there were eight members, two men, six women and two female co-therapists. The members were Fred, Jeff (who was blind), Yvonne, Clary, Mary, Emy, Sue and Olga.

Fred telephoned to say that owing to a court case he had to attend in the morning, his work had been left behind so he wouldn't be able to come. The group began with discussion about the slippers some members were wearing (shoes were taken off because the floor was carpeted).

The leader informed them about Fred.

Yvonne came five minutes late.

MARY: Last time I became conscious that I am still very much a child, and that is why I like playing so much. Also, I feel immature and not responsible.

CLAIRE: Playing is very important to me.

EMY: I am older than you, Mary, and I still like playing.

THERAPIST: You like playing but you also take responsibility for the whole group and get upset when it isn't working together.

YVONNE: We all have a plethora of roles that we take in life. I have certain misgivings about dramatherapy, and I am not quite sure how it works. Why should someone choose a dramatherapy group as opposed to a theatre group?

THERAPIST: Perhaps the word therapy sounds threatening to you.

YVONNE: No, it doesn't.

Jeff came in at 7.15 am.

YVONNE: I just can't make out how dramatherapy works.

SUE: I think that I have now understood how it works.

MARY: I am not sure how much is allowed and how much a person can bring to the group.

JEFF: Why don't we have more time to talk.

THERAPIST: Perhaps if you came on time you wouldn't miss so much.

JEFF: That is beside the point, the fact that I am always late has nothing to do with the group, that's how I am with everything.

A discussion followed about lateness in connection with the group.

THERAPIST: Perhaps the head that had been missing from the group painting from last time, has been brought here today [referring to all the logical talking].

WARM-UP

A balloon exercise took place, where each member was asked to become a balloon and let their body expand and decrease accordingly. Then they were asked to blow each other up. Claire and Olga were not able to blow others up. Jeff had difficulty in taking part. His body was very stiff and he felt self-conscious about it.

This was an exercise given to loosen up the group and allow the members to interplay in a physical way.

ACTION

The group was instructed to make an effigy. All kinds of different materials were supplied. This exercise was chosen to help the members develop group coherency by working together with a specific plan.

All the members assembled round the materials and chose something. It was not discussed who would make what. Jeff took some wire and made a hat. Claire, Mary, Emy, Olga and Sue all got together and it was difficult to see who was doing what. They made a figure which they sat on a chair. Yvonne and Jeff worked alone. Yvonne made a hand out of wire and Jeff made two wire legs. When he was ready he approached the chair and attached his two legs to the effigy not seeing that it already had some. Olga wrapped the two paper legs which had been there round the wire ones Jeff had attached so that both together they made a better picture. Sue drew the facial characteristics and Claire supplied the stuffing for the hands.

THERAPIST: Give your effigy a name and take it round the room.

A brief conversation took place and then all the group members helped hold the effigy and took it round the room chanting 'Old Don Quixote'. Then they put him down in an electrified atmosphere and they all looked at him with a lot of feeling (it was as although through their touch the effigy had become animated). Mary had tears in her eyes and asked him why he made her cry, Jeff said some words which did not make sense, Sue asked him to take her with him, Claire asked him to tell them some stories. Emy, referring to the effigy, said 'You are marginal.'

OLGA: I feel for you and I understand you.

YVONNE: You look like an old ballerina and you are funny.

There were many other things said to Old Don Quixote. What seemed to me unusual was Jeff's request to have a photograph taken. Emy happened to have a camera and took the picture.

FEEDBACK

YVONNE: He didn't stir any feelings in me, and I was both sorry and envious of Mary's feelings.

MARY: I don't want anyone to feel sorry for me.

OLGA: I also wanted to cry because I identified with him.

Emy and Claire both said the same thing.

JEFF: I didn't expect such serious themes to come out, I thought it was just good fun.

Sue was quiet. Olga talked a bit more about her feelings.

OLGA (to JEFF): How do you imagine us making sense of what happened?'

JEFF: I feel both strong and weak as a person and also I have difficulty in allowing my feelings to operate.

SUE: I think he is very old and is about to die but I like him a great deal.

Just before the end of the group the members were asked to dismantle the effigy. They did this with determination. At the end they said he had been a lonely old thing with many experiences.

MARY: I felt that the group worked well together but I also feel lonely.

REFLECTIONS

This session had been very powerful and creative. While watching the members build the effigy, I had wanted to take part and the image of him stayed with me for the rest of the evening.

This was early stages in the development of the group but there were some definite moves towards integration. The value of the group had been discussed openly during the initial sharing, and how much each member was ready to trust the others was apparent by the way they each worked and the feelings this work sparked off.

'Emotion is the moment when steel meets flint and a spark is struck forth, for emotion is the chief source of consciousness. There is no change from darkness to light or from inertia to movement without emotion' (Jung 1964)

As it was a young group, they hadn't reached a stage at which they could plan their movements, but, all the same, they ended up with a group creation to which they also identified as individuals, some more than others.

Having a person with special needs had been discussed before hand at the supervision group, and had caused some feelings of uneasiness. However, in his own group Jeff was treated as an equal who needed a bit of helping on a practical level. Usually this help was provided by the group members and, in the initial planning of the group, by the co-therapists. Only if necessary was he helped out by one of the therapists. However, his habit of being late and any excuse he used because of his handicap, were not accepted either by the therapists or by the group members, with the result that he improved a great deal.

Teasing out group aggression (session 21)

This was a session at the beginning of a closed dramatherapy training group which ran for 90 sessions. The members were Rose, Ann, Gina, Louisa, Helen, Vaso, George, Jenny and Sue. It took place in a small theatre, the space for the audience was used as the main working area and it was carpeted, while the stage had linoleum and was at a higher level.

The group consisted of nine members, eight female and one male, plus one female therapist.

One member, Gina, had called to say she wasn't coming as her child was ill. Three other members were late by between two and six minutes. During the previous session there had been two absent without warning and others late, an indication of unrest. The group was feeling unsettled, sub-groups were operating and there was a feeling of antagonism.

The group began with the therapist giving the information about Gina's absence. George then said that he was concerned about Gina because the house she made out of clay last time was empty and he believed that she was holding out on something. Also, he believed she should be forced to open up as this was a therapy group.

To this the therapist responded that she also believed the absence was connected with previous session and that perhaps Gina's fear of being forced to open up had kept her home.

Louisa asked to be forgiven for not attending the previous session and not warning the group, but she had been to the doctors and believed she would have had time. As it turned out she was delayed and didn't think it worth it to come for 15 minutes. The group told her that her cushion had been kept and that she would have been welcome, however late.

Then the therapist asked group why they hadn't asked Sue about her absence the previous session. George said 'don't push her to speak'. Sue at first replied that she couldn't remember and then mentioned something wrong with her car.

It seemed to me as the therapist that the questions being asked had to do with how much a person can intrude on another, what is intrusion and what is concern? When a member is absent, isn't this also connected to the group issues? I had the feeling that they were testing the sea water with their toes.

WARM-UP

The members were asked to imagine that they were walking on different surfaces ending up on sand with sea in front of them. After testing the waters they had to decide for themselves if they were to go in for a swim. All the members ended up swimming, having taken the plunge in different ways.

ACTION

THERAPIST: I want two persons to become leaders. Any volunteers?

Helen and Louisa came forward. They were asked to walk across the room facing each other, taking turns with each step. The one who's foot ended up stepping on the other's foot was the winner and therefore chose first, her first disciple, the choice then continued in turns. (This is a well-known street game.) The groups were formed as follows:

Group A – Helen with Sue, George and Jenny.

Group B – Louisa with Vaso, Ann and Rose.

Next they were given their instructions which were as follows. Each group represented a rival gang, they each had their particular form of dressing and doing their hair, each had their own slogans plus their own base. When they had determined the above, the two groups would meet. After organising their clothes and their base, the action took place. Group A appeared bored and talked between themselves, staying on the stage area which they chose to be their home and which was at a higher level than the rest of the room. The battle began with Group B out of their home area. Group A gave the impression of being frightened, but at the same time they began by throwing cushions. George and Helen left their base and captured Rose together with Louisa who had gone to the rescue. During the process the therapist had to freeze the group and remind the members of the non-violence rule, as it looked as though they were becoming too physical. When they unfroze George tried to capture Vaso who tried to protect herself with markers. Other gang members captured Sue and some shouting followed. George suddenly dropped out of the action because his track suit had been marked and it had cost him a lot of money. The battle between the two groups continued with each having a hostage. Group A had Vaso and Group B had Sue. Vaso managed to escape. Group B continued to hold Sue hostage, and Helen, the gang leader, asked for help from her mates. However, as George had retired and Jenny appeared indifferent, she went to the fight on her own in order to rescue her protégée, she was like a mad lioness. The fighting was kept at more or less a theatrical level, but once or twice it almost got out of hand. Finally, the therapist asked the groups to freeze, take off their costumes and put the room back into order. After de-roling, the members were asked to write down their feelings on a piece of paper.

FEEDBACK

George refused to come into the circle. He stayed on stage. The therapist asked him to join, but, as he didn't, she asked the other members to close the circle. Ann told him that if he didn't join, he had better also keep his mouth shut.

Louisa began by saying that she had been horrified by the violence which had been expressed. She explained that Group B had only intended to mark the enemy with a small dot from the felt pens while chanting their slogan. However, when they attempted this, the other group attacked them. George then entered the circle, sat down and said that all they wanted to do was avoid the marking. Sue, supporting him, said she felt as though her feelings had been violated. Helen, responding to this, said the violence came from both groups, it was their own and they should accept it as such. Next she accused Jenny of being passive and George for deserting his gang. George talked about his need for cleanliness and that he was wearing a favourite track suit he had especially for the group. Ann asked him why he had it for the group if he wanted it to remain clean. (It was as though the squabbling were continuing out of the action.)

REFLECTIONS

Even although aggression had been expressed in a rather childish fashion on some occasions, this session had been successful in highlighting feelings the group members felt for each other and how these were coped with in a less civilised way. During the following session, at the initial sharing, members were able to address each other about issues which had to do with their relationships in the group, and how these had been lurking unchallenged until then. For the main action of that session the group concentrated on movement and ways of communicating feelings about each other through body language.

King Solomon's judgement (session 77)

This group had been running for two years with the same members and there wasn't a fixed closing date. There were six members and one therapist, all female. The members were Helen, Pat, Shera, Mary, Terry and Christina.

The session began without Pat who was late.

HELEN: My father's tests were OK. I feel cross, however, because of something that happened at work. The headmistress was away for two months and during that time a colleague took over her work. Yesterday when she returned our colleague and the rest of us told her of the work which had been done while she was away and she found fault with it. What made me mad was that we didn't stand up for our colleague.

Pat had come in during this. When questioned by the rest of the group about her feelings, as she also worked at the same school, she said:

PAT: I understand Helen completely. I was not able to respond myself, as I was feeling very low for other reasons.

THERAPIST: You felt too weak to fight back?

PAT: Yes.

TERRY: Today I found out why lately I have been cross for no evident reason. This realisation came to me because of the work done in this group. I suddenly became aware of my tendency to always take on other people's responsibilities as well as my own. When I became conscious of this my anger left me.

SHERA: Tell us Pat about yourself.

PAT: My boyfriend wants us to split up and I am too weak to put up any resistance. He is already seeing another girl. I had done so much for this relationship. I have loved him so much. Will it all go to waste?

THERAPIST: Do you still love him?

SHERA: That isn't enough, if love is one-sided.

CHRISTINA: All this time your actions have been leading towards this, it is only a natural consequence and I feel that you have been expecting it.

WARM-UP

The members were asked to stand and place as many cushions as they liked on their backs. Next to walk around room for a good while. While doing this they were asked to consider what they were carrying and who had placed that load there. Finally when they were ready, they were asked to get rid of the load in any way they wished.

This exercise was carried out with a lot of concentration and feeling.

At the end they were told to find a comfortable place were they could sit in the room.

ACTION

The story of King Solomon and the two mothers was told to the group. In abbreviation: 'When two harlots each claimed to be the mother of the same baby, he determined the real mother by observing each woman's reaction to the prospect of dividing the child into two halves' (*Encyclopaedia Britannica*). They were then asked to choose a role and act the story out.

Mary chose to be the baby, Pat the real mother with the name of Ruth, Terry Solomon, Christine the other mother with the name of Merium, Helen a friend of Pat's with the name of Rebecca and Shera a friend of Christine's with the name of Judith.

SCENE 1

Ruth (Pat) and Merium (Christine) plus the baby (Mary) are asleep in their room, there is another baby wrapped up in a shawl. Ruth is sleeping with her baby. Merium is looking at her own baby and begins to inspect it. She squeezes it, pinches it, listens to it, hits it and when finally she still doesn't get any response she changes it's place with that of Ruth's baby. Ruth wakes up and demands her baby, a fight follows and Ruth takes her baby back from Merium. The other two women arrive and each supports her own friend. As an impasse is reached the friends suggest they go to king Solomon for his opinion. Merium refuses to take her dead baby with her, so Ruth takes it together with hers.

When they reach the king he is not very forceful and tries to relate to the women as a friend. He is very logical and tells them that he feels Ruth was putting on a better fight for the baby than Merium. Finally the king says they should both take the baby home and bring it up together. Ruth says no as she wanted it all to herself, whereas Merium and the others don't speak.

Solomon discharges them without giving them a solution. Merium then takes her dead baby tenderly and starts to cry softly but with a lot of felling. Ruth embraces her. A slow de-roling takes place.

FEEDBACK

PAT: You don't know how hard it is for a child to have two mothers, I have only just discovered this in the last few weeks.

HELEN: I saw the story in connection with Pat and her boyfriend, but also in connection with Christine and her lost baby for which she has never cried, up to now in this group.

THERAPIST: Today she held it in her arms.

MARY: I felt that Pat put up a good fight for me as my mother. Do you feel Helen that you supported her better than you did your friend at work?

HELEN: No.

THERAPIST (to TERRY): By being so democratic you didn't help them that much, were you trying not to take on other people's responsibilities?

TERRY: I wanted them to decide for themselves.

THERAPIST: Is it possible for a baby to have two mothers or a man two women?

CHRISTINE: I wasn't able to support my position.

PAT: I didn't want to upset you.

Shera was crying.

REFLECTION

This was a very moving session, which touched each member separately but also the group as a whole. Helen was able to see how well or not she can support her friend. Pat put herself in her boyfriend's shoes, but also stood up for her baby, something which she had been unable to do for her relationship so far.

Shera, although she didn't say so at the time, told us at a later date that she was reminded of her brother who had died as a baby, and after whom she had been born, and the weight this placed on her shoulders.

Mary, we all knew, had a problem with her mother and grandmother. When she was born she was taken to live with her grandmother in the village while her parents lived and worked in Athens and whom she saw only during the holidays. Only after her brother was born did they take her to live with them in Athens when she was six years old. As a result she felt that her mother had abandoned her and also that she had two half mothers.

Christine had lost her baby while three months pregnant, only a couple of months back.

Terry was a person who found it hard to upset others and would always try to smooth things out. As a king, however, she needed to take a different attitude if she were going to do her job well. Maybe she needed to separate this from taking on other people's responsibilities.

The story lent itself to the group and they were able to work with it on many different levels.

PERSONAL NOTE

This story had always appealed to me from an early age, one of the reasons being that I have a strong feeling about justice being upheld. Being the therapist in the above group, perhaps I was not so satisfied with Solomon's (Terry's) actions as they were acted out. I identified with his role, of having to make decisions and having to find the solution at the given moment, which he avoided. This of course wasn't surprising as Solomon (Terry) was only reacting as a group member and not as the therapist.

Conclusion

I believe that dramatherapy is a ritual one needs to have lived through in order to be able to lead others safely. The personal therapy group is like the twine Ariadne gave to Theseus which guided him back through the labyrinth after he conquered the Minotaur.

Dramatherapy techniques can be used in many different ways, as I have mentioned in the beginning. The knowledge of dramatherapy, however, equips the client with a new way of relating to the world; a way we all knew as children but as adults need to relearn. We need to be able to make believe, to play, to symbolise and to improvise.

> 'People who have difficulty in getting near their centre only really experience themselves when they suffer, when they come to the experience of their real self, and that it does not seem possible for them to get there any other way' (Jung 1964)

A client of mine once told me that she felt that only people who had suffered were really worth anything. Suffering can bring you closer to your centre and it can make you into a gentler person. However, with dramatherapy one can use other means. Getting in contact with an imaginary Minotaur (our centre), outwitting him and still being able to find the way out, is an exhilarating experience, it is cathartic and it gives strength to the person who has undertaken the journey. Through dramatherapy a client can look into all his or her secret parts and have a clearer understanding of them. No one has just one role in life, so getting to know all sides is important. We are heroes and monsters simultaneously and often coming to terms with this is a first step towards self-awareness. Working through dramatherapy the client has the opportunity to explore the creative artist in him as well as the patient artist and the connections these two might have. The client will have the chance to work with these two aspects together or separately, in a protected environment.

Art is universally considered to give vision and culture to those who come into contact with it, where the individual piece becomes collective and the collective individual. 'Art activity provides a concrete rather than a verbal medium through which a person can achieve both conscious and unconscious expression, and can be used as a valuable agent for therapeutic change' (Dalley 1984, p.2). This concrete medium in dramatherapy is action and it can take form in a plethora of expressions. This provides the therapist with the opportunity to choose the medium according to his or her client.

Acknowledgements

Without the people with whom I have shared this work, this chapter could not have been written. I have changed their names as well as certain events in small ways, in order to protect confidentiality. I hope not to offend any person in any way. I have recorded our work together as honestly and as simply as I could. I am grateful to you all and believe that my work with you has made me a richer person.

References

Cavafy, K.P. (1948) *The Complete Poems of Cavafy*, translated by Rae Dalven. A Harvest Book.

Cox, M. and Theilgaard, A. (1987) *Mutative Metaphors in Psychotherapy*. London: Tavistock Publications.

Dalley, D. (1984) *Images in Art Therapy*. London and New York: Tavistock Publications.

Jennings, S. (1990) 'Stages and scripts.' In S. Jennings *Dramatherapy with Families, Groups and Individuals: Waiting in the Wings*. London: Jessica Kingsley Publishers.

Jung, C. (1964) *Man and his Symbols*. London: Picador.

Lahad, L. (1991) Lecture in Athens.

Winnicott, D.W. (1971) *Playing and Reality*. Harmondsworth: Penguin Books.

CHAPTER TWELVE

The Life Cycle

Jayne E. Liddy

In this chapter I explore a 'model' for the dramatherapy process which operates both on behalf of the therapist and the client, by providing a map from which to begin their journey. I have also drawn on the possible reasons why myself and the people with whom I have worked have connected with the language and terminology of this model by making links with psychology, philosophy and anthropology.

I introduce you to the 'life cycle'.

Introductory Visualisation Exercise

To introduce people to the 'life cycle', I do an exercise where I ask people to imagine being in the separate spaces of 'chaos' and 'structure'.

Chaos

So, take a few moments to imagine sitting very still, alone, in a small boat on a vast open ocean. Notice the horizon, empty skies, and that there is only grey water for as far as the eye can see. The cold wind blows back your hair and swirls up the pungent smell of the sea. You sit and stare, far, far away. You are lost in this void. You cannot find your way. You don't know which direction to take, or even where to look.

Return to the present and quickly brainstorm your thoughts and feelings associated with this image.

Now, turn your attention to the next image.

Structure

You are in the middle of a busy city centre. You have to be at a particular place at a given time. You have on a watch, a map in front of you, and there are signposts all around, which clearly show directions. People walk by you slowly, and you are aware that if necessary, you could stop and ask somebody the directions.

Again brainstorm your thoughts and feelings associated with this image. We will return to these images towards the end of the chapter.

Background and Origins

In this chapter we have a direction, and at least for the next few pages or so, I have the map in front of me.

The open ocean was the place in which I found myself as a student dramatherapist. A glimpse of that void left me questioning whether indeed to pursue a career in dramatherapy at all. I have to admit that it frightened me. I had turned to my supervisor and exclaimed, 'If that's what it means to be a dramatherapist then I'm not sure that I want it!', and I was serious.

This place described for me that time in the dramatherapy group when some work has already taken place, but the session requires further development. Being inexperienced, my bag of signposts was severely limited.

It had seemed like it was all my responsibility to find the way. Group members looked to me as their leader. 'Where are we going?', they cried, 'Who knows!' was my reply. 'What if I choose the wrong way?'

A pushing and searching frantically followed this stage coupled with an urgency to come up with the goods... and quickly.

I realised that if I were to pursue dramatherapy as a career, then this was the place which I had to find the courage to confront and to try to understand. This was the 'chaos' which assisted in the development of the life cycle.

I utilised the life cycle initially as a model for charting the dramatherapy process to reassure myself. I then found its application to the dramatherapy group, whilst working in an acute mental health day unit. I believe that the life cycle functions on two levels:

(1) The provision of a structure which allows clients to understand their own individual experience as a member of the dramatherapy group, coupled with a collective understanding of the group's process.

(2) As a way of interpreting behaviour outside the dramatherapy group, faced with life's trials and tribulations.

I have found that clients and anyone who has expressed an interest in the life cycle, have understood and identified with the idea and terminology very quickly. I feel that this is due to its simplicity. The philosophical and anthropological elements of the life cycle, assist the client both on a journey through a return to mental health, as well as on life's pathway.

In my excitement I found myself confronted with the meaning of life, a framework which may provide some key to our existence. A cycle which works on many planes and many levels, presenting an outcome which is inevitable, if only we can accept that to experience each stage in some way, will then lead us on to the next.

Structure/Chaos

The existence of polar opposites has always intrigued mankind. Their co-existence as opposites is as necessary as their complimentary roles.

Creation–Destruction, fertile–barren, light/day–dark/night, Apollo–Dionysius, drought–flood, Earth Mother–Sky Father. Is mental well being about attaining a balance between two extremes?

Rowe (1987), in her book *Beyond Fear* (pp.25–28) explores six aspects of our lives which she believes we are forever striving to achieve a balance between:

Being an Individual	Being a member of a group
Completely valueless/imperfect	Valuable and perfect
Freedom	Security
An infinite choice	No choice at all
Not responsible for anything	Totally responsible for everything
The risk of rejection	The risk of loneliness

She goes on to say, that 'we always risk getting it wrong, but we never give up hope that we'll get it right'.

My interest also lay in the space between the two continuums. What happens when a person crosses this space, if this exercise is employed in the dramatherapy group? Each piece of therapeutic work is a threshold of human experience which is approached, crossed and passed in the sense of being achieved.

Is this where the therapy begins/takes place? Is this the 'order' in the 'chaos'? What is it about the tension between these two opposites? Many ancient civilisations have encompassed them in symbols or Mandalas, for example the union of Yin and Yang.

Mandalas originate from the circle, which appears very early on in human history. Cave and rock drawings found in Australia, Europe, North America and Africa contain spirals and circles which have been important symbols to us for thousands of years.

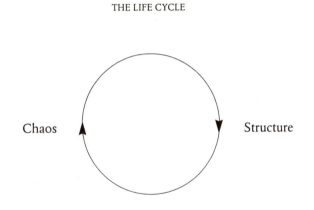

Figure 1 A union of opposing forces

Storr (1972) writes 'It is quite natural, that a union of opposing forces within the psyche should be represented by Mandala patterns in which opposites can be combined and enclosed within a single circle' (p.288).

The word Mandala means centre, circumference or magic circle in Indian traditions. Jung associated the Mandala with the self, a person's centre or total personality. He believed that the Mandala demonstrates an urge to explore our potential, and fulfil the pattern of our whole personality.

The Tibetan Mandala acts as a visual aid in the practice of meditation. Mandalas serve to intensify one's concentration on our inner self and at the same time produce an inner order. They are created over many weeks or months using different coloured sand, only to be gently swirled around and disposed of at the completion of the assigned ritual. This act serves to remind us of impermanence. That nothing is permanent, not even our own mortality. Life cycles, like Mandalas, are impermanent, they are 'for now'.

Storr (1972), goes on to write, 'Every experienced Psychotherapist knows that personality development is a process which is never complete and no sooner is a new integration achieved, a new Mandala painted [a Life cycle completed?] then it is seen as inadequate' (p.289). We are all in the business of creating new life cycles every minute, hour, week, year.

Copeland's statement (1952, p.289) offers an understanding that each added work brings with it an element of self-discovery. I must create in order to know myself, and since self-knowledge is a never-ending search, each new work is only a part answer to the question, 'Who am I?', and brings with it the need to go on to other and different part answers.

I believe that the acceptance of the life cycle allows a union of opposing forces within the psyche and the consequent integration of her/his own personality in the same way as the Mandala.

Emunah (1994), in her book *Acting for Real-Dramatherapy Process, Technique and Performance*, states:

> The circle connotes the cyclical. In dramatherapy the dramatic rituals, beginning and ending in a circle, celebrate the cycles and stages within the groups process. The circle formation contributes to the sense of containment and continuity provided by the ritual, it holds the group – with all its intricacies – in simplicity. (p.23)

Structure

Let us begin by exploring the idea of structure and its role at a universal level. I refer to structure in this instance as providing a framework for our daily existence. Structure relates to routine, safety, security, along with recognised patterns of thinking, feeling and behaving. A sense of 'having found the music to dance to'. People create their own internal structures via belief systems, thought patterns, attitudes, etc. They also create their external behavioural structures of, for example, washing on a Monday, shopping on a Tuesday, fish on Fridays, etc. Here in this example, the days of the week, along with religious beliefs, have assisted in the provision of a structured way of life. Structures, also refer to always making a journey in the same way, going to bed at a certain time. 'All children need routine', is a popular saying. 'Everybody needs routine to a degree', would be my reply. Structure relates to the activities which occur within certain limits of time and space, in a visible order, according to agreed rules. Our world is made up of the structures we have created.

If we compare structure with ritual or rites of passage, we find a shared universal experience in one form or another. Jennings (1983) refers to 'Therapy itself, of whatever sort', as being a rite of passage. All our rituals and 'rites de passage', accompanying us from the womb to the tomb, allow us to mark significant changes in our status. Christenings, initiations/'coming of age', engagements, marriages, retirements, funerals, etc. They make the inner psychological change manageable. Van Gennep (1960) refers to these rites has having three important stages: separation, transition and re-incorporation. These structures/rites of passage act as signposts on our journey. They are prescriptive, in the way that each ceremony is attributed certain rituals via words, actions, objects, songs, chants, behaviour. Certain behaviour follows a rite of passage, for example, being able to go into public houses, some role expectations of husbands, wives, parents and the grieving which accompanies a funeral.

We all require some part of our lives to include doing something which we know and feel comfortable with. As human beings we need to be able to predict our environment in order to feel safe.

White (1961), biographer of the famous composer Stravinsky, wrote of his writing desk as resembling 'a surgeon's instrument case. Bottles of different coloured inks in their hierarchy had each a separate part to play in the ordering of his art' (pp.56–58). Rossini's work space was also his bedroom, which he occupied for many hours a day. Weinstock (1968) described this room with the 'writing table in the centre, and on it set out in perfect order were the papers, his indispensable scrapers, the pens, the inkstand, and whatever else he needed for his writing' (p.59).

This is what I am referring to when I describe the order in the chaos. The order/structure acts as a container for the chaos, and as a 'rite d'entrée'. If we can imagine structure as being the ship's mast, which supports our sails/ideas and ways of being, so that enough of a breeze can be harnessed to allow us to deal with whatever life sends in our direction, then the butterfly mind can be tamed.

Chaos

The word 'chaos', is derived from the Greek root word, meaning to 'gape'. It represents the quality of space or eternal openness and emptiness. As Stewart writes in his book, *Creation Myth* (1989), it was 'originally a cosmic principle without devine characteristics or attributes' (p.45). A later definition which describes chaos as the 'out pouring of disorganised or chaotic energy and matter in space', came from a mistaken derivation from the root word 'to pour'. So it seems that there are two distinct meanings to chaos: 'The pure original cosmic principle of gaping or openness as used by Hesoid'; or 'Confused energies and forms prior to ordered manifestations' (Stewart 1989).

One of the major sources for creation mythology in classical Greek tradition is the 'Theogony' of Hesoid, written in approximately the eighth century BC. Hesoid was said to be a contemporary of Homer.

Chaos is also a word in regular use today, often referring to something being messy, disorganised, primal and is usually attributed negative undertones of destruction or malice.

Gleick (1988), in his book *Chaos* wrote 'Where chaos begins, classical science stops' (p.3). He goes on to present us with an exploration of the chaos theory through the study of chaotic dynamics, such as weather patterns. Results of chaos theory have found that the disorderly behaviour of simple systems, act as a creative process. Photographs of 'The Mandelbrot Set', a series of computer-generated images resulting from the translation of Benoit Mandelbrot's mathematical equations demonstrate the chaos theory in geometric form.

Chaos has always been a part of our lives whether explored as the 'Theogony' or as a natural dynamic occurring in science. Why should it be any different now?

I find it interesting that so often in expressing their mental health problem, people describe feelings of emptiness, desolation, a great void of nothingness. The 'Confused' chaotic emotions associated with this experience may also be interpreted as polar opposites – positive or negative. It is usually the negative aspect which people bring to mental health services, a 'pit of despair', panic, alone and general loss of direction, accompanied somewhere with a notion that the situation could be better.

If we as dramatherapists can know what it is to be alone on that vast empty ocean and feel comfortable with it, then we can begin to accompany our clients in their aloneness, in their chaos.

Chaos is an area much known to practising dramatherapists. Likened to the liminal period in Turner's (1969) *The Ritual Process,* its presence is as inevitable as the natural law of sunrise and sunset. It is impossible to engage in our journey through life and only perceive the positive aspects. We must acknowledge the negative energies in order to progress. The pearl which comes from an oyster is created by the friction of the sand inside its shell. Conflict brings about change and progression. It is a place where initial experiences of fear, darkness and desertion can eventually pave the way for adrenaline, excitement and most of all – creativity.

It is here that creativity knows no boundaries, no shape or form, structure or framework. Jennings (1987) describes a place which 'may feel dangerous at times… and signposts no longer contain coherent messages' (p.15).

Chaos involves itself with the activity of the right brain, such as, imagination, creativity, imagery, intuition and the unconscious, as opposed to the structured left brain which appeals to our intellect, verbal and logic, qualities much revered in our society. To be creative means that we must open ourselves up to the world of chaos.

The Life Cycle

On further analysis of the concept, I discovered three other elements. Figure 12.2 shows how the Life cycle appears. Its movement is clockwise.

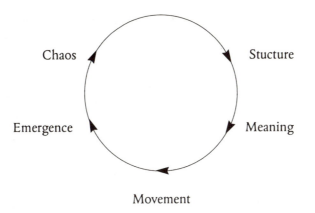

Figure 2 The life cycle

The Life Cycle Explained

Meaning

Structure and meaning are very closely related. They may arrive at the same time, but it is still felt necessary to provide 'meaning', with some separateness. The meaning is derived primarily from the structure which has been chosen. Both go hand in hand in creating the 'purpose' in our lives at any one time.

When Jung (1963, p.237) visited the Pueblo Indians in Mexico, he observed that they performed a daily religious rite which was designed to help the sun to rise. One Indian told him 'After all, we are a people who live on the roof of the world... If we were to cease practising our religion, in ten years the sun would no longer rise. Then the world would be night forever'. The structure here is the ritual and I think the meaning and purpose are obvious.

Movement

If we have undertaken the first two stages of the cycle, then we will automatically find ourselves involved in progression, development and change. Movement relates externally to the passage of time, for example, minutes, hours, months, years or a life time, and internally to our own perceptual shifts, changes and insight learning.

The person is involved in fluctuations between control and surrender, conscious work and passive acceptance. The pace at which this movement takes place is unique to the individual. It is necessary for the group to engage in movement in order to explore further. An acceptance of 'things can never be the same again', accompanies this stage as we are all moving through life. The last minute, hour can never be recreated in exactly the same way and would we really want it to?

Emergence

Although the outcome can never be prescribed, we will usually have some idea of when we have arrived. Here the emergence can refer to an internal process or of having completed a time limit, such as those given to a session or a course.

Emergence refers to a re-birth, achievement and a recognition of having got somewhere. A state of completion has been reached which allows time to reflect on previous perceptions or past events which have now altered in status or value. Everybody involved in this process inevitably experiences change. It is true to say that within the dramatherapy group it is not possible for the therapist to be involved in the journey of the group and their change, without experiencing their own personal change. Several life cycles may be taking place at any one time, for example, one minute, a week, a dramatherapy session, a disagreement, a pregnancy, a lifetime.

So, this is how the life cycle appears when it is complete with all five stages. Symbolism attached to the number five often occurs in nature.

> the number of petals in a blossom, the lobes of a star fish, or the segments of an apple core. Five refers to the physical reality of the body as well. Each of our hands has five digits, as does each foot. When we stand firmly on the ground with feet apart and stretch out our arms, the points of our body number five: hands, feet, and head. (Fincher 1991, p.100)

So we can begin to understand why it may be that the life cycle makes its connections with a person's inner experience so easily.

Some people have asked me why I do not present the life cycle, as in creation myth with a stage in between chaos and structure, of perhaps 'movement'. It has been my experience that the structures are often viewed and explored from the chaotic stage and once recognised, the person takes a leap into the space of structure. The experimentation takes place whilst the person is still in the chaotic phase. Once tried, tested and accepted the person then has the structure firmly in place, ready to commence another life cycle.

So, for example, a person's mental state may be experienced as chaotic on their first contact with psychiatric services. A structure is created by attending a mental health day-centre and choosing from an organised programme of activities. A meaning and purpose to their actions and behaviour is then obtained. The movement is both the passage of time whilst attending the department, along with their own internal perceptual shifts, through acquired knowledge and understanding. Emergence relates to the person having completed their treatment and being able to reflect on their experience. Chaotic emotions arrive once more (all be it of a different nature) as the person leaves the department. They may take up once again their previous employment as their structure or another structure, such as further training.

Application to Mental Health

Negatives and positives of chaos

I have found the negative emotions associated with chaos to be very disabling and disempowering for the person who is experiencing them. I will remind you of vocabulary associated with chaos as being lost, frightened, a void, etc. If, however, people could begin to accept these emotions for what they are and move on to interpret chaos not as the negative 'pit of despair' etc., but as say the positive 'great vessel of nothingness', which can be filled with, and emptied of, whatever ideas we choose, then we may find that we can accept something of the Orphic tradition.

This tradition describes Chaos as being enveloped by night and within this envelope the creative ether-generated cosmic material. The entire organisation became a type of egg, with night as the surrounding shell. If chaos could be seen as the space of a womb-like environment where people can experiment and explore the inner depths of their imagination, examining all possibilities, a place where ideas can be tried on for size, where we may stretch our potential to its limits, rather than freezing at the crossroads, fearing to drop the mask of familiarity, then we can begin to confront the negative associations of chaos and take the opportunity to create appropriate amounts of structure and chaos in our lives.

In 'Theogony', the name chaos is used in the proper sense, immense and shadowy, and present in the Beginning. 'Out of chaos appeared Gaea, the full breasted Earth, and Eros, the fruitful or attracting force that caused the generation of all beings' (Stewart 1989, p.44). It is also a generalised concept of creation myth that patterns of order return to a primal chaos at the completion of a cycle, sometimes described as being a void to which all forms and forces return. Keats (1935) wrote, 'To risk not knowing-not controlling, means making oneself available'. (p.72).

I feel that the creation of appropriate structures does not come by sitting down, thinking hard and then deciding. Oh, if only it were that simple. The creative process relies on elements of humility, passivity and dependence. There is ultimately a need to 'let go'. New structures, directions, life choices cannot be conjured up voluntarily, they 'come to' people. It is true to say that they may be more likely to come if we have created an environment which will encourage them, but there is still no guarantee that they will do so. Storr (1972) writes, 'they must be wooed and waited upon' (p.249). I believe, that to push and search frantically for the structure will only serve to increase and maintain the chaotic response, eventually creating a prison. An old Chinese proverb states, 'There is nothing which cannot be achieved by non-action.' Rowe, in her book *Beyond Fear* (1987), draws on the idea of the emotions surrounding chaos as being ubiquitous, that they are not good or bad but human and universal.

Negatives and positives of structure

As said previously there are many positive words associated with structure, such as safety, routine, direction, predictability, however, feedback from the group activity carried out with the life cycle and described later in the chapter, demonstrated that indeed the balance of these two polarities was of paramount importance if one is to be contented in one's life. So, to experience too much structure in one's life was said to be tedious, boring, generating rigidity, concrete thinking patterns and tunnel vision. Krishnamurti (1976), writes 'control in any form is harmful to total understanding. A disciplined existence is a life of conformity; in conformity there is no freedom from fear. Habit destroys freedom; habit of thought, drinking and so on makes for a superficial and dull life' (p.14). He goes on to state further that 'beliefs, rituals deny the open entry into the vastness of mind. It is only in freedom that creation comes into being'. It is worth contemplating the degree of structure and chaos which we allow into our own personal style as practising dramatherapists. Our own creativity could be seriously hampered by the inability to tolerate the oscillation between the two polarities. An obsession with structure will only serve to keep us captive.

So, just as it is important to be sensitive to these two qualities within the dramatherapy group, it is also my belief now, that some parts of our mental health are derived from the balance and acquisition of adequate amounts of chaos and structure.

Dramatherapy Group Activity

My first explanation of the life cycle began in a dramatherapy group, towards the end of my training whilst working in an acute mental health day-centre. Clients attending the centre have varied mental health problems and chose this group from a diverse programme of activities.

The group were exploring issues around 'risk taking', when I felt it would be useful to communicate the life cycle to them. Jennings (1990) describes every dramatherapy session as having 'a component of ritual risk' (p.61). In this context the risk was related to the group members' own creativity and life choices. They immediately identified with the terminology of the cycle, associating the stages with elements in their own lives. They would take pens and paper and scribble down the drawing, giving their own descriptions of each stage. From that session on, I found that they spoke the language of the life cycle in relation to their own experience as individuals and as a group collectively. I felt encouraged to explore the life cycle further in working with other groups. However, the following research took place with the same group to whom I had initially communicated the life cycle. They asked for another group experience in which to explore the cycle for themselves in greater depth. I was fortunate to be able to organise this. Group One has been the only piece of research where I had chosen beforehand to work with the life cycle. Other pieces of work involved explanation of the cycle at later and appropriate stages in the group's process. The life cycle has two entry points from which to begin, structure or chaos. Group One began from structure.

Group One

This dramatherapy group consisted of eight members. The aims and objectives were to explore the concept of the life cycle over a 12-week period within a group context.

Following the initial warm-up and 'getting to know each other' activities, the clients were asked to explore the issue which had brought them along to the group, with a view to working through this difficulty with the life cycle. They were asked to begin by representing/symbolising the existing 'chaos' in their lives creatively, through clay, paint, spectogram, etc., or by sculpting the group itself.

Each week followed the stages of the life cycle, with the clients representing the elements using creative media. For example, 'structure', and 'what it is that keeps them going when things get difficult', e.g. work commitments, families, social activities, daily routine. 'Meaning', and where/how purpose is achieved in their lives. 'Movement' involved patterns of movement being played around with to see if a particular shape or form became familiar or repetitive. This external movement was used as a theme for the rest of the session, with an acknowledgement of internal movement or perceptual change. Themes around journeys surfaced for some of the group members. By week six, the group was exploring where and how they have 'emerged'. This session inevitably creates a celebratory experience, and even people who felt that they had achieved very little were encouraged by the group to realise their accomplishments. Week seven and people are now engaged in creating their own life cycle, and the possible representation of this in the format of a map, either as a spectogram or by sculpting and using the space in the room.

The rest of the group sessions form the basis for work which any individual may wish to pursue up to the closure. Here, the group focused on termination anxiety and links with chaotic feelings around 'where to next?' These stages have been described as a loose representation of the sessions which took place during this particular piece of research.

Conclusions

I had set out on a journey to explore the elements of the life cycle, with the valued assistance of my co-facilitator, Staff Nurse Paul Greenwood and a group of clients who had expressed an interest in accompanying me in that process. One of the fascinating developments to the life cycle took place during this course. This was the idea of balance. It was the group which highlighted for me, the idea of structure also possessing two qualities of positive and negative.

It became apparent, that some members of the group regarded their mental health difficulties as surfacing as a direct result of their lives being 'over-structured'. That is, that they had developed such rigid routines in their daily lives that to attempt any activity other than the pre-planned, would result in the feelings and emotions associated with what other members of the group described as chaos. These people spoke of wanting to divert from this planned activity and become more spontaneous. They decided that they wanted more chaos in their lives. This theme was explored via the use of continuums, between structure and chaos. Each person attempted to find their own unique sense of balance on the continuum.

So what is this relationship? Ehrenzweig (1967) wrote of *The Hidden Order of Art*. Creativity begins with a primary process which can only become tamed by structure/order. He believes that the psyche contains spontaneous ordering forces which are truly intrinsic to it. So, given what the clients had said and the conclusions which I had arrived at, aspects of mental health could be said to rely on the existence of appropriate amounts of structure and chaos in our lives. The amounts being dependent on individual needs. It is my belief that some of the ingredients of being mentally healthy are about creating enough structure which can enable us to be free and flexible without suffocating us, along with enough chaos to maintain motivation levels, enthusiasm, adrenaline and risk taking. The pendulum swinging too much in one direction creates disharmony.

I wrote earlier about Yin and Yang, and the existence of opposing forces working in unison. I believe that these are natural laws of paradox, which exist inevitably. Perhaps the contents of our daily lives are more to do with to what extent we 'resist' or 'go with the flow', in a continual pushing and pulling action. This piece of research had exposed a very interesting dynamic for me. Chaos and structure as separate entities, coupled with the co-existence and inter-relationship of 'order in the chaos' and 'chaos in the order'.

Feedback about the group, had been that the exploration of each of the elements for the first five weeks had become over-structured. I too had felt the same way and noticed that people had worked very individually and perhaps in an isolated way for the first five weeks. These ideas in retrospect led me to work with the life cycle in a different way for the next research development.

Group Two

The second piece of research using the life cycle experimented with the dynamic of creativity and of 'not knowing'. We were exploring the role of chaos in creativity. There were nine group members over a space of ten weeks.

I decided to begin from a place of chaos. The first research had a clear plan/structure to the group, which was outlined and discussed at the first session. The second group did not have this. The only structure here was related to the group commencing at the same time, same place each week, with the same members, the warm-up/closure, and little else. A local firm had also donated some cardboard materials. These were offered in the first session as possible art materials. The emphasis was on creating 'something', but nobody knew what at that stage.

In the first week, the group were engaged in getting to know each other, being introduced to the idea of creativity, and to the cardboard materials, through the idea of a magic box. People began to create some direction for themselves.

From week two onwards, people worked either alone or in groups developing this direction. Those who 'could not think of anything to do' attached themselves to someone else, either on the same piece of work or using the same theme. For example, someone began to make a small building out of the cardboard materials. This generated a lot of enthusiasm from some other members of the group who then went on to create a small village.

People would constantly check out with me to see if what they were doing was right or wrong, or OK. Sharing and closure centred around recognition of other people's work as well as the idea that we were all working towards creating 'something', and that the links would be found later in the group's process.

Various themes began to emerge, for example, issues around homelessness and mental health, town life and pollution versus country life, male versus female, life and death. One of the clients brought some literature along which described some statistics of the above situations, and a script began to form. Eventually, a small piece of drama emerged which was performed to an invited audience on the final week.

Conclusions

Each session people who were engaged in a piece of work from the previous week, had created a structure from which to re-commence. Others would arrive at the session, having completed something the week before. These people would then sometimes struggle for a while before latching on to an idea/structure and pursuing it.

The middle four weeks of the group followed this action for the most part. Sometimes people would become frustrated with having little direction. Responsibility for this shifted around the group, but was seen as predominantly mine. The life cycle was communicated to the group on week four, primarily as a way of encouraging some understanding of their experience. This created some safety and a structure on which to hang their experience. The structures which the group had created or when chaos had been present in the group were highly debated themes.

Jennings' (1987) statement 'stay with the chaos and the meaning will emerge' (p.15), was for me something to hold on to. At times I felt quite drained, and the group responded with frustration and a searching for direction. When a structure or direction surfaced, the group settled and would work quite intensively from as little as 15 minutes to more than one session at a time.

I found the group quite difficult to facilitate at times. Even my co-facilitator admitted to feeling frustrated with the lack of direction.

The end result of a performance generated feelings around having survived, achieved – of having emerged somewhere. The group had bonded well together, and reflected on their emotions associated with the polar opposites.

Links with personal experiences outside of the group were made. For example, the idea of coping with the fear of what the future may hold for us, the uncertainties of life. Of having the courage to stay with the chaos, knowing that these experiences and emotions are inevitable, and that it is how we respond to them when they arrive. Can we give ourselves permission to sit back and 'not know' for sure, but only guess at what the outcome will be?

Imagine for a moment the fear and anxiety which accompanied Christopher Columbus and his crew as they set sail into unknown territory. They had no way of knowing for sure if the world was flat or round, or when/where they would land. What their journey would be like. If they would return. The crew were bribed with large sums of money to take the risks. All they had was their faith in God, a series of rituals which accompanied each day's activity, singing, music and prayer and their knowledge of how to sail the ships in 'known' weather conditions. These were some of the elements which created a safety and a structure to the voyage. Out of the chaos, came some routine, predictability, known and shared by all at an agreed time.

As the ship's Captain, the crews fears and anxieties were the responsibility of Columbus. At one point, the situation became so arduous, that it resulted in mutiny. The crew had wanted to turn back. Columbus resisted this pressure. He sought support from his colleagues. His reward – when land was finally sighted. This information came to me following this second research group. Consider some of the dynamics and acknowledge the mirror.

I remembered my own training at York. When the therapy/training group looked for direction and blamed the facilitator for not creating one. Cattanach (1994) writes of the therapeutic journey as being 'a process to find our way and the job of the therapist is to make a safe enough place and a safe enough way for the journey to happen' (p.33). The research into this model began as part of the final essay of my dramatherapy training. I have collected ideas, experimented and expanded the concept over four years. I can now reflect on my facilitation of this group. My experience has taught me to respond and be sensitive in creating a 'safe enough place'. I could have made it safer, and I do now.

We can learn from this, that as therapist, it is of paramount importance that we learn to understand the implications and the inter-relationship between structure and chaos in group therapy. For example, if we alter the venue, times, continuity, facilitator of the group, etc., then we are inevitably bringing about a change in the amount of perceived safety/structure in the group. We are playing around with the predictability, the boundaries.

A group particularly susceptible to chaotic emotions, for example, women survivors of sexual abuse as opposed to a creative expressive dramatherapy group, will benefit from a higher degree of in-built structure/direction. Ground rules form part of this structure or the practice of ritualised patterns of activities at the beginning or the end of the group session.

Group Three

This was a self-awareness group, again over ten weeks, with its aims and objectives beint to explore the life cycle within its existing context. They were not introduced to the life cycle until the seventh week, which, once again related to the themes. The group wanted to return to the idea on the following week and it was then that we found a new way of working with the life cycle.

The room was set out in the form of the cycle, using chairs to represent each of the stages. People were asked to stand by each of the stages and experience that part of the cycle by making links with their own lives. When they felt that they had experienced one stage as far as they could they would then continue on to the next. They were encouraged to maintain the clockwise direction as far as possible, but they could experiment in a flexible way once they had completed a cycle.

Read Johnson (1982) claims that the developmental perspective views human disorder as a 'blockage or a halt in development' (pp.183–90). Assessment involves exploration of where the person has stopped themselves. 'The journey then recommences with the therapist acting as a companion and guide', (Cattanach 1994, p.29). Members of the group could explore their 'blockage or halt in development', using both the therapist and the life cycle as a companion and guide.

One woman's experience/block was of having always viewed the 'chaos' in her life as a disabling 'pit of despair', treated as depression. Her view had changed identity to become a place of re-birth, the 'womb-like' environment in which to germinate new ideas, directions, structures, etc. She spoke about becoming more involved with her grandchildren as a way of 'structuring' her life and therefore, creating more 'meaning' to her existence. Her chaos would allow her to experiment with ideas of how she would do this.

Another person described his 'chaos' as bereavement. He had lost his wife and had taken up night school in order to increase his social life. This had helped and he had made some friends whilst attending. The class had generated some 'meaning' for him. The 'movement' was the time he spent with his friends both at the class or in the pub afterwards, along with his improved self-image.

He 'emerged', having found a new skill, completed the course, with some changed opinions about his own self-worth. His 'chaos' was around the course having finished, what to do next? Would he still be able to continue the friendships without the structure of the course? Having identified in the group the value of his choice, he chose to repeat the experience knowing that one life cycle had been completed and the new one would inevitably be different.

The overall response, as in other group work, was very positive and allowed people to feel hopeful about their situation. The language of the life cycle formed the themes to the closure, which invariably focused around where they had emerged.

Theatre provides a vehicle which enables us to condense a story, allowing us to take it in as a whole, and emerge with a different perspective. The play has a beginning, a middle and an end.

This is what the life cycle can provide us with. Our own story is condensed into the stages of the cycle, so that we may ultimately develop a new perception or understanding. Each time a play is performed, there is a difference and a new cast of actors will only serve to change it further. Given that 'all the world's a stage', I believe it is this difference at each performance' which is instrumental in creating some of the chaos.

The life cycle, like the script, acts as a construction which holds the session together, so that a beginning, a middle and an end can be made overt. Developmental psychologists believe that an early dependence on both physical and emotional external structures will go on to facilitate growth in the individual. The life cycle helps us to perform rite of passage between our own personal issues, the dramatherapy group and the drama of life in general. The chaotic hyperactivity of mania and the structured stillness of depression can be encompassed in one circle.

Life Cycle in Relation to Individual Work

It is useful to give an example of a life cycle in relation to my career as a way of demonstrating that the cycle can be used in individual work. So, imagine I am the person with whom you are working.

On leaving school, I experienced a feeling of 'chaos' at not knowing the kind of career I wanted to follow. The 'structure' at that time developed as further education to take A levels. This provided a temporary 'meaning' to my life. I 'moved' through the two years, acquiring new knowledge and maturity, eventually to 'emerge' with some qualifications. I spent some time exploring opportunities, trying out new ideas, until the 'structure' of my nurse training came along. Once again, I had 'meaning' to my life. I experienced a 'moving' through three years, three months of training and personal development, to qualify as an Registered Mental Nurse (RMN). A qualified nurse, but once again 'chaos' about where to go next. Then the 'structure' of dramatherapy. This lasted for two years, with both the passage of time as well as the inevitable learning and changes in perception about myself and my world. I 'emerged' as a qualified dramatherapist. Perhaps my understanding of this cycle has allowed me to remain in the chaos a little while longer, whilst I decide the next course of action for my career. But, for now, this life cycle is complete and will be taken up again at another time. Meanwhile other life cycles are continuing their completion, such as acquired knowledge in the field of dramatherapy. Given this concept then, what would your life cycle look like?

The Life Cycle and Supervision

The life cycle is a useful supervision tool. The supervisee describes their own process using the language and terminology of the cycle. They also describe the process of the group and apply it to any clients with whom they may be working.

In this way, the worker can observe the completion of cycles, both in the individual sessions as well as overall. A beginning, a middle and an end to the therapy is established. These shifts can then be checked out with the group/client.

I have found that this triangular model works well in association with the life cycle during the supervision process.

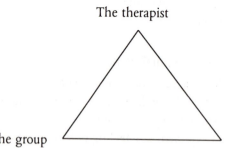

The therapist

The group

The individual

Figure 3 Facilitator's model

The supervisee is encouraged to explore their own life cycle in relation to their individual/group practice. The life cycles of the client's individual experience, along with the whole group's collectively, can link with supervision in forming the closure of the final session. The life cycle once again uses the shared language, framework and terminology.

As the life cycle is an approach and a philosophy, each supervisee/facilitator is encouraged to explore their own cycle, examining the amounts of chaos and structure in their lives, and the implications their response has on the group's process. The shared language, framework and terminology form a bridge for the space between continuums and facilitator/client. If we are to assist the client in working through their life cycle, then we have to acknowledge our own.

Return to the Images

I would now like to return to the words which were brainstormed in the exercise at the beginning. With your developed understanding of the life cycle, I invite you to compare the two lists of words. Do you have a negative/positive concept of chaos? What do you notice about structure?

Conclusion

I don't pretend that the information I have presented here is new to us. Such ideas around polarities have surfaced in many ancient cultures in the form of religious and worship practices.

The life cycle could assist both the student and the newly qualified dramatherapist in mapping their personal and professional development in the way that it has my own. The life cycle has its roots in our ability to be creative. Acknowledgement of our own creativity gives us control and responsibility for our own destiny on this journey through life. We can create our own signposts, it is how we interpret, perceive and ultimately understand them that counts.

To be creative means to open oneself up to the world of chaos – to see it, hear it, smell it, touch it and taste it with all our sensory equipment.

The Chapter as a Life Cycle

We have now completed the journey. The chaos associated itself with opening the book and wondering what the contents of this chapter might be. The structure arrived when you began to read and engage in the material being presented, which then went on to provide a meaning. The movement has been the number of pages and the internal questioning, agreement/disagreement with the content. Finally, you have emerged in a different place, having read the literature. Your emergence is inevitable, your response is not. Chaos is present once more as you move into the next chapter or decide what to do next. Will it be to make a cup of tea, make your complaints to the editor or put your own thoughts and feelings into a structure? Who knows?

Finally, although there is not the time or space here to journey any further in this life cycle, (I have gone as far as I can, for now), I intend at a later stage to explain and evaluate the role of the cycle in relation to obsessional behaviour and the ritual/structure of repetitive behaviour patterns.

I would like to acknowledge the valued assistance of the brave crew who accompanied me on this journey (they did not require bribes), Paul Greenwood, John Casson, Simon Liddy, Mark Huxley and the support of many clients.

References

Cattanach, A. (1994) 'The Developmental Approach of Dramatherapy.' In S. Jennings, A. Cattanach, S. Mitchell, A. Chesner and B. Meldrum *The Handbook of Dramatherapy.* London: Routledge.

Copeland, A. (1952) *Music and Imagination.* London: Oxford University Press.

Ehrenzweig, A. (1967) *The Hidden Order of Art.* London: Weidenfield & Nicolson.

Emunah, R. (1994) *Acting for Real – Dramatherapy Process, Technique and Performance.* Published by Brunner/Mazel inc, New York.

Fincher, S. (1991) *Creating Mandalas.* Boston, MA/London: Shambhala Publications.

Gleik, J. (1988) *Chaos.* London: Cardinal by Sphere Books.

Jennings, S. (1983) *Creative Arts Therapies in Psychiatry.* Paper presented to the Royal College of Psychiatry and the College of Occupational Therapy.

Jennings, S. (1987) 'Dramatherapy in Groups.' In S. Jennings, A. Cattanach, . S. Mitchell, A. Chesner and B. Meldrum *Dramatherapy, Theory and Practice for Teachers and Clinicians.* London: Croom Helm.

Jennings, S. (1990) *Dramatherapy with Families, Groups and Individuals: Waiting in the Wings.* London: Jessica Kingsley Publishers.

Jung, C.G. (1963) *Memories, Dreams, Reflections.* London: Collins.

Keats, J. (1935) *The Letters of John Keats.* M.B. Forman. (ed). London: Oxford University Press.

Krishnamurti, J. (1976) *Krishnamurti's Notebook.* London: Victor Gollancz Ltd.

Read Johnson, D. (1982) 'Developmental approaches in drama.' *Arts in Psychotherapy 9.* Oxford: Pergamon Press.

Rowe, D. (1987) *Beyond Fear.* London: Fontana.

Stewart, S. (1989) *Creation Myth.* Shaftesbury, Dorset: Element Books Ltd.

Storr, A. (1972) *The Dynamics of Creation*. Harmondsworth: Penguin Books.

Turner, V.W. (1969) *The Ritual Process*. London: Routedge and Kegan Paul.

Van Gennep, A. (1960) *The Rites of Passage*. London: Routledge and Kegan Paul.

Weinstock, H. (1968) *Rossini*. London: Oxford University Press.

White, E.W. (1961) 'Stravinsky.' In H. Hartog (ed) *European Music in the Twentieth Century*. Harmondsworth: Pelican Books.

CHAPTER THIRTEEN

The Business
One Dramatherapist's View of a Business Plan

Lorraine Fox

This chapter will define the parameters of one particular business plan. It has to be stated that this plan is not mutually exclusive to dramatherapists, nor is it indeed intended to be. It is merely one dramatherapist's experience of having to devise a business plan for a particular hospital. This plan will no doubt differ from many other dramatherapists' own experiences but will hopefully prove useful at some level.

A business plan in simple terms determines:

- what a dramatherapist does;
- what you've got;
- what you need to do it;
- who you work with.

Briefly, it's a summary of what happens where and with whom, who you work with and the resources that are required. This provides a comprehensible framework, it is only the details that are quite specific.

This chapter will therefore use a particular framework, detailed as follows:

- Philosophy – current perspectives
- Mission statement
- Profile of current operations
    a) service management
- Resource profile
- Financial Profile

- Forward service plan

    a) projected service levels

    b) resource projections

    c) cost projections

- Manpower plan

    a) manpower projections

    b) employee resourcing

    c) education, training and development

- Quality assurance programme

    a) clinical quality initiatives

    b) non-clinical quality initiatives

- Estate plan

    a) condition and suitability of estate

    b) condition of infrastructure

The business plan involves the administrative, clinical and non clinical aspects of a service provision. Unfortunately, within the present economic climate, a cost-effective and efficient service is of vital importance. As has happened in the world of drama and theatre, it is vital that there is a full house at each performance and that customer satisfaction is seen as important. Theatre companies offer backstage tours to see the rehearsal process as one method of attracting 'punters' and at the same time putting money in the 'coffers'. This could sound like the 'Scrooge' from *A Christmas Carol*. Dramatherapy is a different process. It is important that a dramatherapist who believes in the use of dramatherapy is able to use the same language as the organisation and business managers. I am also of the opinion that it is impossible to 'categorise' the people referred for dramatherapy. However, it is important to ascertain what dramatherapists know, that it is possible to justify a cost-effective service because 'it' works, proving this often adds to the administrative nightmare.

As the notion of business plans in the dramatherapy world is a fairly new concept, I do hope that this provides the reader with what could be termed a 'ready knowledge', if, for example, they were asked to compile a mission statement and aims of the service for management. I also hope that this chapter provides dramatherapists with some ready knowledge for other areas of work, for example, the voluntary sector and local authority. I therefore propose to discuss this framework and provide what will in effect be useful ideas that are helpful to dramatherapists wherever they are working.

The Business Plan

Philosophy – current perspectives

This has to be a brief and succinct paragraph, understandable to anyone who has little or no knowledge of dramatherapy and involves:

- what dramatherapy is;
- who the client population is;
- the available research;
- is it an exclusive treatment or can dramatherapy be utilised alongside other treatments?

What the dramatherapist states about dramatherapy depends on their particular area of work. For example, in an adult mental health directorate which is predominantly 'medical model', the word 'healing' would probably be best left out. This is a purely personal viewpoint due to my experience of working in this area. The dramatherapist would know better than anyone what language their colleagues are familiar with.

Client population relates to the particular area of work, for example, adult mental health, child and adolescent, continuing care and the elderly. Research available is somewhat limited in dramatherapy, however, Grainger's (1990) book, *Drama and Healing: The Roots of Drama Therapy*, is an excellent example.

Whether dramatherapy is an exclusive service or can be utilised with other treatments depends on where the dramatherapist is employed – as part of a multidisciplinary team based in, for example, a day hospital, rehabilitation unit or as part of the continuing care of the elderly. Dramatherapy would in these examples, be used alongside other treatments. However, this is not to say that dramatherapy cannot be a specialist service if no other treatments are being utilised.

As the reader is becoming aware, dramatherapy is flexible, which is the beginning of 'good business'. No longer is it possible to be 'mutually exclusive', an openness and flexibility is essential. After all, within the world of the 'supermarket' it is possible to have child-care facilities, something to eat, have your hair done, post letters and have your clothes dry-cleaned. People have now come to expect these services. Again, I feel I must explain the fact that we all know that dramatherapy is a clinical service and as such differs greatly from the supermarket, but it is still a customer service which will be purchased by the provider, which, for example, may be the GP and as such, places it firmly in the 'market place'.

Mission statement

This can be viewed from two perspectives. The first being that the mission statement is set by the dramatherapist's employers. Most business concerns these days have their own mission statement. The dramatherapist needs to be aware of what the mission statement is and how the dramatherapist will work towards achieving this.

The second perspective is that the dramatherapist needs to be able to provide a mission statement which highlights the high quality of clinical service provided. This is maintained by stating the aim in meeting the mission statement. This could include what the service promises to achieve within the next financial year and what standards will be in place to ensure that these needs are met.

Profile of current operations

This is a 'thumbsketch' of where the dramatherapist works, which involves the service management and clinical work. This includes some or all of the following:

SERVICE MANAGEMENT

This has to take into account the dramatherapist's own role, whether as an independent practitioner or part of a department. This may be part of an arts therapy department or a team. This section needs to detail the meetings that require the attendance of the dramatherapist. An example of this could be a business, clinical or staff support meeting.

CLINICAL WORK

This should take into account:

- specialist service;
- client population;
- who refers;
- assessment – what type;
- identification of problems;
- what types of therapeutic intervention are used;
- which model and when;
- methods of evaluation;
- discharge policies.

SERVICE MANAGEMENT

What is the role of the dramatherapist? Is this an individual who provides a service as part of a unit in one directorate or part-time in one unit and providing a service across directorates. The following example may help to illustrate this.

A dramatherapist, who is cited in one directorate, say adult mental health, works in a day hospital for four sessions and one session in a ward. Therefore, if the post is full time, the dramatherapist may provide a further five sessions to another directorate, say the child and adolescent. This would result in 'cross-charging'. That is, the budget holder for the child and adolescent directorate would pay the budget holder for the adult mental health directorate for the clinical services of the dramatherapist. This is a simplistic example which involves other practicalities such as service level agreements. This allows for the service of a dramatherapist and outlines what the dramatherapist would do whilst working in this directorate. Therefore in the service management the dramatherapist would define the following:

Adult Mental Health Directorate

0.4 sessions day hospital at . . . .

0.1 sessions ward based a . . . .

Child and Adolescent Directorate

0.5 sessions child and adolescent unit at. . . . .

The dramatherapist in this section would define their role as part of a multidisciplinary team and taking a case-load as a key worker or as an independent practitioner. The dramatherapist may have both these roles as a provider of a clinical service.

The following have to be detailed in service management:

- Attendance at meetings whether clinical such as team meetings when cases are reviewed; business meetings of the team or as an arts therapies department – in other words, at any time when they sit down with an agenda. An example of this may be the following. A team may have a weekly clinical meeting to discuss referrals, assessment and reviews; a weekly or monthly business meeting which may discuss future developments, community resources and 'day-to-day' team business; a support meeting usually fortnightly or monthly when a team may sit down to discuss personal issues pertaining to the team; an audit meeting where new initiatives are formulated to ascertain that specific tried and tested methods of working are successful.

- An in-service training session where members of the team share skills or have an outside speaker who is able to share relevant information with them.

CLINICAL WORK

This section includes where the dramatherapist obtains their referrals, client population and diagnoses. For example, a dramatherapist in an adult mental health directorate may receive referrals from consultant psychiatrist, psychologist, community psychiatric nurse, social worker, GP or multidisciplinary team.

Diagnosis is made by consultant psychiatrist which should be defined in the plan. For example, a consultant psychiatrist may use different coding for specific criteria. I have had experience of a consultant psychiatrist using ICD 10 (1994) coding. This offers specific methods of recording a patient's diagnosis, useful for audit purposes.

Assessment – what type of assessment a dramatherapist uses. If for example the dramatherapist works with a team, assessment may be formalised. An example of this could be the following:

- reason for referral;
- history of presenting problem;
- family history including psychiatric history;
- medical history including medication;
- personal history;
- social/financial/living circumstances;
- mental state examination;
- expectations of treatment;
- provisional diagnosis;
- conclusions.
- problems;
- key worker;
- review date;
- ICD 10 coding.

This enables the dramatherapist to begin an intervention by dramatherapeutic assessment. However, other forms of assessment are detailed by Meldrum (1994, p.187) in her chapter which discusses the various forms available at this present time. This would also be useful for the information regarding which model and when. For example with social-skill work, the task-orientated method described by Jennings (1990) could be outlined (p.32).

Evaluation – what types of evaluation are used and with whom. For example, the group defined above may have a client evaluation skill score sheet which has self-scoring between one and five. A client may then tick or state whether they feel that their skills have improved. Alternatively, the system whereby a multiple choice question is used may be more useful. An example of this may be:

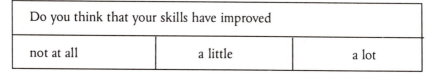

Do you think that your skills have improved		
not at all	a little	a lot

Evaluation is a difficult concept in dramatherapy. One reason being, that it is almost impossible to measure whether a person is better than they were prior to treatment. One option and simple method of comparative evaluation is where the client has a range of categories which are from the least that they could have improved, to the most improved. Somewhat simple, but nevertheless effective.

If the dramatherapist is part of a team, they may have methods in place which the dramatherapist has to adopt for the purposes of clinical audit.

DISCHARGE POLICIES

This section includes what type of discharge policies the dramatherapist uses. If working as part of a team there may be documentation which requires specific information. This may include:

- name;
- address;
- GP;
- discharge code;
- length of treatment;
- what type of model was used and what it achieved;
- the client's self-evaluation (if required);

- where a person is discharged to, for example, a GP or consultant psychiatrist.

This process is invaluable for clinical audit, enabling the collection of clear, precise information. Therefore within the business plan the dramatherapist may provide evidence of a discharge document which determines, for example, what is being termed 'seemless care', with details of communication with other agencies. The dramatherapist is able to ensure patient care as part of their discharge policy.

Having examined the management and clinical work of the dramatherapist, it is important to determine what is needed to provide an efficient and effective service.

Resource profile

What resources are needed to provide a dramatherapy service? They include the following:

- the dramatherapist;
- where the dramatherapist is based;
- room for clinical work;
- what items are currently held on the inventory.

It is important to state whether a desk/telephone is primarily for the dramatherapist's use or if the office is shared, if so with whom. It must also be made clear where the dramatherapist works, whether there are rooms available within the setting or whether the work is community based.

Items the dramatherapist uses to enable them in their clinical work must be enumerated. A simple detailed inventory of equipment appears tedious but is vital for the management, who wish to know what the dramatherapist needs as a service provider.

Financial profile

The financial profile includes the following:

- dramatherapist's salary;
- administrative time;
- secretarial support;
- administrative costs of this system;
- hire of rooms if working in the community;
- travel expense budget;

- training budget;
- equipment budget;
- petty cash.

A dramatherapist in a single department may receive a detailed monthly print out of salary, travel expenses and equipment budget. This will help in compiling this particular section.

However, it may be important to provide a breakdown of the costs detailed above. Administrative time is possibly unavailable, but a dramatherapist should have some knowledge of the administrative time within their clinical service. For example, how long does it take to complete therapy notes for individuals and groups? Does the dramatherapist have to 'up-date' multidisciplinary case notes? Writing letters to referring agents takes time which needs to be accounted for in the service provision.

In terms of a clinical service, the preparation and administrative time for one group is almost equal to working time. Therefore in the progress of a dramatherapist's working week of, say, ten sessions, two of these sessions may have to be utilised administratively and would need to be costed as such for service provision to the purchaser.

HIRE OF ROOMS

A dramatherapist may have to use community services if applicable to where they are working. In the present economic climate most church halls and community rooms have to be paid for. This needs to be added to the financial profile in such a way that proves a viable venture. If for example the cost of hire of a room was £10.00 for two hours and eight people attend, cost per person is minimal within the overall cost of seeing eight individual patients.

Another facet that needs to be accounted for in using community rooms, is the need for refreshments. As a dramatherapist, refreshments form an integral part of the clinical service. A budget for this or a supply from the hospital needs to be highlighted.

TRAVEL EXPENSE BUDGET

This is the cost incurred by the dramatherapist for driving, or indeed transportation to provide sessional work in the community. As community care becomes 'on-line', more funds will have to be made available. A dramatherapist who holds individual or group sessions in different directorates or in the community will have to realise the implication of cost for the service.

TRAINING BUDGET

It is important to continue to strive for training needs. The Annual Conference of the British Association for Dramatherapists provides an excellent
example of what would be needed to ensure professional practice and to be
kept informed of new developments. Supervision should also be highlighted
in this section as an important and vital element of a dramatherapist's clinical
work.

EQUIPMENT BUDGET

List what a dramatherapist needs to function, such as paper, pens, plays,
cushions, etc. A recurring budget for equipment needs to be realised to
replace and obtain new items.

PETTY CASH

Often, what a dramatherapist needs cannot be purchased from the suppliers.
An example may be music cassettes, material, postcards, etc. These are freely
available in shops but the management will refuse to take a hospital invoice
when the total is under £50.00. Therefore access to a £20.00 fund will enable
the dramatherapist to purchase these items when and where required.

Analysis of recent trends

This section has to explain evidence of the service functioning, which may
involve the use of questionnaires as part of the evaluative process.

The dramatherapist would be able to determine that the people who had
been referred for dramatherapy had for example, improved their confidence,
self-esteem or communication skills depending on what the initial referral
stated. These concepts are difficult to measure, but a self-assessment ques-
tionnaire completed by an individual or group attender provides some form
of evidence that a dramatherapist can use.

If the dramatherapy service is an entirely new venture then terms such as,
service provision was deemed improved in these areas, would suffice. After
all, there are specific dramatherapy terms that 'business-speak' people can
understand. Included in this section would be the statistics, that is, the
number of patients seen for individual and group work. The numbers should
also include people referred for specific interventions and whether they
attended or not. An example might be S. who was to attend for specific work.
S. may have been able to attend nine sessions, been on holiday for two of
the sessions and did not attend for one session.

This would be shown in the following format:

	GROUPS	ABA	DNA
S.	9	2	1

ABA is 'absence allowed' (the holiday) and DNA is 'did not attend', when patient fails to notify of absence. If for example S. had telephoned the total would have been three under ABA.

Statistics are best collected weekly and monthly. The annual score would then be used for the business plan. For example, a dramatherapist who has had say a total number of patients attended for a year at a guess might be 730. This total number would be quantified by the number of groups and individual sessions. These may be detailed as follows:

Assertiveness group 10 weeks x 8 attenders	80
Womens group with 6 referrals	180
Ongoing therapy group with 6 referrals x40	240
Individual sessions for 10 patients	230
Total	730

Detailed analysis could also include attenders, absences allowed and did not attend. I hope this example illustrates the value of statistics. These provide valuable evidence of a dramatherapist's flexibility and workload.

Forward service plan

PROJECTED SERVICE LEVELS

What in an 'ideal world' would a dramatherapist need to function as a service provider? Referrals from different sectors of the directorate? The dramatherapist may be able to offer a service to the rehabilitation or continuing care unit. This would enable a wider service option for the provider, therefore benefiting the purchaser.

RESOURCE PROJECTIONS

These detail what equipment would be needed if a service was available in the units mentioned above.

COST PROJECTIONS

An increase in budget for the extra travel and equipment needs to be presented here. This is obviously less detailed than the financial profile but some consideration of the content could help complete this section.

Manpower Plan

MANPOWER PROJECTIONS

This section enables the dramatherapist to state whether other dramatherapists are required and on what basis – sessional, part or full time. It may also be important to state that agreements across directorates would perhaps develop the dramatherapy service. It may be important to highlight the range of work a dramatherapist has with other voluntary sectors.

EMPLOYEE RESOURCING

This is the 'as if' scenario which is familiar to all dramatherapists. If a vacancy should occur, what specialisms would be preferable to the directorates.

EDUCATION, TRAINING AND DEVELOPMENT

A dramatherapist should highlight that this section is essential to professional practice. Research days, attendance at the meetings of the Professions Allied to Medicine and the Annual Conference are essential. Another example might be that if the dramatherapist were to receive a budget to train as a supervisor, it would be a cost-effective venture for the employer, enabling other dramatherapists to receive 'in-house' supervision.

Quality assurance programme

Quality assurance is not an easy concept for dramatherapy. Perhaps, I should quantify this statement. There has not been to my knowledge any quality assurance programme written by and for dramatherapists relating to their clinical practice. I would also stress that the code of ethics and dramatherapy practice is always provided to the highest clinical degree by any dramatherapist. As dramatherapists, we know that whatever we do is of the highest quality and we are able to assure the client or group of clients of our intentions at all times. However, dramatherapists, unlike other professions, do not have specific criteria. In the Report to the Department of Health, quality assurance is described as 'the process in which achievable and desireable levels of quality are described, the extent to which these levels are achieved and the action to enable them to be reached is taken' (Report to the Department of Health, A Pilot Study, p.6).

Often professions set standards to ensure good practice. These standards are defined for both clinical practice and service management. These standards would in one sense qualify for quality assurance. As this chapter is concerned with the business of dramatherapy it would confuse the reader should I begin to define what standards are, other than to state that they are essential for clinical audit. However, to return to quality assurance, this is in two parts, clinical quality initiatives and non clinical quality initiatives.

CLINICAL QUALITY INITIATIVES

This is the dramatherapist's clinical practice. One important part of this process is supervision. The guidelines set by the British Association for Dramatherapists provide an excellent example for the dramatherapist to include in this section. Other factors include:

- patients'/clients' knowledge of dramatherapy;
- issues of confidentiality;
- patients/clients assessment and review process if part of a team;
- up-to-date therapy notes and/or multidisciplinary case notes;
- informing referring agent at regular interval;
- set guidelines if informing the referring agent should the dramatherapist be concerned about the client;
- monitoring mechanisms in place to determine a high standard of quality assurance;
- awareness of new developments and research in dramatherapy practice;
- informing other professions what dramatherapy can achieve;
- ensuring waiting times for referrals are 'in line' with the Patients Charter determined by individual health boards;
- ensure that patient/client is seen on time or within the Patients Charter;
- keep record of attendances up to date;
- ensure efficient collection of statistics;
- attendance at clinical meetings;
- an efficient communication network if part of a team.

This is what all dramatherapists 'do' in their clinical practice and will I'm sure be surprised that they have a quality assurance programme. It may not be standardised within the department but evidence will be available.

NON-CLINICAL QUALITY ASSURANCE

This section includes the management of the dramatherapy service and administrative practices, such as secretarial services. Basically, the time span that, for example, the dramatherapist has between seeing a new patient/client and informing the referrer of the outcome.

Health and safety is also important, for instance in the dramatherapist's working space. If, for example, the dramatherapist had a group in the community, it would be the responsibility of the dramatherapist to ensure that these premises were safe, had adequate fire exits and that any materials used met safety standards. Also that adequate monitoring mechanisms were in place to ensure that articles were checked and up-dated as required.

Any problems that affect the use of certain rooms for dramatherapy should be outlined. If, for example, a room contained other equipment that had to be moved each time a session commenced, this should be stated in the report. A dramatherapist's clinical practice is affected, if the place designated for dramatherapy is entirely unsuitable.

Estate Plan

CONDITION AND SUITABILITY OF ESTATE

This section includes the building where the dramatherapist has, for example, an office and a work room. If a dramatherapist works in several areas then this should be stated. At the time of writing this there has not been any separate financial comparison of itemised costs for particular buildings. However, if the present economic climate continues, the cost of up-dating buildings will become part of a department's plan.

CONDITION OF INFRASTRUCTURE

This is the up-date and renewal of the inside of buildings. For example, painting inside a studio or office would eventually become part of the financial burden for the dramatherapist.

Conclusion

This chapter outlined one dramatherapist's viewpoint of a business plan. Whilst the framework offered one perspective, it was my intention that each section could be taken and used in different contexts. Whilst the business of being a dramatherapist who has had to adopt this methodology was certainly problematic, it was also necessary. As we all know, this is the world of the 1990s, when mission statements are the 'norm' and methods of achieving the aims are predominant. Dramatherapists need to ensure that they understand and can function within this 'world', whilst still enjoying their clinical 'world'.

Reference

Grainger, R. (1990) *Drama and Healing, The Roots of Drama Therapy*. London: Jessica Kingsley Publishers.

ICD. 10 Classification of Mental and Behavioural Disorders (1994) Geneva: World Health Organisation.

Meldrum, B. (1994) 'Evaluation and assessment.' In S. Jennings, A. Cattanach, S. Mitchell, A. Chesner and B. Meldrum. *The Handbook of Dramatherapy*. London: Routledge.

Jennings, S. (1990) *Dramatherapy with Families, Groups and Individuals, Waiting in the Wings*. London: Jessica Kingsley Publishers.

Report to the Department of Health on a Pilot Study (undated) *Clinical Audit in Professions Allied to Medicine and Related Therapy Professions. Health and Care Research Unit*. Belfast: The Queens University of Belfast.

Contributors

Christopher Appolinari has been working in psychiatry for 21 years, both in the health service and in the voluntary sector. He has been a practising dramatherapist in East Anglia since 1988, and also works in Cambridge.

Madeline Andersen-Warren is currently employed as a dramatherapist within an NHS Trust. She is coordinator of Dramatherapy North West, a regional network of the British Association for Dramatherapists, and has published work on Dramatherapy with elderly people and dramatherapy and Jacobean theatre.

Katerina Couroucli-Robertson is a dramatherapist and a teacher in special education. As a dramatherapist she works both privately and also at the dramatherapy training centre 'Theatre and Therapy' in Athens, as director of studies. She has been involved in the training of dramatherapists since 1987. She also works at a vocational school for adolescents with learning difficulties where she runs the silk screen printing workshop. She has been in special education since 1973. Finally she coordinates a theatrical and musical group for people with different handicaps for Very Special Arts Hellas.

Ditty Dokter is a senior lecturer in dramatherapy and course leader in dance movement therapy at the University of Hertfordshire, England. Most recently, her clinical work has been based at Addenbrook's Teaching Trust, Cambridge, in a specialist psychiatric unit for clients with affective and/or eating disorders. Her Ph.D research is on transcultural issues in arts therapies (registered since 1992). She is editor of *Arts Therapies and Clients with Eating Disorders: Fragile Board.* (Jessica Kingsley Publishers 1994).

Judy Donovan is the course director for the diploma in dramatherapy and certificate in supervision for dramatherapists and groupworkers at the University College of Ripon and York St John. She has had 17 years experience working as a dramatherapist within a health trust counselling and psychotherapy unit and has experience working with offenders and adults with learning difficulties.

Lorraine Fox is a dramatherapist, supervisor, trainer, qualified dance teacher and social worker. She is treasurer of the British Association for Dramatherapists; has experience of working as a dramatherapist with a community mental health team in the NHS, in the mental health directorate and has extensive experience of working with people who have learning disabilities. She is currently in freelance practice.

Di Grimshaw is a freelance dramatherapist working in schools and day centres for children and adults with emotional and behavioural difficulties. Di is also employed at the NSPCC Child Sexual Abuse Consultancy in Manchester. She is a dramatherapy supervisor and convenor of the Supervision Sub-Committee for the British Association for Dramatherapists. Di is also a registered playtherapist and teaches at the Institute of Dramatherapy, Roehampton Institute, London, and the College of Ripon and York St John.

Pete Holloway works as a full-time senior dramatherapist for Canterbury and Thanet Community Healthcare. Working in an acute psychiatric day-patient facility he has developed a special interest in techniques which will provide containment and a problem-solving focus. He also currently teaches on the Institute of Dramatherapy graduate diploma training programme at Roehampton Institute, London.

Jocelyne James graduated in drama and English literature at Roehampton Institute, London, before training initially as a Sesame practitioner and later an integrative arts psychotherapist. She has a wide variety of experience in many different clinical and educational contexts. She is currently the course leader for the Central/Sesame Training in Drama and Movement Therapy at Central School of Speech and Drama, and a tutor at the Institute for Arts in Therapy and Education. She has a private practice in north London working with both adults and children.

Jayne E. Liddy until recently was manager of the mental health day centre at the Royal Oldham Hospital. During her time in this role, she was instrumental in introducing a dramatherapeutic approach to psychiatric services. She is currently employed as a nurse specialist attached to the Additional Support Team within Learning Disabilities for Oldham NHS Trust.

Steve Mitchell is a full-time dramatherapist for Lancaster Priorities Health Trust Lancaster, and Course Director of Dramatherapy Programmes at the Institute of Dramatherapy at Roehampton, London. For the past 30 years he has explored the interface between theatre and therapy, first as a theatre director, then after his degree at Dartington, as director of Pathfinder Studio. This gave rise to 'The Theatre of Self-Expression' a therapeutic theatre he describes in *The Handbook of Dramatherapy* (Jennings 1994, Routledge).

Brenda Rawlinson came into dramatherapy from professional theatre and Drama-in-Education, where she worked with Brian Way. She later became co-director of Northcott Youth Theatre. She is head therapist at the Creative Therapy Unit, which is situated in Exeter, Devon, where she works as both clinician and coordinator. The unit offers art, music, drama and dance movement therapy, providing a generic service to health service community trust users. She is also involved in related teaching and training work within the Devon area and Exeter University.

Subject Index

Numbers in italic indicate figures or tables

abuse 10, 15, 72
    see also sexual abuse
adults with learning disabilities 15–31
aggression 209–12
alchemy 154, 159
All's Well That Ends Well 25
anger 131
anorexia nervosa 180, 182, 185
    medical criteria 181
    dramatherapy group 185–92
anxiety 151, 156, 168
art therapy 58, 196
assessment 35, 73–4, 112, 245
autism 15

Bacchae, The 156, 158–9
behaviour 52–2
behaviour modification 17
bereavement 224–5
body image 179, 182, 185
body language 23, 130, 212
bulimia nervosa 180, 182, 185
    medical criteria 181
    dramatherapy group 185–92
business plans 240–54
    financial profile 243–4
    manpower plan 251
    resource profile 247
    service profile 243–4
    structure 240–1

catharsis 144, 148, 216
chaos 185, 220, 223–4, 227, 231, 234
characterisation 116
child abuse *see* abuse
children with emotional and behavioural difficulties 51–69
Christmas Carol, A 113, 122–34
Cinderella 144, 172
clinical audit 245, 246, 247
co-working 39, 44, 191
Commedia dell'Arte 79

communication, non-verbal 22–3, 25, 130, 190
community theatre 111
confidentiality 134, 141

delinquency 52–3
depression 151, 156, 161, 166, 168, 171–2, 234
development of self 91, 98, 100, 106
Dionysus 152, 155, 156, 157, 158–9, 165
Down's Syndrome 15
drama 138, 198
dramatherapist, roles of 100, 105, 120, 137, 189–90, 195, 203, 233, 244
dramatherapy
    benefits of 111, 123, 216
    customer service 244
    definition of 194, 197
    integrative approach 20
    profession of 198–9
    see also individual dramatherapy
dramatherapy groups
    appropriateness 13, 140
    boundaries 4, 6, 7, 13, 38, 41, 43, 234
    case studies 92–106, 203–15, 229–30, 231–2, 234–5
    creating dependency 157
    developmental stages 187
    duration 186, 187, 191, 201
    evaluation 45–8
    forming a group 18, 34, 108–9, 141, 202
    functions 31, 137, 149
    group coherency 206–7
    leadership 18
    meeting places 34
    referrals 34–5, 67
    size 185, 201
    structure 39, 137, 195, 219–20
    techniques 187–8, 196, 199
    thematic work 200–1
dramatherapy group settings
    day treatment unit 136–150
    educational unit 50–69
    out-patient group 33–48
    psychiatric hospital 108–35
dramatic distance 87, 102, 115–6, 139, 149
dramatic space 141

dreams 7, 26, 151, 152–4
    and alchemy 154–5
    and Jung 155, 198

eating disorders
    and the female body 182–3
    and men 183
    treatment of 183–4
    see also anorexia nervosa and bulimia nervosa
Emperor's New Clothes, The 95–104
empty chair technique 11–12, 85–6, 131
evaluation 45–8, 110, 112, 123, 191, 246

fairy tales 26, 56, 66, 105, 144, 200
    see also myths
false memory syndrome 173
forum theatre 139, 140, 145–6, 146–8
fragile board 180

games 12
Gestalt therapy 21
Greek mythology 26–7
    see also myths
group dynamics 92–4, 202–3
group exercises 73, 142–3, 199, 207
group focal conflict model 92, 94
group tension 94, 103

humanistic psychology 20, 177

image theatre 139, 140, 145–6
impasse 82–3
improvisation 93, 126, 166, 187
incest 1
individual dramatherapy 3, 64–7, 72–89
    advantages and disadvantages of 72, 88–9
    duration 86
    role of therapist 76–7
    ritual 77–82
    stages of 73–86
    termination of 84–8
individuation 159
integrative therapy
    existential 21
    regressive 20–1
    transpersonal 21
introjects 29–30

King Lear 80
King Solomon's Judgement 212–15

learning disability 15–16
life crises 140
life cycle *221, 225*
    stages of 224–7
life map 73–4

mandalas 220–1
maskwork 95, 203
melodrama 114–5, 116, 120
mental health 228, 231
motherhood, images of 168–70
myths 26, 27, 72, 200
    see also fairy tales

narcissism 91, 96, 99, 102

object relations 53–4, 67

Pan 165
panic 151, 165–6, 168
    treatment of 166
personality disorder 1–14
    definition 2
play 5, 6, 18, 19, 54, 66, 95,
    142
    developmental play 55, 67
    embodiment play 15, 67, 145
    projective play 56, 67, 145
play space 81, 99, 103–4, 106
poetry 185, 187, 194
political theatre 128
projection 56
psychiatric hospitals 13
psychiatric drugs 6, 9, 139
psycho-social development
    stages 91, 96, 98
psychology 20

quality assurance 251–3

referral process 34, 67
relationship of client and
    therapist 19–20
reparation 99, 102
'revolving door' syndrome 108
ritual 77–82, 149, 215, 222,
    229
    threshold ritual 77–8
    transformation ritual 79–81
    transitional ritual 78–9
role play 67

sandtray therapy 151, 162–75,
    201

sculpting 6, 77, 93, 95, 115,
    123, 124, 127, 146, 166,
    185–9
Sesame Method 2, 25
    and the 'oblique approach'
    25–6
sexual abuse 5, 11, 174, 234
shame 91, 102, 106
singing 133
sleep 160–1
story making 28, 45, 58, 74,
    93, 98, 113, 123, 144, 187,
    189
supervision 4, 8, 23, 62, 191,
    203, 236, 249

team work 17–18, 68, 141, 186
Tempest, The 152, 159–61, 165,
    169, 171, 173, 175–6, 177,
    178
theatre 71, 138–9, 235
theatre of self-expression 89
theatre model of dramatherapy
    39, 41, 80, 197–9
theatrical exercises 115, 126–7
therapist, role of 18, 53
transference 12, 138, 191
transitional object 56, 67, 96

Ugly Duckling, The 104–5

Author Index

Ayto, J. 69

Badrinath, B.R. 182, 192
Baker, T. 185, 193
Bannister, A. 69
Baring, A. 164, 178
Berger, J. 92, 103, 106
Berne, E. 19
Berry, P. 170, 178
Bettelheim, B. 56, 69
Bleakley, A. 177, 178
Boal, A. 79, 127, 138, 139,
    140, 143, 144–5, 147, 148
Bosnak, R. 154, 178
Brecht, B. 128
British Association of
    Dramatherapists 194, 249
Brook, P. 71
Bruch, H. 182, 192
Brumberg, J.J. 180, 192
Buber, M. 19, 32
Butler, G. 31

Campbell, J. 14, 26, 27, 32, 72
Casement, P. 23, 32
Cashford, A. 164, 178
Cattanach, A. 18, 32, 49, 89,
    149, 193, 233, 234, 238
Chesner, A. 49, 89, 149, 193
Clarkson, P. 19, 20, 24, 29
Cobb, N. 159, 178
Copeland, A. 221, 238
Cox, M. 194, 207

Dalley, D. 216
Dekker, K. 29, 32
Department of Education and
    Science 52, 69
Dokter, D. 180, 181–2, 185,
    192
Dryden, W. 149

Ehrenzweig, A. 230, 238
Emunah, R. 71, 89, 222, 238
Erikson, E. 32, 59, 91, 96, 98,
    102, 106
Estés, C.P. 26, 32, 53, 69, 104,
    106
Euripides 156, 178
Ewing, C.P. 140, 149

Fincher, S. 226, 238
Fransella, F. 140, 149
Freud, S. 54, 153

Gardner, D.M. 182, 184, 186, 188, 192
Gersie, A. 28, 32, 60, 69, 83, 96, 106, 189
Goffman, E. 138, 149
Grainger, R. 41, 49, 135, 242, 254
Grateful Dead, The 14
Grimshaw, D. 51, 69
Grotowski Laboratory Theatre 83
Guy's Hospital 22

Hansen, T. 82, 89
Heal, M. 192
Hesse, H. 14
Hillman, J. 32, 178
Hoffman, B. 87, 89
Holden, N.L. 182, 192
Holmes, P. 62, 69
Hornyak, L. 185, 193

Jennings, S. 41, 43, 45, 49, 51, 55, 74, 85, 89, 94, 106, 137, 145, 149, 182, 187, 193, 198, 217, 222, 224, 229, 232, 238, 254,
Johnson, D. 187, 193
Johnstone, K. 95, 98, 106
Joines, V. 32
Jung, C. 19, 21, 26, 27, 32, 61, 72, 155, 159, 198, 199, 209, 216, 217, 221, 225, 238

Kaufman, G. 91, 102, 106
Keats, J. 227, 238
Keleman, S. 21, 32
Kelly, G.A. 71, 89, 138, 140, 149, 150
King, N. 32, 106
Klein, M. 51, 53, 69
Kohut, H. 91, 99, 100, 106
Kopp, S. 3, 14
Krishnamurti, J. 228, 238
Kumiega, J. 90

Lahad, M. 69, 74, 90, 200, 217
Laing, R.D. 14, 17
Landy, R. 53, 54, 98, 106
Lawrence, M. 183, 193
Levens, M. 185, 193

Liebermann, M. A. 92, 94, 95, 107
Lindkvist, M. 22
Lopez-Pedraza, R. 165, 178
Luzzato, P. 183, 193

Magarshack, D. 135
Mahrer, A.L. 53, 70
Margo, J.L. 193
Maslow, A. 21, 71, 90
Meldrum, B. 49, 89, 91, 98, 106, 150, 193, 246, 254
Meredith, C. 114
Miller, A. 3, 14, 51, 70, 90
Miller, H. 3
Mitchell, S. 41, 42, 49, 85, 89, 90, 149, 193, 197
Mitchelson, M. 25, 32
Molik, Z. 83
Mollon, P. 91, 99

Neelands, J. 138, 150

Opera North 111
Orbach, S. 182–3, 193

Parad, H.J. 1140, 150
Parad, L.G. 140, 150
Paris, G. 156, 157, 173, 178
Parry, G. 91, 99, 107
Plant, F. 21, 32
Polster, E. 21, 32
Polster, M. 21, 32
Prior, M. 174–5
Proper Job Theatre 108, 110
Puddy, J. 3

Read Johnson, D. 43, 234, 238
Rebillot, P. 71–2, 90
Rhead, A. 52, 70
Robinson, P.H. 182, 192
Rogers, C. 71
Roscher, W.H. 178
Roth, G. 90
Rowan, J. 20, 32, 70
Rowe, D. 220, 228, 238
Rust, M.J. 185, 193

Sampson, F. 169, 178
Samuels, A. 21, 32
Schraven, J. 184, 193
Sesame Institute 22
Seymour, A. 121
Shorter, B. 21, 32
Shakespeare, W. 80–1, 152, 159, 178
Sloboda, A. 183, 193

Stewart, I. 32
Stewart, S. 223, 238
Storr, A. 221, 228, 238
Styron, W. 151–2, 161, 178
Sunderland, M. 21, 32

Taylor, G. 115, 135
Theilgaard, A. 194, 217
Therapeutic Theatre Group 112–35
Tsu, L. 18, 32
Turner, V.W. 224, 238

van Gennep, A. 222, 239

Watts, P. 26, 32
Warriner, E. 180, 190, 192
Weinstock, H. 223, 239
Whitaker, D.S. 92, 94, 95, 107
White, E.W. 223, 239
Wigram, T. 192
Williams, D. 90
Winnicott, D. 51, 54–6, 57, 67, 70, 91, 96, 99, 100, 101, 103–4, 105, 106, 107, 183, 193, 196, 217
Wiseman, G. 41, 49
Woodman, M. 171, 178
World Health Organisation 245, 254

Yalom, I. 3, 14, 88
Young, M. 185, 187, 190, 193